INTERNET & JAVA PROGRAMMING

INTERNET
&
JAVA PROGRAMMING

By

HARISH KUMAR TALUJA

MCA, M.Sc. (IT), 'A' Level, AJCP
*MST, M. Tech (IT)**
HOD., MCA
H.R. Institute of Technology, Ghaziabad
Uttar Pradesh

FIREWALL MEDIA
(An Imprint of Laxmi Publications Pvt. Ltd.)
An ISO 9001:2015 Company

BENGALURU • CHENNAI • GUWAHATI • HYDERABAD
KOCHI • KOLKATA • LUCKNOW • RANCHI
NEW DELHI

Printed and bound in India
First Edition : 2008, Reprint : 2010, Edition : 2026
ISBN : 978-81-3180-367-7
FIN-2963-449-INTERNET & JAVA PROG-TAL

Price: ₹ 449.00

Branches

✆	Bengaluru	080-26 75 69 30
✆	Chennai	044-24 34 47 26
✆	Guwahati	0361-254 36 69
✆	Hyderabad	040-27 55 53 83
✆	Kochi	0484-405 13 03
✆	Kolkata	033-40 04 77 79
✆	Lucknow	0522-430 36 13
✆	Ranchi	0651-224 24 64

PUBLISHED IN INDIA BY

FIREWALL MEDIA
(An Imprint of Laxmi Publications Pvt. Ltd.)

An ISO 9001:2015 Company
113, GOLDEN HOUSE, GURUDWARA ROAD, DARYAGANJ,
NEW DELHI - 110002, INDIA

Corporate Office : B-33, Sector-5, Noida,
Gautambuddha Nagar (U.P.) - 201 301, INDIA
Telephone : +91-120-44 46 900
www.laxmipublications.com
info@laxmipublications.com

CONTENTS

PREFACE

There have been rapid developments in Information Technology and Communication Engineering during the recent years. Keeping in mind the changing scenario in software development and the recent advances in communications, this book has been primarily the written for the use in first level course on Internet and Java Programming. The book is self-contained and contains basic knowledge on Internet and its applications. An attempt has been carefully made to present the subject in as simple manner as possible with sufficient number of illustrations and required explanations.

The book would serve as an extremely useful text for MCA, M.Sc. (Information Technology/ Computer Science), B.Tech (Information Technology/Computer Science) and DOEACC 'A' Level students as well as practicing programmers, who would also find this book to be a valuable reference source.

Chapters 1, 2 and 3 explain the basic of Internet. The essential rudiments of object oriented programming have been furnished in chapter 4. Details of Java Programming are divided into chapters 5 and 6. Chapter 7 and 8 present a galaxy of basic elements, control statement and keywords in Java. Chapter 9 and 10 present a basic knowledge of Classes, Object and Inheritance. Chapter 10 to 15 discuss the Java Package, Exception Handling, String Handling, Multithreading, File Handling. Chapter 16 and 17 describe the Applet, AWT, and Swing in Java.

Suggestions for further improvements will be thankfully acknowledged and duly incorporated in the next edition.

—Author

ACKNOWLEDGEMENT

I acknowledge the debt I owe to my respected father Shri Amar Nath Taluja and My mother Smt. Shakuntla Taluja, ex-Vice Principal, CDDP College Modinagar. I am also thankful to my dear wife Mrs. Anuradha Taluja, my dear daughter Seejal for making venture of writing this book very comfortable.

I am also thankful to Er. Anil Agarwal Ji, Chairman, HRIT, Dr. V.K Jain, Director General, HRIT, Dr. K.K. Tripathi, Director, HRIT and Dr. S.D. Sharma, Additional Director, HRIT for providing me academic guidance and inspiration for writing this book.

—Author

CHAPTER 1

THE INTERNET

INTRODUCTION

The Internet is a worldwide network of network. It is a collection of networks. It can also be described as information highway. It is the world largest network of computers. It consists of over 40,000 networks around the world. Around the world each country has at least one backbone network that operates at very high speed and carriers the bulk of the traffic. Other smaller network connects to that backbone. Networks are relocated to the academics, research, and government and include users of all types of profiles *i.e.*, corporate, individual professionals, children's, schools, institutes etc. It may be remembered that computer is not located at a single site, not controlled by any central authority. The networking in the Internet are not directly connected but interconnected.

WHY WE USE INTERNET?

The Internet has revolutionized the communication methods around the world. Sitting at a workstation or PC, One can get any kind of information one wants. The latest technology advances have the result that companies are today spending considerable amount of money on Internet research. The amalgamation of computer and communication technology have resulted in the integration of data, sound and video on the Internet, which in turn has made it a powerful tool for reengineering business process the world over. One can use the Internet from for the following purposes.

(*a*) To exchange electronic mail with friends all over the globe for a small price.

(*b*) To participate in-group discussion on topics of interest, thorough public news groups.

(*c*) To find educational tools. Universities around the world, Book stores and Libraries are sharing online information.

(*d*) To shop-commercial electronics showrooms are growing in number in the USA and Europe. One can order different product over the Internet.

(*e*) In the case of business one can get technical support for products one in using. One can publish information such as technical or marketing literature.

(*f*) The Internet has becomes the first global venue for publishing information. This network has enough users now and is benefiting from the positive feedback loop.

(*g*) Internet's main asset is freedom. An alternative to controlling its freedom is to train and educate the user.

BRIEF HISTORY

A network is a group of connected communicating devices such as computers and printers. An internet (note the lowercase letter *i*) is a two or more network that can communicate with each other. The most notable internet is called the Internet (upper – case letter I), a collaboration of more than hundreds of thousands interconnected networks. Private individuals as well as various organizations such as government agencies, schools, research facilitates. Corporations, and libraries in more than 100 countries use the Internet. Millions of people are users. Yet this extraordinary communication system only came into being in 1969.

In the mid-1960s, mainframe computers in research organizations were standalone devices. Computers from different manufacturers were unable to communicate with one another. The Advanced Research Projects Agency (ARPA) in the Department of Defense (DOD) was interested in finding a way to connect computers so that the researchers they funded could share their findings, thereby reducing coasts and eliminating duplication of effort.

In 1967, at an Association for Computing Machinery (ACM) meeting, ARPA presented its ideas for ARPANET, a small network of connected computers. The idea was that each host computer (not necessarily from the same manufacturer) would be attached to a specialized computer, called an INTERFACE MESSAGE PROCESSOR (IMP). The IMPs, in turn, would be connected to one another. Each IMP had to be able to communicate with other IMPs as well as with its own attached host.

January 1969, ARPANET was a reality. Four nodes, were connected via the IMPs to form a network. Software called the network control protocol (NCP) provided communication between the hosts.

In 1983, ARPANET was reserved for civilian use, while MILNET was created for Military use. Communication between two networks is possible and this network came to be known as the Internet.

INTERNET REQUIREMENTS

Hardware Requirements for Internet

- IBM PC or compatible
- Intel Pentium 233 MHz or better
- 32 MB (recommended 64 MB or more)
- 56 KB PS (or better) modem
- 15″ or 17″ SVGA monitor
- 10 MB free hard disk space

Software Requirements for Internet

- Windows 95, Windows 98 or Windows NT
- Internet provider
- Netscape Navigator or Internet Explorer
- E-mail capabilities

Others Requirement

A telephone Line or Dedicated Internet line

MODEM

The process of modulation and demodulation, that is the conversion of digital data to analog form and vice-versa, is carried out by a special device called a Hence, when an analog facility is used for data communication between two digital devices (say a terminal and a computer), two modems are required, one near each digital device. As shown in Fig. 1.1, the digital signal generated at the terminal is converted to analog form by the modulator of the modem placed near it. The analog signal is transmitted through the telephone lines and then converted to digital form by the demodulator of the modem placed near the computer. This digital data is processed by the computer. The processed digital information is modulated to analog form and returned via the telephone lines to the terminal where the analog signals are demodulated to digital form for display on the terminal.

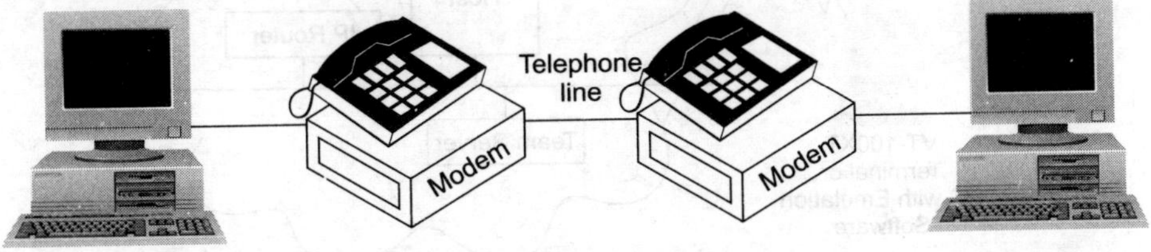

Fig. 1.1

WHY USE MODEMS?

There are two main reasons for using modems. They allow higher speeds of transmission on a given analog line, and they reduce the effects of noise and distortion. Modems can do a lot more than simply transport data across telephone lines. A good modem can also perform tests and checks on how it is operating. Some modems are able to vary their transmission rate, commonly measured in baud. While the typical baud rate is 300, some modems can transmit at 1 1200 baud or even 9600 baud. Some of the more expensive modems actually contain microprocessors that allow them to operate and function under a large number of different circumstances. These modems are called smart modems.

INTERNET CONNECTION OPTIONS

There are several ways to connect to the Internet. The more expensive services provide more features, more flexibility, and greater data transfer capacity. Large companies choose dedicated Internet access or LAN dial-up. Smaller organization are happy with PC dial-UI) access and terminal emulation, which provides E-mail and other services through a service provider's computer.

PC DIAL-UP AND TERMINAL EMULATION

This is the simplest and cheapest type of connection to Internet. All you need is a computer with a modern (attached to a phone line) and any of the popular telecommunications packages. The individual user dials-in to an Internet service provider. Each user has an account on the provider's Internet Services host computer to the Internet.

Many Internet access providers also allow dial-up users to interactively roam the Internet in real-Lime, logging on to remote hosts with TELNET, searching indexed databases with WAIS, and locating esoteric information with Gopher.

The equipment and software for PC dial-up is essentially the same—whether the user is dialing from a stand alone computer at home, or from a networked computer equipped with a local modem, or from a networked computer using a communications server and a shared pool of network modems.

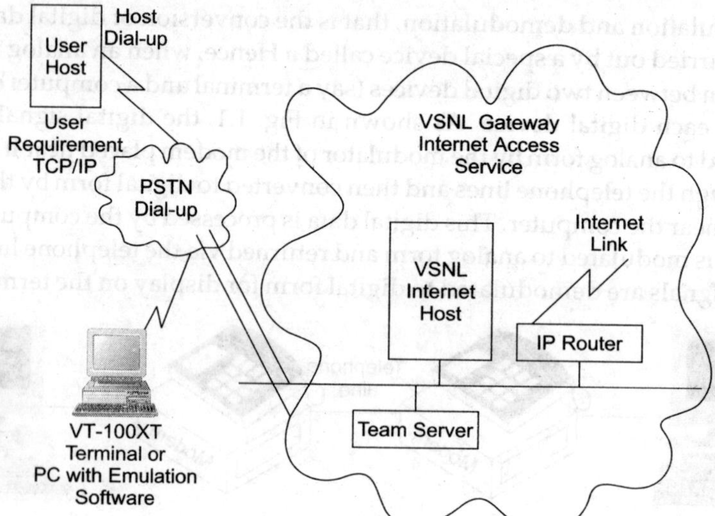

Fig. 1.2

The computer uses terminal emulation software, and not TCP/IP to talk to the Internet host computer. The Internet host computer uses TCP/IP to talk to the rest of the Internet. Ordinary modems and telephone lines provide adequate throughput for PC dial-up access, though fast modems make the experience more pleasant.

DEDICATED INTERNET ACCESS

The most popular Internet access for companies and institutions is a dedicated phone line connecting your LAN to the Internet 24 hours a day. However, a dedicated Internet access also requires substantial initial investment in equipment. The main continuing cost is a flat monthly fee for the use of the line. It varies with line capacity, and line capacity determines how many users can connect to Internet simultaneously.

INTERNET SERVICE PROVIDERS

After deciding what kind of Internet connection you need, look for a service provider. A wide variety of providers support a wide variety of Internet connection services. Here are some hints. If you want to connect an individual PC to the Internet, you can choose a national provider. If you want to connect several geographically scattered sites, contact one of the major national and regional Internet providers. To get a dedicated line into the Internet, contact one of the leased line; the more traffic it can carry, the more expensive it will be. A final word of caution before connecting your network to the Internet. A large number of people have made it their pastime to break into computer networks. There are many stories of companies that have plugged their networks into the Internet, not realizing that at that point, anyone from Russia to the Fiji Islands could look at their files.

Whichever system you choose, make sure it is implemented. It is easy to believe that you are invisible, but that is not true. Tools are now available to automatically scan for new IP addresses as well as weak points in your defenses. Set your security properly before you connect to the Internet for the first time.

WORLD WIDE WEB

World Wide Web also called the WEB, www, and W3 is an interlink collection of hypertext documents (Web pages) residing on Web servers and other documents, menus, and databases, available via URLs (uniform resource locators). Web documents are marked for formatting and linking with hypertext markup language (HTML) and Web servers use hypertext transport protocol to deliver Web pages.

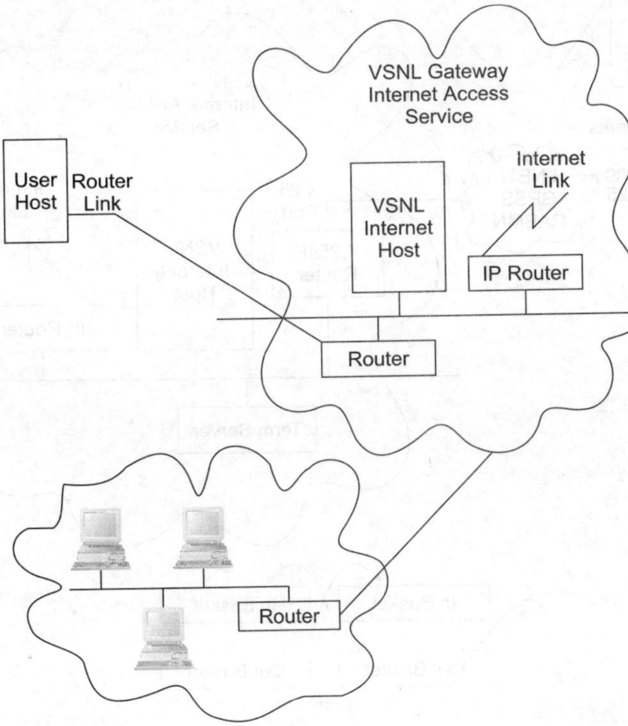

Fig. 1.3

ELECTRONIC MAIL

Electronic mail or E-mail is used to send messages on the Internet. E-mail is fast, flexible and reliable E-mail systems may Fe confirmed to a single computer s1ystem or network or enable users to send

E-mail anywhere in the world. The sent messages are stored in electronic mailboxes until the recipient gets them. The messages should specify the recipient's address. You çan also send the message to several users at once. To send any E-mail you need an address. Internet has an addressing scheme *i.e.*, aname@aserver.com. Here name identifies a user, is pronounced "at" and aserver.com identifies the location of the server computer.

E-MAIL ARCHITECTURE

Electronic Mail (e-mail) is a system whereby a computer user can exchange messages with other computer users or group of users via a communications network. The backbone of an electronic mail system is a communications network that connects remote terminals to a central system or a local area network that interconnects personal computers. Users can send mail to a single recipient or they can broadcast it to any number of selected users on the system.

The method for receiving mail depends on the sophistication of the system. When multitasking personal computers and workstations are used, mail can be delivered to users while they are working on something else. Otherwise, users have to interrogate their mailboxes (disk space) in a central system, or file server.

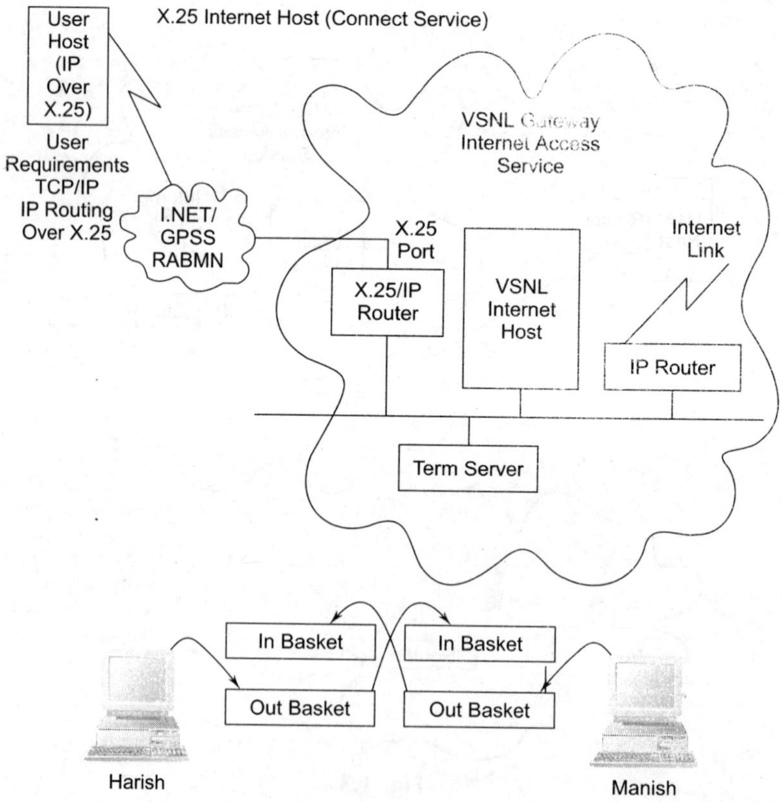

Fig. 1.4

Electronic mail programs often come with local area network software or as add-on options. Or, they may be independent programs designed to work with a particular network environment. A simple form of electronic mail is the use of facsimile (fax) terminal in remote locations, which uses the public telephone network for transmission. The advantage of fax is that an form of information printed on paper can be transmit.

Electronic mail eliminates most of the problems and delays of getting a physical document from one person to another. Like a telephone call, the message becomes available to the addressee as soon as it is sent. But unlike a telephone call, both parties need not be available simultaneously for communication to succeed. Thus electronic mail effectively eliminates "telephone tag" when two parties try to communicate–invariably when one of them is out the office.

A computer-based message system (CBMS) such as a local area network electronic mail, has many advantages over terminal-based electronic delivery systems. LAN electronic mail allows users to create, send, receive, and store messages. Mail can be sent to individuals or groups. In addition to supporting direct communications, the CBMS permits computers to store messages for reference, forwarding, and for a variety of other purposes.

LANs that are user—defined, not device-defined yet another advantage in a mail system. A user-defined system enables a user with a password to log on to any convenient PC. That PC will have the same access privileges, file directories, and mail addresses as the user's own workstation. Therefore, in a user-defined LAN, a person can send and receive personal messages from any place in the network, as long as the proper password is given. Unauthorized people cannot read personal mail or send messages.

WEB SEARCH ENGINES

Today, Internet acts as a big repository of information. Searching for Information on the web is quite difficult because of its large size. A number of search engines are available which uses the databases and index them to locate the sites that meet the criteria.

Some popular search engines are

- Google
- Yahoo
- MSN

EXERCISE

1. Explain Internet and why we use Internet?
2. Define Modem.
3. Explain E-Mail Architecture.
4. What are the Hardware and Software requirement of Internet?
5. Explain the term Web Search Engine.

CHAPTER 2

CLIENTS AND SERVER

CLIENTS AND SERVER

The term client refers to the application involved in a communication that actively initiates the contact and the term server refers to the application that passively waits for contact.

Characteristics of Client's Software

- An application program that performs computations locally
- Is needed temporarily for remote access
- Is invoked directly by a user
- Executes only for one session
- Runs locally on users computer
- Can access multiple services
- Doesn't require special hardware.

Characteristics of Server Software

- Is invoked automatically at the time of booting
- Runs on a shared computer
- Accepts requests from clients
- Require special hardware and operating systems
- Can handle multiple clients at the same time.

HOST AND TERMINALS

Host: A host is a main computer that has all the programs, data and the processing elements. It has its own method of connection. A terminal may connect to the host and may or may not have the store and forward capabilities. To connect computers in a network, cables, connector cards and software's are needed.

TCP/IP

TCP (Transmission Control Protocol) and IP (Internet Protocol) are the two types of protocol. A protocol is defined as a set of standard rules that lets communication between computers takes place. The first one TCP (Transmission Control Protocol) is a reliable, connection-oriented protocol that allows stream of bytes from the sender to be delivered to the receiver without error this is the protocol of the transport layer. The Internet layer defines a protocol called IP (Internet Protocol) to specify an official packet format. Its job is to deliver IP packets to the destination.

The TCP/IP model has five layers:

- Application
- Transport
- Network
- Data link
- Physical

WWW: WORLD WIDE WEB

WWW is a worldwide hypermedia system. It is the most important feature of the Internet. This is commonly called web and is the main reason of popularity of the Internet. WWW is a system of Internet servers responsible for supporting specially formatted pages and documents. The document follows HTML and support links to the other documents, graphics, audio and videos.

All the Internet servers are not essentially the part of WWW. The Internet and worldwide web are redefining the global community. Businesses have found a new venue for two-way communication with customers in the web site. Not only can businesses advertise, but they also can provide much more information that customers, students and investors usually wouldn't be able to obtain easily. WWW is a graphical representation of information on Internet.

HYPERTEXT

The web consists of client and server computers that are capable of handling multimedia documents. The client computers use browser software (like Internet Explorer or Netscape Navigator) to view documents. WWW uses HTTP (Hypertext Transfer Protocol) as its underlying protocol HTTP defines the way messages are formatted and transmitted HFT'P is a stateless protocol. The commands are executed without caring for the previous commands HTML is an acronym for Hypertext Markup Language. This is the language used to create www pages. The hypertext objects refer to the text and object linked to each other.

URL (UNIFORM RESOURCE LOCATOR)

URL is an addressing system that is used by WWW as a standard system for specifying a particular site or file on web. it combines information about the type of protocol being used, the address of the site where the resource is located, the sub-directory location and name of the file.

For each web page a URL is specified. This gives a worldwide name of the page. A URL has three parts

- the scheme (protocol)
- domain name server (DNS) where the page is located
- the filename for the page

When the URL is given, the browser searches for the host name using the DNS and then establishes the connection with the host. The filename is then send over the connection using the protocol specified. The host then returns the page.

The URL scheme is open-ended and can be used for other protocols besides being used for web pages.

Other protocols used in URLs are

- HTTP
- FTP
- News
- GOPHER
- File for files at local end
- Telnet
- Mailto

WEB BROWSERS

Because the web is a hypertext environment, special browser is required to use hypertext capability.

A software application used to locate and display web pages. The important browsers are

- Microsoft Internet Explorer
- Netscape Navigator
- Spyglass Mosaic

These browsers display graphics as well as text and also present multimedia information.

Internet Explorer

This browser is by Microsoft and is distributed free. This enables you to view web pages. The Internet explorer supports Active X and VB script. It runs only under windows. It also supports Java and Java script.

Netscape Navigator

It is a web browser by Netscape Communications Corporation. Earlier it was given free but now it is sold commercially. This is most popular as it can run on all the major platforms like Windows, Macintosh's and Unix.

Mosaic

It was originally produced by National Centre for Supercomputing Applications (NCSA). It was distributed as freeware. Later the commercial development of the program was given to spyglass.

IP ADDRESS AND DNS (DOMAIN NAME SYSTEM)

There are many users of Internet. There is a need to have a system of naming in which the names are managed centrally so that there are no naming conflicts. That is why DNS was evolved. DNS is a hierarchical domain based naming scheme. When a name is given its IP address is returned by a program known as resolver. The IP addresses are then used for establishing the connection to the required destination.

DNS domain is hierarchically structured to manage it with ease. At the top level, domains are of two types

- **Generic**
  - *.com (commercial)*
  - *.edu (educational)*
  - *.gov (government)*
  - *.mil (military)*
  - *.net (networking)*
  - *.org (non-commercial organisations)*
- **Country**
  - *uk (United Kingdom)*
  - *ni (Netherland)*
  - *ca (Canada)*
  - *in (India)*

The domain name forms the last part of the name.

ISP (INTERNET SERVICE PROVIDER)

Nobody truly owns the Internet. It is maintained by a group of volunteers. Control of this is through ISP, which comprises a number of limited central locations responsible for assigning Internet addressed to users, and for making connections between valid users.

INTERNET SECURITY

There are a number of methods that aim at providing security over the Internet.

- Cryptograph systems: This involves coding messages so that only authorized users can read them.
- Authentication: This is the process of verifying that the concerned person is the user of the account and that he has the rights of particular services on a network.
- Use of SIM (Subscriber Identity Module)
- Digital Signatures
- Using a digital certificate issued by a CA (Certificate of Authority)
- Use of firewalls: Firewall is used by the source host to limit access.

WEB SEARCH ENGINES

Today, internet acts as a big repository of information. Searching for Information on the web is quite difficult because of its large size. A number of search engines are available which uses the databases and index them to locate the sites that meet the criteria.

Some popular search engines are

- yahoo
- lycos
- altavista

- netscape
- webcrawler

NET SURFING

This term is used for going through the web pages on the Internet by using hyperlinks.

FTP

This is File Transfer Protocol needed for sending files on the Internet. The files can be uploaded or downloaded by using FTP. The term acronym' FTP is used for downloading public files using FTP. Some anonymous FTP sites do not even prompt for name and you don't need to identify yourself. Some FTP sites are protected. These restrict the unauthorized access to individuals not having a valid id. File Transfer Protocol (FTP), a standard Internet protocol, is the simplest way to exchange files between computers on the Internet. Like the Hypertext Transfer Protocol (HTTP), which transfers displayable Web pages and related files, and the Simple Mail Transfer Protocol (SMTP), which transfers E-mail, FTP is an application protocol that uses the Internet's TCP/IP protocols. FTP is commonly used to transfer Web page files from their creator to the computer that acts as their server everyone on the Internet. It's also commonly used to download programs and other files to your computer from other servers.

As a user, you can use FTP with a simple command line interface (for example, from the Windows MS-DOS Prompt window) or with a commercial program that offers a graphical user interface. Your Web browser can also make FTP requests to download programs you select from a Web page. Using FTP, you can also update (delete, rename, move, and copy) files at a server. You need to logon to an FTP server. However, publicly available files are easily accessed using anonymous FTP

Basic FTP support is usually provided as part of a suite of programs that come with TCP/IP. However, any FTP client program with a graphical user interface usually must be downloaded from the company that makes it.

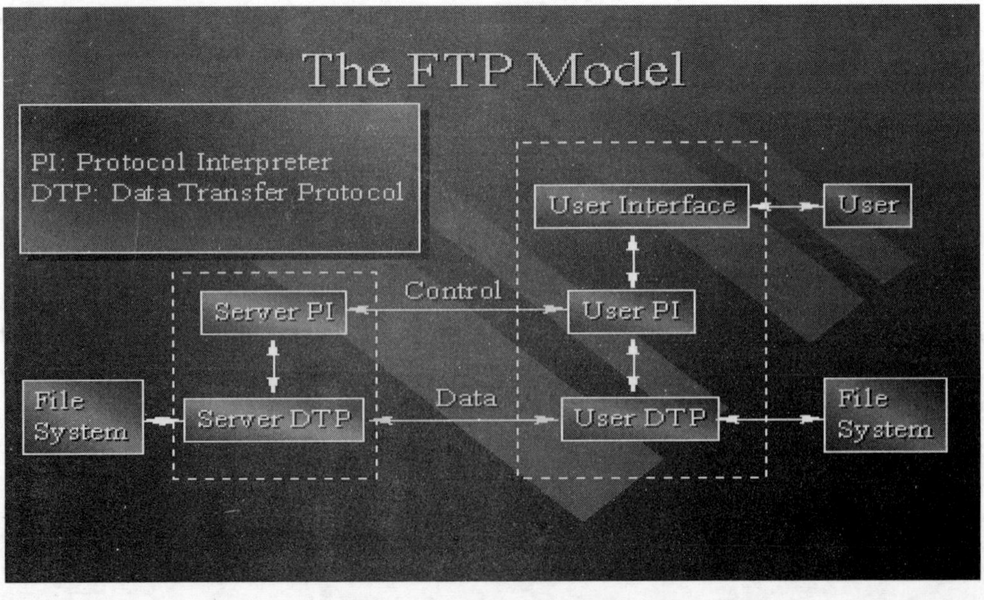

SIMPLE MAIL TRANSFER PROTOCOL (SMTP)

What is SMTP?

SMTP or Simple Mail Transfer Protocol is a way to transfer e-mail reliably and efficiently. SMTP is a relatively simple, text-based protocol, where one or more recipients of a message are specified (and in most cases verified to exist) and then the message text is transferred. You can think of SMTP as the language that mail servers use to communicate among themselves.

Since this protocol started out as purely ASCII text-based, it did not deal well with binary files. Standards such as MIME were developed to encode binary files for transfer through SMTP. SMTP is used to send mail to the recipient's mailbox. The recipient may use various methods to access the emails in his mailbox. A couple of methods that are very popular are POP and IMAP. These protocols allow a user to access his messages stored on a remote mail server.

Basics of SMTP

When the user wants to send a message to someone, the sender-SMTP establishes a two-way transmission channel to a receiver-SMTP. SMTP commands are generated by the sender-SMTP and sent to the receiver-SMTP. SMTP replies are sent from the receiver-SMTP to the sender-SMTP in response to the commands. In case a direct connection does not exist between the sender and the final destination, the message may be sent via one or more relay SMTP-servers. The relay SMTP-servers first acts as receivers and then relays the message to the next SMTP. To be able to provide the relay capability the SMTP-server must be supplied with the name of the ultimate destination host as well as the destination mailbox name.

Once the transmission channel is established, the SMTP-sender sends a MAIL command indicating the sender of the mail. If the SMTP-receiver can accept mail it responds with an OK reply. The SMTP-sender then sends a RCPT command identifying a recipient of the mail. If the SMTP-receiver can accept mail for that recipient it responds with an OK reply; if not, it responds with a reply rejecting that recipient (but not the whole mail transaction). The SMTP-sender and SMTP-receiver may negotiate several recipients. When the recipients have been negotiated the SMTP-sender sends the mail data, terminating with a special sequence. If the SMTP-receiver successfully processes the mail data it responds with an OK reply. The dialog is purposely lock-step, one-at-a-time.

SMTP Commands

Given below are some basic commands with their brief descriptions. The SMTP standard defines many more commands, most of which are optional to implement. For a detailed study, the user should see RFC 821.

HELLO (HELO)

This is the first command that is sent when a connection is established. It is used to identify the sender-SMTP to the receiver-SMTP. The argument field contains the host name of the sender-SMTP.

```
HELO <SP> <domain> <CRLF>
```

Note: <SP> stands for a space and <CRLF> stands for a combination of Carriage Return and Linefeed.

The receiver-SMTP identifies itself to the sender-SMTP in the connection greeting reply, and in the response to this command.

MAIL (MAIL)

There are three steps to SMTP mail transactions. The transaction is started with a MAIL command, which gives the sender identification. A series of one or more RCPT commands follows giving the receiver information. Then a DATA command gives the mail data. And finally, the end of mail data indicator confirms the transaction.

The first step in the procedure is the MAIL command. The <reverse-path> contains the source mailbox.

```
MAIL <SP> FROM:<reverse-path> <CRLF>
```

If accepted, the receiver-SMTP returns a 250 OK reply. The <reverse-path> can contain more than just a mailbox. The <reverse-path> is a reverse source routing list of hosts and source mailbox. The first host in the <reverse-path> should be the host sending this command.

RECIPIENT (RCPT)

This command gives a forward-path identifying one recipient. If accepted, the receiver-SMTP returns a 250 OK reply, and stores the forward-path. If the recipient is unknown the receiver-SMTP returns a 550 Failure reply. This second step of the procedure can be repeated any number of times.

```
RCPT <SP> TO:<forward-path> <CRLF>
```

The <forward-path> can contain more than just a mailbox. The <forward-path> is a source routing list of hosts and the destination mailbox. The first host in the <forward-path> should be the host receiving this command.

DATA (DATA)

The third step in the procedure is the DATA command.

```
DATA <CRLF>
```

If accepted, the receiver-SMTP returns a 354 Intermediate reply and considers all succeeding lines to be the message text. When the end of text is received and stored the SMTP-receiver sends a 250 OK reply.

Since the mail data is sent on the transmission channel the end of the mail data must be indicated so that the command and reply dialog can be resumed. SMTP indicates the end of the mail data by sending a line containing only a period.

The mail data includes the memo header items such as Date, Subject, To, Cc, From etc. To see details about possible memo headers and their formats, read RFC 822 - Standard for the format of ARPA Internet text message

VERIFY (VRFY)

This command asks the receiver to confirm that the argument identifies a user. If it is a user name, the full name of the user (if known) and the fully specified mailbox are returned.

```
VRFY <SP> <user name> <CRLF>
```

RESET (RSET)

This command specifies that the current mail transaction is to be aborted. The receiver must send an OK reply.

```
RSET <CRLF>
```

NOOP (NOOP)

This command does not affect any parameters or previously entered commands. It specifies no action other than that the receiver send an OK reply.

```
NOOP <CRLF>
```

QUIT (QUIT)

This command specifies that the receiver must send an OK reply, and then close the transmission channel.

```
QUIT <CRLF>
```

In order to make SMTP workable, the following minimum implementation is required for all receivers:

MAIL

RCPT

DATA

RSET

NOOP

QUIT

Relaying of Messages

The sender specifies the forward-path of the recipient while sending the mail. This forward-path includes not only the address of the recipient but also the route that is to be taken to reach there. This information is useful if there is not direct link between the sender and the recipient. The forward-path may be a source route of the form "@ÇNE,@TWO:VARUN@THREE", where ONE, TWO, and THREE are hosts. ONE is the name of the host who is receiving this command. ONE will forward this message to host TWO. TWO will in turn forward the message to THREE, which is the host on which the user VARUN has a mailbox.

Conceptually the elements of the forward-path are moved to the reverse-path as the message is relayed from one server-SMTP to another. The reverse-path is a reverse source route, (*i.e.,* a source route from the current location of the message to the originator of the message). The reverse-path is used in case a reply has to be sent to the sender.

If a server-SMTP has accepted the task of relaying the mail and later finds that the forward-path is incorrect or that the mail cannot be delivered for whatever reason, then it must construct an "undeliverable mail" notification message and send it to the originator of the undeliverable mail (as indicated by the reverse-path).

TELNET

This is a utility needed to log on another system and use various services on that host. You can use telnet to host computers all around the world in a cost-effective way. The telephone charges are at the local rates and you can connect to remote computers.

IRC (INTERNET RELAY CHAT)

This is basically a chat program that allows users to chat and participate in discussions. People can go to different channels representing common 'topics. The user can see the list of available channels and select the one of his choice. You can also create your own room. IRC was developed in 1988 as a replacement for the old Unix program, talk users specific channels in which a specific subject or theme is usually predominant. Channels can be either public, where anybody on Internet can Join, or private, in which two people can carry on a private conversion.

USENET NEWS

It is a group of 5000 newsgroup, or discussion groups on every conceivable subjects. This is like a massive distributed bulletin board service with hundreds of newspapers. People subscribe to newsgroups for worldwide discussions on specific topics. They can also post articles for automatically posting to all the subscribers.

At the top level of newsgroup hierarchies are

- comp (for computer related issues)
- sci
- humanities
- news
- rec (for recreational activities)
- soc (for social activities)
- talk
- misc

MAILING LISTS

Corporate managers often need to send a message to each of their subordinates, customers or suppliers. This gives rise to the idea of a mailing list. A mailing list is a list of email addresses. When a message is sent to the mailing list, copies are delivered to all members in the list.

INTERNET TALKING

This includes services like diapad. Here the user can talk over the existing Internet connection and can save his telephone bill.

GOPHER

This is a menu driven program that used by users of Internet to find files and other resources. The users can go all around looking for information on various servers and in libraries of information.

'Gopherspace' is the term used for the space made up of interconnected Gopher libraries. Browser allow access to gopher servers in the, same way as they allow access to www pages. Gopher pages may lack rich formatting.

ARCHIE

Archie is a search program that helps the users to locate files they want by looking through hundreds of different anonymous FTP sites. It is a collection of servers' responsible for keeping track of file locations in several anonymous FTP sites. The Archie Servers talk to each other and collect the information in a huge, global database that is updated periodically.

JUG-HEAD

Jug-head is similar to veronica, however it searches only a confined area of Gopherspace. Jughead server maintains a database of all the menu items within the part of gopherspace specified by the system administrator. A Jug-head search is faster than a veronica search.

VERONICA

Veronica is 'Very Easy, Rodent-Oriented, Netwide Index to computer Archieves'. This is also a search tool that allows the user to quickly scan Gopherspace for specified files and directories.Veronica is accessed using Gopher. The search specification are given in veronica and then thousands of Gopher servers are searched and files and directories that satisfy the criteria are filtered and returned to the user.

WAIS

WAIS or Wide Area Information Service consists of a few designated servers that keep the directory of servers having the actual information. WAIS maintains a master index proceeding the links to all sites related to the request specified by the user and identifies the links most closely related to the topic. WAIS programs can work independently of the web can be reached using special gateway software's available on the web pages.

HTTP

Hyper Text Transfer Protocol (HTTP) is needed when a browser interacts with a web server. HTTP allows a browser to request for items and the server then returns there unambiguously in the exact format as specified by the request.

HTML

Each browser must contain an HTML interpreter to display pages. HTML is Hyper Text Markup Language. Web pages use this representation. This includes the general guidelines to display a page and allows a browser to choose the details. Therefore, two browsers can display an HTML document in different ways.

The HTML details are provided by using TAGS.

A tag specifies an action that takes effect immediately. Some tags may provide formatting details.

```
<HTML>
<HEAD>
<TITLE>
</TITLE>
</HEAD>
<BODY>
Body of doc
</BODY>
</HTML>
```

INTRANETS

The use of internet-based technology is the internal usage of organizations is known as intranets. These are basically "baby" Internets. They use the same network facilities that Internet does, but restrict the access to confine it to the company itself. The intranet client is a universal browser using TCP/IP protocol. The server in the organization may use any operating system as long as they support TCP/IP, they are part of the intranet.

The services may include

- Mail
- File transfers
- Web services
- Audio services
- Video services

The enhanced services lead to the term "Full Service Intranets". The components of the intranet include

- Network
- TCP/IP
- Hardware for hosting intranet services
- Software
- Mail servers
- Browsers
- Others like HTML editors, CGI, Active X.

Usefulness of Services

- Reduced cost of printing, paper, mailing software distribution etc.
- Reduced telephone expenses
- Easier, faster access to marketing information
- Access to remote locations
- Latest and up-to-date information
- Easier access to customers, partners
- Accurate and timely information
- Reduced information search time
- Reduced support cost and development costs
- Sharing of resources and skills
- Cheaper and faster creation
- Revising of tools and information.

Intranet Implementation

The emphasis during intranet implementation is on creating a system that will be subjected to constant change and updating. The existing databases and software's should be used. The important steps during intranet implementation include taking care of the following issues:

- Planning
- Servers and software platforms
- Operating system selection
- Proxy server requirement
- HTML editors and other content creation software
- Training
- Study of existing databases
- Web publishing needs.
- Subnet details

Intranet Administrator

Intranet administrator is also called Webmaster. The responsibilities of **Webmaster include:**

- Setting up and maintaining of the companies internal or external websites
- Maintain the functionality of intranet servers and services
- Updating the contents of mail directories
- Integrating with databases
- Connecting with the internet
- Knowing the organization's business, network technology and programming languages.
- Working with intranet committee.

In larger organizations, several people collectively act as the Webmaster or as an intranet team.

EXERCISE

PART A:

Fill in the Blanks

1. A computer on the internet is called ____________.
2. ____________ language is used in web pages.
3. ____________ is called binary file.
4. ____________ searches presenting everything to you in the form of menus.
5. ____________ is a collective name for all Gopher servers on the net.
6. Modems that understands Hayes At instruction are called ____________
7. ____________ is a brand name for modem make.
8. Free software available for downloading on the net is called ____________
9. ____________ enables a user to log into a remote computer.
10. Gopher is the electronic equivalent of ____________
11. TCP/IP has ____________ layers.
12. Jughead helps to find specified information on Gopher directions.

13. Cyberspace is a virtual universe of ____________ and ____________.
14. ____________ is a software program that connects to another computer and gets data from it.
15. E-mail is the method of ____________ with other users in the ____________.
16. Network of network is ____________.
17. Last part of an E-mail address is ____________.
18. Software to search for web resources is called ____________.
19. ____________ connect web pages.
20. An IP address is a ____________ bit number.

PART B:

1. Write a short note on SMTP and FTP.
2. Define TCP/IP in detail.
3. What is Gopher?
4. What is Internet Relay Chat?
5. What is Telnet?
6. Explain DNS with suitable example.

3 CHAPTER

Object Oriented Programming

INTRODUCTION

Object oriented programming focuses on defining a hierarchy of classes of objects, each with associated data fields and methods. Subclasses inherit data fields and methods from their parent and ancestor classes.

Object oriented programming is generally considered good for software re-use and maintenance as objects, with clearly defined interfaces can be used and modified with relatively little effort. It has been widely used in creating user interface libraries and toolkits.

OBJECT ORIENTED PROGRAMMING

OOP is a programming language that is based on the Object Orientation methodology. The major advantages of OOP are its capabilities for creating flexible, modular programs and its abilities of code reuse.

Object orientation provides a new paradigm for software construction. In this new paradigm, objects and classes are the building blocks, while methods, messages and inheritance produce the primary mechanisms object oriented programming is a programming method that combines data and instructions into a self-sufficient "object". In an object-oriented program, the design is represented by objects. Objects have two sections, fields (instance variables) and methods. Fields represent what an object is.

Methods represent how an object is used. These fields and methods are closely tied to the real world characteristics and use the object. An object is used by means of its methods.

BASICS OF OOP

Some characteristics of object-oriented programming are

- Objects

- Classes
- Encapsulation
- Abstraction
- Inheritance
- Polymorphism

Objects

An object is a concrete instance of some classes. Objects are the basic entities in an object-oriented system. Each object is denoted by a name and has a state. The variables within the object express everything about the object (state) and the methods specify how it can be used (behavior). For example, a bicycle has a state (the number of wheels and the current gear), and behavior (breaking, accelerating, slowing down, changing gears).

Method

A method is a function or a procedure that access to the internal state of the object needed to perform some operation. So, methods are functions defined inside the classes that operate on instances of those classes.

Classes

A class is a blueprint or a prototype that defines the variables (data) and methods (code) common to all objects of certain kind. The class serves as a user-defined type. A class thus defines a data type that behaves like the built-in types of a programming language. An object is an individual instance of a class.

Access to the variables and methods declared in a class depend on whether they are declared in private or public. A variable declared as public is visible everywhere. A variable declared as private is not visible outside the class.

Encapsulation

One of the fundamental principles of object technology is that the internals of an object are private to that object and may not be accessed or even examined from outside the object.

Encapsulation is a simple yet reasonably effective building tool. It is a way of packaging information. Encapsulation allows the programmer to present clearly specified interfaces around the services they provide. The programmer can decide what should be hidden and what is intended to be visible.

Some advantages of encapsulation are:

- Managing complexity
- Managing change
- Protecting data

Message	:	The communication media of objects.
Subclass	:	A class inheriting another class's properties.
Data hiding	:	Protecting data by preventing direct access to it. This is done by making the data, private or protected members of a class.

Abstraction

Abstraction refers to the act of representing essential features without including the background details or explanations. It is the art of concentrating on the essential thing and ignoring the non-essential things.

Classes that use the concept of data abstraction are known as "abstract data types". Abstract data types are achieved by making certain variables and methods in a class as private. Abstraction makes an objects look either unique, similar to or different from other objects depending on viewers.

For example, people do not think of a computer as a set of thousands of individual parts. They can ignore the details of how the CPU, Monitor and Keyboard work.

Inheritance

A class can inherit characteristics from another class. Classes embody coherent and cohesive concepts. Classes can be used to create more specialized classes via inheritance. For example, a bicycle can be specialized to a kind built by a given manufacturer.

Inheritance is the mechanism that allows the programmer to derive new classes from existing classes. The derived classes inherit the methods and data structures of the parent class. One can add new methods or override the inherited methods to make them more specific. The parent methods will not be affected because of these modifications.

For example, different kinds of bicycles like bikes can inherit the common properties from a bicycle class and can override the methods in the parent class to suit local properties. For example, some racing bikes have an extra set of gears with a lower gear ratio.

Polymorphism

Polymorphism is a feature that allows one interface to be used for a general class of actions. The concept of polymorphism is often expressed by the phrase "one interface, multiple methods". It basically refers to the ability of giving the same name to methods in different subclasses. The individual methods may implement similar tasks but can be differentiated by the type of arguments passed to them.

By using polymorphism different methods can be created with the same name but with different parameters.

Dynamic Binding

Dynamic binding means, when a method is called within a program are associated with the program at runtime rather than at compile time.

FUNDAMENTAL CHARACTERISTICS OF OOP

1. Everything in a object oriented paradigm is an object.
2. Each object is an instance of a class.
3. A class is the definition of methods and data, which are other objects.
4. An object of a class encapsulates its own state (data values) but the same behavior (methods).
5. A class may communicate with others via messages, which requests associate with required arguments. By this way, a class can ask other classes to perform actions without knowing the details of the work under those actions. This is called Information Hiding.

6. A class may inherit another class properties. Let class A inherits from class B. Then, class A is a subclass of class B and, on the other way around, class B is a super class of class A.
7. All classes can be arranged into an inheritance hierarchy, which is a single root tree. These specifications belong to the interface part of a new OOP learning environment.
8. A class can override behaviors inherited from its superclass.
9. More than one class may share some common interface but embed different details inside. This is called Polymorphism, which means many forms.

BENEFITS OF OBJECT ORIENTED PROGRAMMING

OOP provides a better system structure in modeling the real world. The abstract data type concept, along with its associated encapsulation and information hiding principles, increases software reliability and modifiability by decoupling object specification and object implementation. Polymorphism and dynamic binding increase flexibility and reusability of code by allowing the creation of generic software components and new classes using existing code.

Inheritance allows software code to be extensible and reusable, since new attributes and new operations can be added through the creation of new child object classes without modifying the original code. OOP facilitates prototyping and an iterative approach to software development that more closely follows software life cycle. OOP permits the use of reusable software component libraries to build modules/units of new software applications.

THE USAGE OF THE KEYWORDS PUBLIC, PRIVATE AND PROTECTED

Public

The data members and methods declared as public can be used by its own methods and also by other classes.

Protected

Data members are made accessible to derived classes but private to other classes.

Private

The data members and methods declared as private can only be used by the methods of its own class.

APPLICATIONS OF OOP

The following areas are example for application of OOP:

- Simulation and modeling.
- User interface design and Windowing System.
- OOD (Object Oriented Database).
- Artificial Intelligence and Expert System.
- Neural Networks.
- Web Designing.
- CAD/CAM system.

EXERCISE

1. What is an Object Oriented Programming ?
2. Explain the Basic Concepts of OOP.
3. What is the difference between a Class and an Object ?
4. What are the advantages of OOP ?
5. List any five applications of OOP technology.
6. Compare and Contrast Structured Procedural Programming (SPP) and OOP.
7. Explain the fundamental characteristic of OOP.
8. Write short notes on
   (*a*) Inheritance
   (*b*) Dynamic Binding
   (*c*) Abstraction
   (*d*) Encapsulation
   (*e*) Polymorphism

4

CHAPTER

INTRODUCTION TO JAVA

INTRODUCTION TO JAVA

Java is an object-oriented programming language with a built-in application-programming interface (API) that can handle graphics and user interfaces and that can be used to create applications or applets. Because of its rich set of API's, similar to Macintosh and Windows, and its platform independence, Java can also be thought of as a platform in itself. Java also has standard libraries for doing mathematics. Much of the syntax of Java is the same as C and C++. One major difference is that Java does not have pointers. However, the biggest difference is that you must write object-oriented code in Java. Procedural pieces of code can only be embedded in objects. In the following we assume that the reader has some familiarity with a programming language. In particular, some familiarity with the syntax of C/C++ is useful.

In Java we distinguish between applications, which are programs that perform the same functions as those written in other programming languages, and applets, which are programs that can be embedded in a Web page and accessed over the Internet. Our initial focus will be on writing applications. When a program is compiled, a byte code is produced that can be read and executed by any platform that can run Java.

Features of Java

1. Simple
2. Object-Oriented
3. Java is safe and secure
4. Interpreted and High performance
5. Multi-Threaded
6. Garbage Collection
7. Platform Independent
8. Dynamic

Java is Simple

Java was designed to make it much easier to write bug free code. Assuming that you have some programming experience, you will not find Java hard to master. If you already understand the basic concept of Object Oriented Programming, learning java will be easier. Because Java is simple, it is easy to read and write. Obfuscated Java isn't nearly as common as obfuscated C. There aren't a lot of special cases or tricks that will confuse beginners.

About half of the bugs in C and C++ programs are related to memory allocation and de allocation. Therefore the second important addition Java makes to provide bug-free code is automatic memory allocation and deallocation. The C library memory allocation functions malloc () and free () are gone as are C++'s destructors.

Java is an excellent teaching language, and an excellent choice with which to learn programming. The language is small so it's easy to become fluent. The language is interpreted so the compile-run-link cycle is much shorter. The runtime environment provides automatic memory allocation and garbage collection so there's less for the programmer to think about. Java is object-oriented unlike basic so the beginning programmer doesn't have to unlearn bad programming habits when moving into real world projects. Finally, it's very difficult (if not quite impossible) to write a Java program that will crash your system, something that you can't say about any other language.

Java is Object Oriented

Object oriented programming is the catch phrase of computer programming in the 1990's. Although object oriented programming has been around in one form or another since the Simula language was invented in the 1960's, it's really begun to take hold in modern GUI environments like Windows, Motif and the Mac. In object oriented programs data is represented by objects. Objects have two sections, fields (instance variables) and methods. Fields tell you what an object is. Methods tell you what an object does. These fields and methods are closely tied to the object's real world characteristics and behavior. When a program is run messages are passed back and forth between objects. When an object receives a message it responds accordingly as defined by its methods.

Object oriented programming is alleged to have a number of advantages including:

- Simpler, easier to read programs
- More efficient reuse of code
- Faster time to market
- More robust, error-free code

Java is Safe

Java was designed from the ground up to allow for secure execution of code across a network, even when the source of that code was untrusted and possibly malicious. This required the elimination of many features of C and C++. Most notably there are no pointers in Java. Java programs cannot access arbitrary addresses in memory. All memory access is handled behind the scenes by the (presumably) trusted runtime environment. Furthermore Java has strong typing. Variables must be declared, and variables do not change types when you aren't looking. Casts are strictly limited to casts between types that make sense. Thus you can cast an int to a long or a byte to a short but not a long to a boolean or an int to a String. Java implements a robust exception handling mechanism to deal with both expected and unexpected errors. The worst that an applet can do to a host system is bring down the runtime environment. It cannot bring down the entire system.

Most importantly Java applets can be executed in an environment that prohibits them from introducing viruses, deleting or modifying files, or otherwise destroying data and crashing the host computer. A Java enabled web browser checks the byte codes of an applet to verify that it doesn't do anything nasty before it will run the applet.

Java is High Performance

Java byte codes can be compiled on the fly to code that rivals C++ in speed using a "just-in-time compiler." Several companies are also working on native-machine-architecture compilers for Java. These will produce executable code that does not require a separate interpreter, and that is indistinguishable in speed from C++.

While you'll never get that last ounce of speed out of a Java program that you might be able to wring from C or Fortran, the results will be suitable for all but the most demanding applications.

Java enables the creation of Cross-platform programs by compiling into an intermediate representation called Java Bytecode. This code can be interpreted on any system that provides a Java Virtual Machine. As explained earlier, while it is true that Java was engineered for interpretation, the java Bytecode was carefully designed so that it would be easy to translate directly into native machine code for high performance by using just-in-time compiler.

It is certainly possible to write large programs in Java. The HotJava browser, the Eclipse integrated development environment, the LimeWire file sharing application, the jEdit text editor, the JBoss application server, the Tomcat servlet container, the Xerces XML parser, the Xalan XSLT processor, and the javac compiler are large programs that are written entirely in Java.

As explained earlier, while it is true that Java was engineered for interpretation, the java Bytecode was carefully designed so that it would be easy to translate directly into native machine code for high performance by using just-in-time compiler.

Java is Multi-Threaded

Java is inherently multi-threaded. A single Java program can have many different threads executing independently and continuously. Three Java applets on the same page can run together with each getting equal time from the CPU with very little extra effort on the part of the programmer.

This makes Java very responsive to user input. It also helps to contribute to Java's robustness and provides a mechanism whereby the Java environment can ensure that a malicious applet doesn't steal all of the host's CPU cycles.

Unfortunately multithreading is so tightly integrated with Java, that it makes Java rather difficult to port to architectures like Windows 3.1 or the PowerMac that don't natively support preemptive multi-threading.

There is a cost associated with multi-threading. Multi-threading is to Java what pointer arithmetic is to C, that is, a source of devilishly hard to find bugs. Nonetheless, in simple programs it's possible to leave multi-threading alone and normally be OK.

Java is Garbage Collected

You do not need to explicitly allocate or deallocate memory in Java. Memory is allocated as needed, both on the stack and the heap, and reclaimed by the *garbage collector* when it is no longer needed. There's no malloc (), free (), or destructor methods. There are constructors and these do allocate memory on the heap, but this is transparent to the programmer.

The exact algorithm used for garbage collection varies from one virtual machine to the next. The most common approach in modern VMs is generational garbage collection for short-lived objects, followed by mark and sweep for longer lived objects. I have never encountered a Java VM that used reference counting.

Platform Independent

Java is a platform for application development. A platform is a loosely defined computer industry buzzword that typically means some combination of hardware and system software that will mostly run all the same software. A Windows program will not run on a computer that only runs DOS. A Mac application can't run on a Unix workstation. VMS code can't be executed on an IBM mainframe, and so on. Therefore major commercial applications like Microsoft Word or Netscape have to be written almost independently for all the different platforms they run on. Netscape is one of the cross-platformest of major applications, and it still only runs on a minority of platforms.

Java solves the problem of platform-independence by using byte code. The Java compiler does not produce native executable code for a particular machine like a C compiler would. Instead it produces a special format called *bytecode*. Java byte code written in hexadecimal, byte by byte, looks like this:

CA FE BA BE 00 03 00 2D 00 3E 08 00 3B 08 00 01 08 00 20 08

This looks a lot like machine language, but unlike machine language Java byte code is exactly the same on every platform. This byte code fragment means the same thing on a Solaris workstation as it does on a Macintosh PowerBook. Java programs that have been compiled into byte code still need an interpreter to execute them on any given platform. The interpreter reads the byte code and translates it into the native language of the host machine on the fly. The most common such interpreter is Sun's program java (with a little j). Since the byte code is completely platform independent, only the interpreter and a few native libraries need to be ported to get Java to run on a new computer or operating system. The rest of the runtime environment including the compiler and most of the class libraries are written in Java.

All these pieces, the javac compiler, the java interpreter, the Java programming language, and more are collectively referred to as Java.

Dynamic

Java programs carry with them substantial amounts of run-time type information's that is used to verify and resolve accesses to objects at run time. This makes it possible to dynamic link code in a safe and expedient manner. This is crucial to the robustness of the applet environment, in which small fragments of bytecode may be dynamically updated on a running system.

Java's Magic : The Byte Code

The key that allows java to solve both the security and the portability problems just described is that the output of a java Compiler is not executable code. Rather it is Bytecode. Bytecode is highly optimized set of instructions designed to be executed by the Java run time system, which is called the Java Virtual Machine (JVM). That is in its standard form, the JVM is an interpreter for Bytecode.

Firstly, the JVM must accept Bytecode instructions. Bytecode defines the instruction set that executes the user's application program. Each of the JVM'S stack based instruction consists of a one-byte opcode immediately follwed by Zero or more operands. The JVM's instruction set defines 200 standard opcode, 25 quick variation of some opcode (to support dynamic binding), and three reserved opcode. The opcode dictated to the JVM what action to be perfomed.

Secondly, a binary format known the class file format must be used to convey Bytecode and related class infrastructure in a platform-independent manner. Static tools such as class file viewers can look at this representation.

Finally, a verification algorithm must be used for identifying programs that will not compromise the integrity of the JVM. A verifier is a key component of the Java security architecture. It will check that the code respects the syntax of the Bytecode language and that it respects the language rule.

The Difference between C++ and Java

1. Java does not include structure and union.
2. Java does not support operator overloading.
3. It is not possible to declare unsigned integer in Java.
4. Java does not allow goto, size of and typedef.
5. Pointers don't exist in java.
6. Java object are passed by reference only.
7. Java does not allow default argument.
8. Java does not allow automatic type conversion.
9. Java does not have a preprocessor.
10. There are no header files and delete operators.
11. Java does not support the multiple inhritance, but we can accomplish through the feature called "interface".
12. Java is Platform Independent.

The Execution of a Java Program

A Java program is a collection of class definitions written in the Java language (3). A Java compiler then complie or translate this into a collection of bytes that are represented in a form known as the *class* file format. This is a platform independent intermediate representation of the program. As an alternative to being stored in a file these bytes can also be kept in a database, across a network or as part of a Java Archive File (JAR).

The *class* file contains bytecode instructions for the JVM [32]. This file will have the same semantics as the original Java source code. The JVM will execute these instructions to produce executable code. Figure 4.1 illustrates the steps involved in the execution of a Java program. As long as the original semantics of the instructions are obeyed, the JVM is free to perform the actions specified by the bytecode in any way it sees fit. There are a number of implementation techniques a JVM has to choose from and the memory layout is also determined by the JVM implementation. The bytecode instructions can be interpreted or alternatively the JVM can translate them into native machine code.

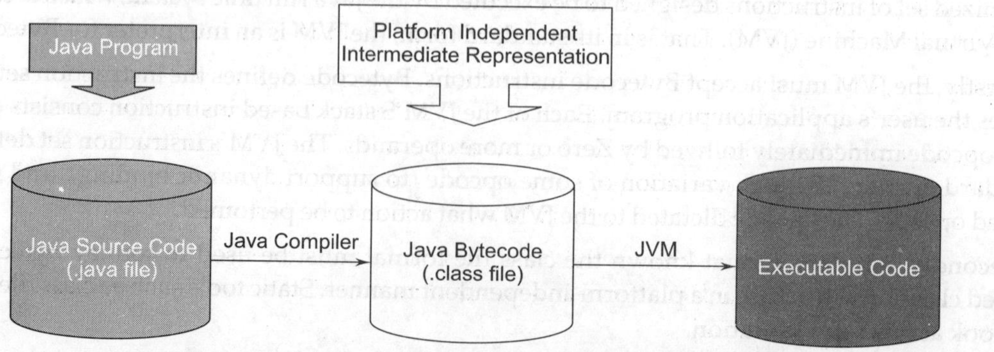

Fig. 4.1 Steps in the execution of a Java program.

EXERCISE

1. Explain the characteristics of Java.
2. What is Byte code?
3. List any five difference between C++ and Java.
4. Java is 100% Object Oriented Programming Language Comment on it.
5. Define Java Virtual Machine.

5 CHAPTER

BEGINNING OF JAVA PROGRAMMING

INTRODUCTION

This chapter lays a firm groundwork to Java, Explaining in brief about Java Programming.

Before Developing our java program we must know the following things

1. Java is case sensitive.
2. Java program must be entered in a file with file name as the class name.
3. Every statements end with a semicolon.
4. Every program must have a main.
5. Any editor must be required (DOS Editor, Notepad, etc).

THE HELLO WORLD APPLICATION

```
class HelloWorld {
  public static void main (String args[]) {
    System.out.println("Hello World!");
  }
}
```

Hello World is very close to the simplest program imaginable. When you successfully compile and run it, it prints the words "Hello World!" on your display. Although it doesn't teach very much programming, it gives you a chance to learn the mechanics of typing and compiling code. The goal of this program is not to learn how to print words to the terminal. It's to learn how to type, save and compile a program. This is often a non-trivial procedure, and there are a lot of things that can go wrong even if your source code is correct. To write the code you need a text editor. You can use any text editor like Notepad,

You should not use a word processor like Microsoft Word or WordPerfect since these save their files in a proprietary format and not in pure ASCII text. If you absolutely must use one of these, be sure to tell it to save your files as pure text. Generally this will require using Save As... rather than save. If you have an integrated development environment like BlueJ 1.0 or Borland JBuilder that will include a text editor you can use to edit Java source code. It will probably change your words various colors and styles for no apparent reason. Don't worry about this yet. As long as the text is correct you'll be fine.

A CLOSER LOOK AT THE FIRST JAVA PROGRAM

```
class HelloWorld
{
```

This line uses the keyword class to declare that a new class is being defined. Example is an identifier that is the name of the class. The entire class definition, including all of its member, will be between the opening curly braces ({) and the closing curly brace (}). The use of the curly braces in Java is identical to the way they are used in C,C++, and C#.

The next line of code is

```
public static void main (String args[]) {
```

This line begins the **main ()** method. The public keyword is access Specifiers, which allow the programmer to control the visibility of class members. When a class member is proceed by **public,** then that member may be accessed by code in which it is declared. In this case **main ()** is declared as a **public,** since it must be called by code outside of its class when the program is started. The keyword void simply tells the compiler that **main ()** does not return any value. **String args []** declares a parameter named **args,** which is an array of type string object of type string stores character string. In this case, **args** receives any command line arguments present when the program is executed.

When you've chosen your text editor, type or copy the above program into a new file. For now type it exactly as it appears here. Like C and unlike Fortran, Java is case sensitive so **System.out.println** is not the same as **system.out.println.** CLASS is not the same as class, and so on.

SAVING FILES ON WINDOWS

Some Windows text editors including Notepad add a three letter "*.txt*" extension to all the files they save without telling you. Thus you can unexpectedly end up with a file called "HelloWorld. java.*txt*." This is wrong and will not compile. If your editor has this problem, you should get a better editor. However in the meantime enclose the filename in double quotes in the Save dialog box to make editor save the file with exactly the name you want.

Save it by : C:\jdk1.3\bin\ HelloWorld.java

COMPILING AND RUNNING HELLO WORLD

To compile the program ,we must run the java compiler javac , with the name of source file.

```
C:\Javac HelloWorld.java
```

If your computer responds with

```
error: Can't read: HelloWorld.java
```

Now we check it, the class path variable by typing the following command.

C: \javac

C: \java

```
javac: Command not found
java: Command not found
```

It probably means your CLASSPATH environment variable isn't properly set up. Assuming that Java is properly installed on your system there are three steps to creating a Java program:

1. writing the code
2. compiling the code
3. running the code

Under Unix, compiling and running the code looks like this:

```
$ javac HelloWorld.java
$ java HelloWorld
Hello World
$
```

Under Windows, it's similar. You just do this in a DOS shell. (if your class path is set)

```
C:> javac HelloWorld.java
C:> java HelloWorld
Hello World
C:>
```

Notice that you use the .java extension when compiling a file, but you do not use the .class extension when running a file.

CLASSPATH PROBLEMS

If you get any message like this,

```
javac HelloWorld
Can't find class HelloWorld
```

It probably means your CLASSPATH environment variable isn't properly set up. Make sure it includes the current directory as well as the location where the classes.zip file was installed. Type the following command.

C:\ set path=D:\jdk1.3\bin; (if java (jdk1.3) folder is in D:)

And check

C:\javac

It produces the following output.

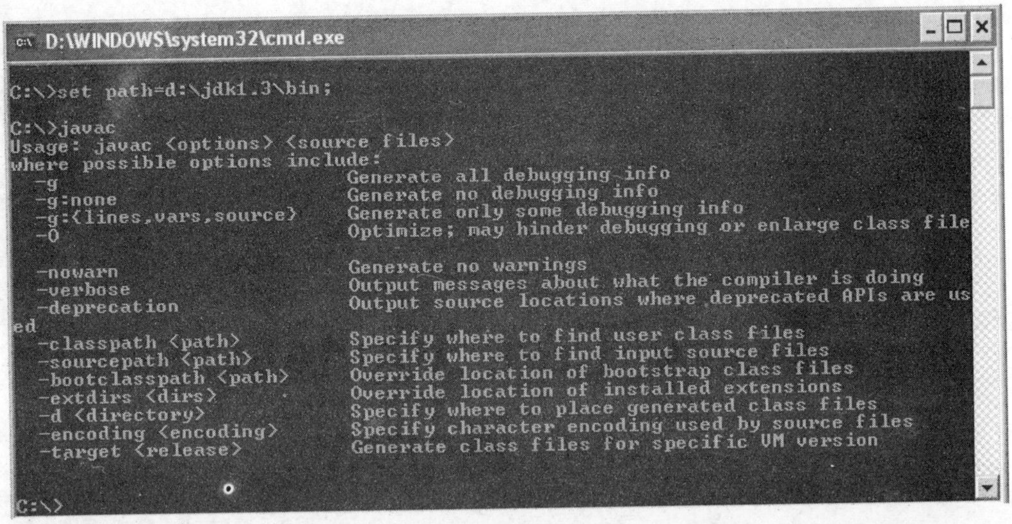

To Run and Compile

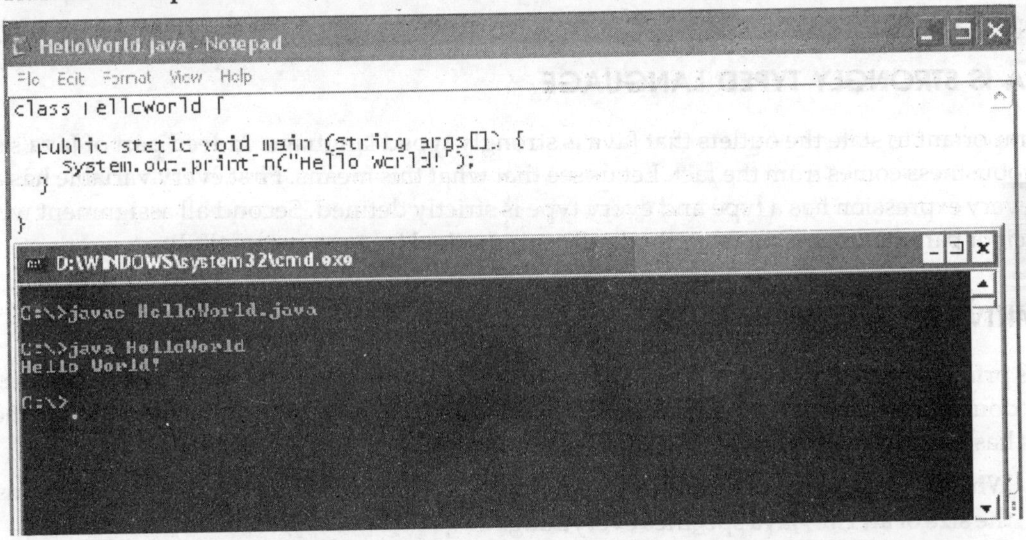

EXERCISE

1. Write a Java program to display your name, roll number, and subjects.
2. Write the steps for running and compiling a Java program.
3. What do you understand by public static void main (String args[]).

6 CHAPTER

DATA TYPE VARIABLES AND ARRAY

JAVA IS STRONGLY TYPED LANGUAGE

It is important to state the outlets that Java is strongly typed language. Indeed part of Java's safety and robustness comes from the fact. Let us see that what this means. First every variable has a type and every expression has a type and every type is strictly defined. Second all assignment whether explicit or parameter passing in method calls, are checked for type compatibility.

PRIMITIVE DATA TYPES IN JAVA

Java's primitive data types are very similar to those of C. They include boolean, byte, short, int, long, float, double, and char. The boolean type has been added. However the implementation of the data types has been substantially cleaned up in several ways.

1. Where C and C++ leave a number of issues to be machine and compiler dependent (for instance the size of an `int`) Java specifies everything.
2. Java prevents casting between arbitrary variables. Only casts between numeric variables and between sub and superclasses of the same object are allowed.
3. All numeric variables in Java are signed.

`sizeof` isn't necessary in Java because all sizes are precisely defined. For instance, an `int` is always 4 bytes. This may not seem to be adequate when dealing with objects that aren't base data types. However even if you did know the size of a particular object, you couldn't do anything with it anyway. You cannot convert an arbitrary object into bytes and back again.

JAVA'S PRIMITIVE DATA TYPES

`boolean`

1-bit. May take on the values `true` and `false` only.

`true` and `false` are defined constants of the language and are not the same as `True` and `False`, `TRUE` and `FALSE`, zero and nonzero, 1 and 0 or any other numeric value. Booleans may not be cast into any other type of variable nor may any other variable be cast into a boolean.

byte

1 signed byte (two's complement). Covers values from -128 to 127.

short

2 bytes, signed (two's complement), -32,768 to 32,767

int

4 bytes, signed (two's complement). -2,147,483,648 to 2,147,483,647. Like all numeric types int may be cast into other numeric types (byte, short, long, float, double). When *lossy* casts are done (*e.g.* int to byte) the conversion is done modulo the length of the smaller type.

ADDITION OF INTEGERS IN JAVA

```
class AddInts {
  public static void main (String args[]) {
    int i = 1;
    int j = 2;
    System.out.println("i is" + i);
    System.out.println("j is" + j);
    int k = i + j;
    System.out.println("i + j is" + k);
    k = i - j;
    System.out.println("i - j is" + k);
  }
}
```

Here's what happens when you run AddInts:

```
C:\javac AddInts.java
C:\ java AddInts
i is 1
j is 2
i + j is 3
i - j is -1
```

long

8 bytes signed (two's complement). Ranges from -9,223,372,036,854,775,808 to +9,223,372,036,854,775,807. This makes it useful when big, whole number are needed. For example

```
// compute Distance light travels using long variable.
class light
{
public static void main (String args[ ])
{
    int speedoflight;
    long days;
    long seconds;
    long distance;
    speedoflight=18600;
    days=1000;
    seconds= days * 24 * 60 * 60;
    distance= speedoflight *seconds;
    System.out.println("\nDistance"+ distance+" miles");
}}
```

Output

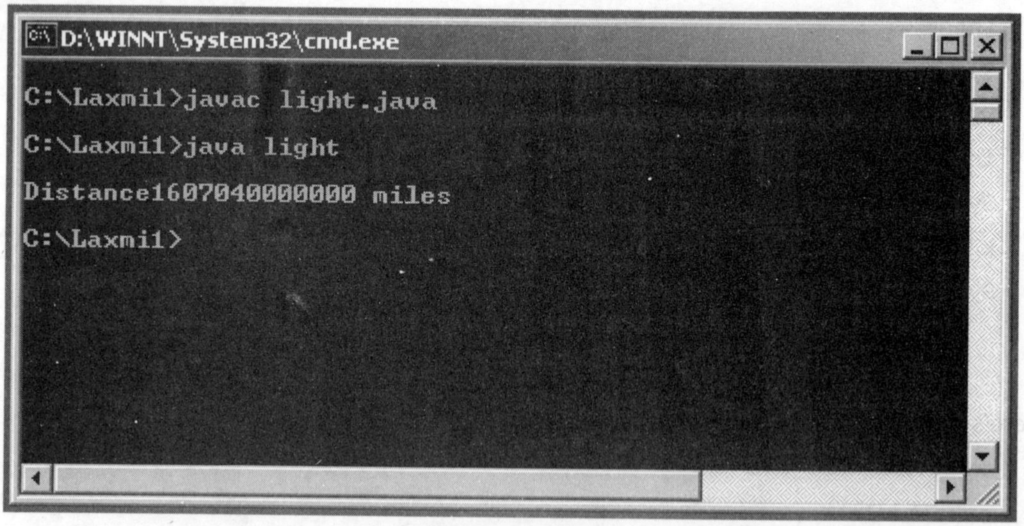

`float`

4 bytes, IEEE 754. Covers a range from 1.40129846432481707e-45 to 3.40282346638528860e+38 (positive or negative).

Like all numeric types floats may be cast into other numeric types (`byte`, `short`, `long`, `int`, `double`). When *lossy* casts to integer types are done (*e.g.* `float` to `short`) the fractional part is truncated and the conversion is done modulo the length of the smaller type.

`double`

8 bytes IEEE 754. Covers a range from 4.94065645841246544e-324d to 1.79769313486231570e+308d (positive or negative).

ADDITION OF DOUBLES IN JAVA

Doubles are treated much the same way, but now you get to use decimal points in the numbers. This is a similar program that does addition and subtraction on doubles.

```
class AddDoubles {
  public static void main (String args[]) {
    double x = 7.5;
    double y = 5.4;
    System.out.println("x is " + x);
    System.out.println("y is " + y);
    double z = x + y;
    System.out.println("x + y is " + z);
    z = x - y;
    System.out.println("x - y is " + z);
  }
}
```

Here's the result:

```
% javac AddDoubles.java
% java AddDoubles
x is 7.5
y is 5.4
x + y is 12.9
x - y is 2.0999999999999996
char
```

2 bytes, unsigned, Unicode, 0 to 65,535

Chars are not the same as bytes, int, shorts or Strings.

```
// Char demo program
class Chardemo
{
public static void main (String args[ ])
{
char c1,c2;
c1 = 65;
c2 = 'A';
System.out.println ("C1 and C2");
System.out.println (c1+" "+c2);
```

```
    }
}
```

output:

c:\javac Chardemo.java

c:\java Chardemo

C1 and C2

A A

LITERALS

Literals represent the value of a certain type where the type describes the behavior of the value. Literals are pieces of Java source code that mean exactly what they say. For instance `"Hello World!"` is a string literal and its meaning is the words Hello World!

The string `"Hello World!"` looks like it's several things; but to the compiler it's just one thing, a `String`. This is similar to how an expression like 1,987,234 may be seven digits and two commas but is really just one number.

There are different types of literals. They are

- Number Literals
- Character Literals
- Boolean Literals
- String Literals

1. Number Literals

There are several Integer literals such as int long, octal, hexadecimal etc. Numbers can also be literals. `34` is an `int` literal and it means the number thirty-four. `1.5` is a `double` literal. `45.6`, `76.4E8` (76.4 times 10 to the 8th power) and – 32.0 are also `double` literals.

`34L` is a `long` literal and it means the number thirty-four. `1.5F` is a `float` literal. `45.6f`, `76.4E8F` and -32.0F are also `float` literals.

2. Character Literals

`char` literals are similar to string literals except they're enclosed in single quotes and must have exactly one character. For example `'c'` is a `char` literal that means the letter c. Table 1.1 shows the special codes that represent non-printable character and character from Unicode character set.

Escape	Meaning
\n	New line
\t	Tab
\b	Backspace
\r	Carriage Return
\f	Form Feed
\\	Backslash
\'	Single Quote
\"	Double Quote
\ddd	Octal
\xdd	Hexadecimal
\udddd	Unicode character

3. Boolean Literals

`true` and `false` are boolean literals that mean true and false.

4. String Literals

The double quote marks tell you this is a string literal. A string is an ordered collection of characters (letters, digits, punctuation marks, etc.). Although the String may have meaning to a human being reading the code, the computer sees it as no more than a particular set of letters in a particular order. It has no concept of the meaning of the characters. For instance it does not know that "two" + "two" is "four." In fact the computer thinks that "two" + "two" is "twotwo"

The quote marks show where the string begins and ends. However the quote marks themselves are not a part of the string. The value of this string is Hello World!, not "Hello World!" You can change the output of the program by changing Hello World to some other line of text.

A string in a Java program has no concept of italics, bold face, font family or other formatting. It cares only about the characters that compose it. Even if you're using an editor like NisusWriter that lets you format text files, **"Hello World!"** is identical to *"Hello World!"* as far as Java is concerned.

VARIABLES

Variables are the basic unit of storage in a program. A variable is defined by the combination of identifiers, a type and an optional initializer. In addition all variable having scope, which defines their visibility, and a lifetime.

Syntax:

Type identifier [=value];

IDENTIFIERS IN JAVA

Identifiers are the names of variables, methods, classes, packages and interfaces. Unlike literals they are not the things themselves, just ways of referring to them. In the HelloWorld program, `HelloWorld`, `String`, `args`, `main` and `println` are identifiers.

Identifiers must be composed of letters, numbers, the underscore _ and the dollar sign $. Identifiers may only begin with a letter, the underscore or a dollar sign.

Each variable has a name by which it is identified in the program. It's a good idea to give your variables mnemonic names that are closely related to the values they hold. Variable names can include any alphabetic character or digit and the underscore _. You cannot begin a variable name with a number. It is important to note that as in C but not as in FORTRAN or Basic, all variable names are case-sensitive. `MyVariable` is not the same as `myVariable`. There is no limit to the length of a Java variable name. The following are legal variable names:

- `MyVariable`
- `myvariable`
- `MYVARIABLE`
- `x`
- `i`

- `_myvariable`
- `$myvariable`
- `_9pins`
- `andros`
- `This_is_an_insanely_long_variable_name_that_just_keeps_going_and_going_and_going_and_well_you_get_the_idea_The_line_breaks_arent_really_part_of_the_variable_name_Its_just_that_this_variable_name_is_so_ridiculously_long_that_it_won't_fit_on_the_page_I_cant_imagine_why_you_would_need_such_a_long_variable_name_but_if_you_do_you_can_have_it`

The following are not legal variable names :

- `My Variable // Contains a space`
- `9pins // Begins with a digit`
- `a+c // The plus sign is not an alphanumeric character`
- `testing1-2-3 // The hyphen is not an alphanumeric character`

TIP: HOW TO BEGIN A VARIABLE NAME WITH A NUMBER

If you want to begin a variable name with a digit, prefix the name you'd like to have (*e.g.* 8ball) with an underscore, *e.g.* _8ball. You can also use the underscore to act like a space in long variable names.

Dynamic Initialization

Java allows variable to be initialize dynamically, using any expression valid at the time the variable is defined. For Example

```
// Dynamically variable declaration
class variableDyn
{
public static void main(String args[])
{
    double a=3.0,b=4.0;
    double c=Math.sqrt(a*a + b*b);
    System.out.println("value of C" + c);
}
}
```

ARRAY

An array is a group of like-types variable that are referred to a common name. Array of any type can be created and may have one or more dimensions. A specific element in an array is accessed by its index.

One dimensional array:

A one dimensional array is, essentially a list of like–typed variables.

Declaring Arrays

Like all other variables in Java, an array must have a specific type like `byte`, `int`, `String` or `double`. Only variables of the appropriate type can be stored in an array. One array cannot store both int and Strings, for instance. Syntax for array is

Type[] var-name;

or

type var-name[];

Like all other variables in Java an array must be declared. When you declare an array variable you suffix the type with `[]` to indicate that this variable is an array. Here are some examples:

```
int[] k;
float[] hkt;
String[] names;
```

This says that `k` is an array of int

hkt is an array of floats

`name` is an array of Strings.

In other words you declare an array like you declare any other variable except that you append brackets to the end of the type.

You also have the option to append the brackets to the variable instead of the type.

```
int k[];
float yt[];
String names[];
```

However, unlike in C, you cannot include the length of the array in the declaration. The following is a syntax error:

```
int k[3];
float hkt[7];
String name[100];
int k[];
float hkt[];
String name[];
```

Creating Arrays

Declaring arrays merely says what kind of values the array will hold. It does not create them. Java arrays are objects, and like any other object you use the `new` keyword to create them. When you create an array, you must tell the compiler how many components will be stored in it. Here's how you'd create the variables declared on the previous page:

```
k = new int[3];
hkt = new float[7];
name = new String[50];
```

The numbers in the brackets specify the length of the array; that is, how many slots it has to hold values. With the lengths above k can hold three int, hkt can hold seven floats and `name` can hold fifty Strings. **This step is sometimes called allocating the array since it sets aside the memory the array requires.**

Initializing Arrays

Individual components of an array are referenced by the array name and by an integer which represents their position in the array. The numbers you use to identify them are called subscripts or indexes into the array.

Subscripts are consecutive integers beginning with 0. Thus the array `k` above has components `k[0]`, `k[1]`, and `k[2]`. Since you start counting at zero there is no `k[3]`, and trying to access it will throw an `ArrayIndexOutOfBoundsException`. You can use array components wherever you'd use a similarly typed variable that wasn't part of an array. For example this is how you'd store values in the arrays above:

```
k[0] = 2;
k[1] = 5;
k[2] = -2;
hkt[17] = 7.5f;
name[7] = "HARISH";
```

This step is called **initializing the array or, more precisely, initializing the components of the array.** Sometimes the phrase "initializing the array" is used to mean when you initialize all the components of the array.

For even medium sized arrays, it's unwieldy to specify each component individually. It is often helpful to use for loops to initialize the array. Here is a loop which fills an array with the squares of the numbers from 0 to 100.

```
float[] squares;

squares = new float[101];

for (int i=0; i <= 100; i++) {

squares[i] = i*i;

}
```

Two things you should note about this code fragment:

1. Watch the fencepost! Since array subscripts begin at zero you need 101 components if you want to include the square of 100.
2. Although i is an int, it is promoted to a float when it is stored in squares, since squares is declared to be an array of floats.

System.arraycopy()

Although copying an array isn't particularly difficult, it is an operation which benefits from a native implementation. Therefore `java.lang.System` includes a static `System.arraycopy()` method you can use to copy one array to another.

```
public static void arraycopy(Object source, int sourcePosition, Object destina-
tion, int destinationPosition, int numberOfElements)
```

`System.arraycopy()` copies `numberOfElements` elements from the array `source`, beginning with the element at `sourcePosition`, to the array `destination` starting at `destinationPosition`. The `destination` array must already exist when `System.arraycopy()` is called. The method does not create it. The `source` and `destination` arrays must be of the same type.

For example,

```
int[] unicode = new int[65536];

for (int i = 0; i < unicode.length; i++) {

unicode[i] = i;

}

int[] latin1 = new int[256];

System.arraycopy(unicode, 0, latin1, 0, 256);
```

MULTI-DIMENSIONAL ARRAYS

So far all these arrays have been one-dimensional. That is, a single number could locate any value in the array. However sometimes data is naturally represented by more than one number. For instance a position on the earth requires latitude and a longitude.

The most common kind of multidimensional array is the two-dimensional array. If you think of a one-dimensional array as a column of values, you can think of a two-dimensional array as a table of values like this

	c0	c1	c2	c3
r0	0	1	2	3
r1	1	2	3	4
r2	2	3	4	5
r3	3	4	5	6
r4	4	5	6	7

Here we have an array with five rows and four columns. It has twenty total elements. However we say it has dimension five by four, not dimension twenty. This array is not the same as a four by five array like this one:

	c0	c1	c2	c3	c4
r0	0	1	2	3	4
r1	1	2	3	4	5
r2	2	3	4	5	6
r3	3	4	5	6	7

We need to use two numbers to identify a position in a two-dimensional array. These are the element's row and column positions. For instance if the above array is called `J` then `J[0][0]` is 0, `J[0][1]` is 1, `J[0][2]` is 2, `J[0][3]` is 3, `J[1][0]` is 1, and so on.

Here's how the elements in a four by five array called `M` are referred to:

M[0][0]	M[0][1]	M[0][2]	M[0][3]	M[0][4]
M[1][0]	M[1][1]	M[1][2]	M[1][3]	M[1][4]
M[2][0]	M[2][1]	M[2][2]	M[2][3]	M[2][4]
M[3][0]	M[3][1]	M[3][2]	M[3][3]	M[3][4]

Declaring, Allocating and Initializing Two Dimensional Arrays

Two dimensional arrays are declared, allocated and initialized much like one dimensional arrays. However you have to specify two dimensions rather than one, and you typically use two nested for loops to fill the array.This example fills a two-dimensional array with the sum of the row and column indexes

```
// Double dimensional Array
class FillArray
```

```
{
   public static void main (String args[]) {
      int[][] matrix;
      matrix = new int[4][5];
      for (int row=0; row < 4; row++)
       {
          for (int col=0; col < 5; col++)
            {
               matrix[row][col] = row+col;
            }
       }
      for (int row=0; row < 4; row++)
         {
            for (int col=0; col < 5; col++)
            {
               System.out.print( matrix[row][col]+" ");
            }
            System.out.print("\n");
         }
}}// End of Class
```

Output:

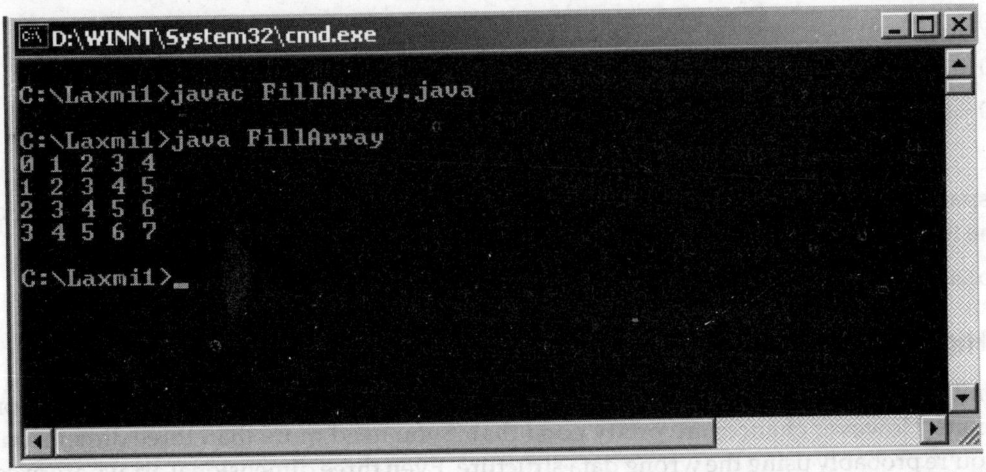

Of course the algorithm you use to fill the array depends completely on the use to which the array is to be put. The next example calculates the identity matrix for a given dimension. The identity matrix of dimension N is a square matrix which contains ones along the diagonal and zeros in all other positions.

```
class IDMatrix {
   public static void main (String args[]) {
     double[][] id;
     id = new double[4][4];
     for (int row=0; row < 4; row++) {
       for (int col=0; col < 4; col++) {
         if (row != col) {
          id[row][col]=0.0;
          }
         else {
          id[row][col] = 1.0;
          }
       }
     }
   }
}
```

In two-dimensional arrays `ArrayIndexOutOfBoundsExceptions` occur whenever you exceed the maximum column index or row index.

You can also declare, allocate, and initialize a two-dimensional array at the same time by providing a list of the initial values inside nested brackets. For instance the three by three identity matrix could be set up like this:

```
double[][] ID3 = {
{1.0, 0.0, 0.0},
{0.0, 1.0, 0.0},
{0.0, 0.0, 1.0}
};
```

The spacing and the line breaks used above are purely for the programmer. The compiler doesn't care. The following works equally well:

```
double[][] ID3 = {{1.0, 0.0, 0.0},{0.0, 1.0, 0.0},{0.0, 0.0, 1.0}};
```

Even Higher Dimensions

You don't have to stop with two dimensional arrays. Java permits arrays of three, four or more dimensions. However chances are pretty good that if you need more than three dimensions in an array, you're probably using the wrong data structure. Even three dimensional arrays are exceptionally rare outside of scientific and engineering applications.

The syntax for three dimensional arrays is a direct extension of that for two-dimensional arrays. The program below declares, allocates and initializes a three-dimensional array. The array is filled with the sum of its indexes.

```
class Fill3DArray {
  public static void main (String args[]) {
    int[][][] M;
    M = new int[4][5][3];
    for (int row=0; row < 4; row++) {
      for (int col=0; col < 5; col++) {
        for (int ver=0; ver < 3; ver++) {
          M[row][col][ver] = row+col+ver;
        }
      }
    }
  }
}
```

You need the additional nested `for` loop to handle the extra dimension. The syntax for still higher dimensions is similar. Just add another pair of brackets and another dimension.

Unbalanced Arrays

Like C Java does not have true multidimensional arrays. Java fakes multidimensional arrays using arrays of arrays. This means that it is possible to have unbalanced arrays. An unbalanced array is a multidimensional array where the dimension isn't the same for all rows. In most applications this is a horrible idea and should be avoided.

EXERCISE

1. Explain the literals in detail with suitable example.
2. Write a program to compute division of 2 without using any arithmetical operators.
3. Write a program to print the ASCII value of 'A' and 'Z'.
4. Write a program in java to swap the two variables without using the third variable.
5. Explain the Identifies of java with suitable example.
6. What is an Array? What are the uses of array?
7. Can an array support elements of different type? Justify your answer.
8. Write a program to store the three names and print them in sorting order.
9. Write a program in java for merge sort and Bubble sort.
10. Write a program to check whether a string is Palindrome or not.
11. Write a program in java to display four by four identity matrix.
12. List the Primitive Data Types of java.
13. Explain the three type of Integer constant.

CHAPTER 7

OPERATORS

JAVA OPERATORS

Java provides a rich operator environment. An operator is a symbol that operates on one or more arguments to produce a result. The Hello World program is so simple it doesn't use any operators, but almost all other programs you write will use operators.

Operator	Purpose
+	addition of numbers, concatenation of Strings
+=	add and assign numbers, concatenate and assign Strings
–	Subtraction
–=	subtract and assign
*	Multiplication
*=	multiply and assign
/	Division
/=	divide and assign
%	take remainder
%=	take remainder and assign
++	increment by one
––	decrement by one
>	greater than
>=	greater than or equal to
<	less than
<=	less than or equal to
!	boolean NOT

!= not equal to

&& boolean AND

|| boolean OR

== boolean equals

= Assignment

~ bitwise NOT

?: Conditional

instanceof type checking

| bitwise OR

|= bitwise OR and assign

^ bitwise XOR

^= bitwise XOR and assign

& bitwise AND

&= bitwise AND and assign

>> shift bits right with sign extension

>>= shift bits right with sign extension and assign

<< shift bits left

<<= shift bits left and assign

>>> unsigned bit shift right

>>>= unsigned bit shift right and assign

Most of its operator can be divided into four groups.

1. Arithmetic operator
2. Bitwise operator
3. Relational operator
4. Logical operator
5. Unary operator
6. Instance of operator
7. New ( ) operator

1. **Arithmetic operators :** Arithmetic operators are used in mathematics expression in the same way that they are used in algebra. Some Arithmetic operators are…

	Operator	Result
1.	+	Addition
2.	-	Subtraction
3.	*	Multiplication
4.	/	Division
5.	%	Modulus
6.	+ +	Increment
7.	+ =	Addition assignment
8.	- =	Subtraction assignment
9.	* =	Multiplication assignment
10.	/ =	Division assignment

11.	% =	Modulus assignment
12.	- -	Decrement

The Basic Arithmetic operators are:

1. Addition
2. Subtraction
3. Multiplication
4. Division

Addition and Subtraction and Division of Integers in Java

```
class AddInts {
  public static void main (String args[]) {
      int i = 1;
      int j = 2;
     System.out.println("i is " + i);
     System.out.println("j is " + j);
      int k = i + j;
     System.out.println("i + j is " + k);
      k = i - j;
     System.out.println("i - j is " + k);
      i= 10;
      j=5;
      K=i / j ;
     System.out.println("i / j is "+ k);
   }
}
```

Here's what happens when you run AddInts:

```
javac AddInts.java
java AddInts
i is 1
j is 2
i + j is 3
i - j is -1
I / j is 2
```

THE MODULUS OPERATOR

The Modulus operator % returns the remainder of a division operation. It can be applied to floating point as well as Integer type.

class modulusoperator

{

```
public static void main(String args[])
{
        int x = 42;
        int y = 10;
        z = x% y;
       System.out.println(" The Value of Z is " + z);
}}
```

Output:

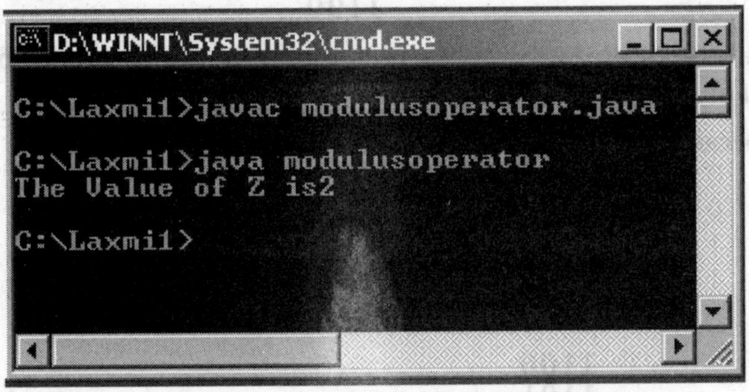

THE BITWISE OPERATORS

Java defines the several bitwise operators which can be applied to integer type such as long, int, short and byte. These operator acts on individual bits of their operands.

	Operator	Result
1.	~	Bitwise unary NOT
2.	&	Bitwise AND
3.	|	Bitwise OR
4.	^	Bitwise exclusive OR
5.	>>	Shift Right
6.	>>>	Shift Right zero fill
7.	<<	Shift Left
8.	&=	Bitwise AND assignment
9.	|=	Bitwise OR assignment
10.	^=	Bitwise exclusive OR assignment
11.	>>=	Shift right assignment
12.	>>>=	Shift right Zero fill assignment
13.	<<=	Shift left assignment

Bitwise Operator

Bitwise NOT : Also called the bitwise complement, the UNARY NOT operator, ~, inverts all of the bits of its operand. If the operand bit is 1 the result is 0 and if the operand bit is 0 the result is 1.

Operator	Result
0	1
1	0

Example :

~ (110010) = 001101

Bitwise AND : The AND operators, &, produces a 1 bit if both operands are also 1. A zero is produced in all other cases. Here is an example.

Operand 1	Operand 2	Result
0	0	0
0	1	0
1	0	0
1	1	1

Example :

```
  1100
& 1101
------
  1100
```

Bitwise OR : The bitwise operator is represented by the symbol | pipe symbol. It is an inclusive. Inclusive means that if either the two bits are 1 the result is 1.

Operand 1	Operand 2	Result
0	0	0
0	1	1
1	0	1
1	1	1

Example : 12 1 13

```
1100
1101
----
1101  The result is 13 in decimal.
```

Bitwise XOR : The bitwise XOR is represented by the symbol. It is called an exclusive or operation. It means if the two operators are different, the result is 1 otherwise the result is zero.

Operand 1	Operand 2	Result
0	0	0
0	1	1
1	0	1
1	1	0

Bitwise XOR Example :

```
1100
1101
----
0001  The give the result 1.
```

```
// Demonstration of Bitwise Operator
class bitwise
{
public static void main (String args[])
{
    int a = 1;
    int b = 2;
    int c = 3;
    a = a | 4;
    b>> = 1;
    c << = 1;
```

```
      a = a^c;
      System.out.println(" a =" + a);
      System.out.println(" b =" + b);
      System.out.println(" c=" + c);
   }
}
```

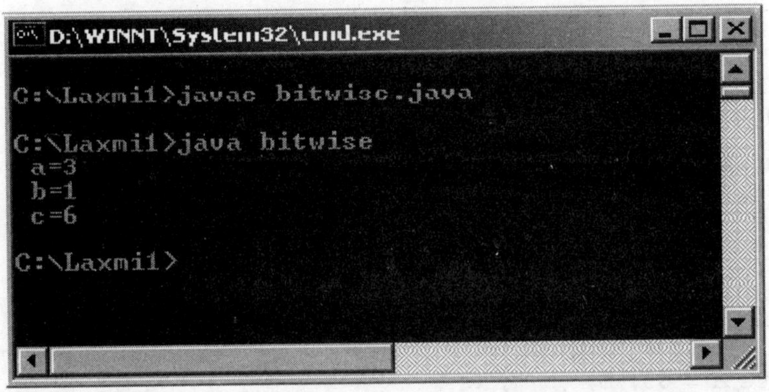

The Left shift : The left shift operator, <<, shift all of the bits in a value to the left a specified number of times. Syntax

Value << num

Here, num specifies the number of positions to left-shift the value in value. The << moves all of the bits in the specified value to the left by the numbers of bit positions specified by num.

Eq ⇒

0 0 0 0 1 1 0 1 (13)

left shift 1.

0 0 1 1 0 1 0 (26)

⟵

shift by 1 digit.

```
|| Left shift operator
class left shift
{
  public static void main (string args [])
  {
    byte a = 65, b ;
      b = a << 2 ;
    System.out.println ("Before shifting value of a" + a)
    System.out.println ("After shifting value of b" + b) ;
  }
}
```

The Right shift : The right shift operator, >>, shift all of the bits in a value to the right a specified number of times. Syntax.

Value << num

Here, num specifies the number of positions to right-shift the value in value. The >> moves all of the bits in the specified value to the right by the number of bits position specified by num.

Eq ⇒

0	0	0	0	1	1	0	1	(13)

⟶

Shift by 1 digit.

0	0	0	0	0	1	1	0	(6)

```
  || right shift operator.
class right shift
{
  Public static void main (String args [])
  {
        byte a = 65, b, ;
        b = a >> 2 ;
        system.out.println ("Before shifting the value of a = " + a),
        system.out.println ("After shifting the value of b = " + b) ;
  }
}
```

RELATIONAL OPERATORS

The relational operators determines the relationship that one operands has to the other.

Java support six relational operators

Operator	Result
= =	Equal to
!=	Not equal to
>	Greater than
<	Less than
> =	Greater than or equal to
< =	Less than or equal to

The outcomes of there operators are Boolean value Relational operators are more frequently used with conditional statement. eq⇒

```
  || Relation operators.
Class Relation
{
Public static void Main (string args [])
{
```

```
int a = 4 ;
string name ;
if (a = = 10)
{
  system.out.println ("Name is Harish"),
}
else
  system.out.println ("Name is Anuradha"),
 }
}
```

Relational Operators

x < y Less than	True if *x* is less than *y*, otherwise false.
x > y Greater than	True if *x* is Greater than *y*, otherwise false.
x <= y Less than or equal to	True if *x* is less than or equal to *y*, otherwise false.
x >= y Greater than or equal to	True if *x* is Greater than or equal to *y*, otherwise false.
x == y Equal	True if *x* is equals *y*, otherwise false.
x != y Not Equal	True if *x* is not equal to *y*, otherwise false.

Here are some code snippets showing the relational operators.

```
boolean test 1 = 1 < 2; // True. One is less that two.
boolean test 2 = 1 > 2; // False. One is not greater than two.
boolean test 3 = 3.5 ! = 1;   // True. One does not equal 3.5
boolean test 4 = 17*3.5 >= 67.0 - 62;    // True. 59.5 is greater than 5
boolean test 5 = 9.8*54 <= 654;    // True. 529.2 is less than 654
boolean test 6 = 6*4 == 3*8; // True. 24 equals 24
boolean test 7 = 6*4 <= 3*8; // True. 24 is less than or equal to 24
boolean test 8 = 6*4 < 3*8;   // False. 24 is not less than 24
```

This, however, is an unusual use of booleans. Almost all use of booleans in practice comes in conditional statements and loop tests. You've already seen several examples of this. Earlier you saw this

```
If (args. Length > 0) {
  system.out.println ("Hello" + args [0]);
}
```

`args.length > 0` is a Boolean value. In other words it is either `true` or it is `false`. You could write

```
boolean test = args.length > 0;
if (test) {
```

```
    system.out.println ("hello" + args [0]);
  }
```

instead. However in simple situations like this the original approach is customary. Similarly the condition test in a `while` loop is a boolean. When you write `while (i < args.length)` the `i < args.length` is a boolean.

RELATIONAL OPERATOR PRECEDENCE

Whenever a new operator is introduced you have to ask yourself where it fits in the precedence tree. If you look back at the example in the last section, you'll notice that it was implicitly assumed that the arithmetic was done before the comparison. Otherwise, for instance

```
boolean test 8 = 6*4 < 3*8;   // False. 24 is not less than 24
```

4 < 3 returns false which would then be multiplied by six and eight which would generate a compile time error because you can't multiply booleans. Relational operators are evaluated after arithmetic operators and before the assignment operator. == and != have slightly lower precedences than <, >, <= and >=. Here's the revised order :

1. *, /, % Do all multiplications, divisions and remainders from left to right.
2. +, - Next do additions and subtractions from left to right.
3. <, >, >=, <= Then any comparisons for relative size.
4. ==, != Then do any comparisons for equality and inequality.
5. = Finally assign the right-hand side to the left-hand side.

For example,

```
boolean b1 = 7 > 3 == true;
boolean b2 = true == 7 > 3;
b = 7 > 3;
```

TESTING OBJECTS FOR EQUALITY

<, >, <= and >= can only be used with numbers and characters. They cannot be used with Strings, booleans, arrays or other compound types since there's no well-defined notion of order for these objects. Is true greater than false? Is "My only regret is that I have but one life to give for my country" greater than "I have a dream" ?

Equality is a little easier to test however. `true` is equal to `true` and `true` is not equal to `false`. Similarly "My only regret is that I have but one life to give for my country" is not equal to "I have a dream." However you might be surprised if you ran this program :

```
class JackAndJil    {
  public static void main (String args []) {
    String s1 = new String ("Jack went up the hill.") ;
    String s2 = new String ("Jack went up the hill.") ;
    if (s1 ==s2)    {
      System.out.println ("The strings are the same.") ;
```

```
    }
    else if (s1 != s2)   {
      System.out.println ("The strings are not the same.") ;
    }
  }
}
```

The result is

```
The strings are not the same.
```

TESTING FOR EQUALITY WITH EQUALS()

That's not what you expected. To compare strings or any other kind of object you need to use the `equals (Object o)` method from `java.lang.String`. Below is a corrected version that works as expected. The reasons for this odd behavior go fairly deep into Java and the nature of object data types like strings.

```
class JackAndJill   {
  public static void main (String args [])      {
    String s1 = new String ("Jack went up the hill.") ;
    String s2 = new String ("Jack went up the hill.") ;
    if (s1.equals (s2))  {
      System.out.println ("The strings are the same.") ;
    }
    else {
      System.out.println ("The strings are not the same.") ;
    }
  }
}
```

LOGICAL OPERATORS IN JAVA

The relational operators you've learned so far (<, <=, >, >=, !=, ==) are sufficient when you only need to check one condition. However what if a particular action is to be taken only if several conditions are true? You can use a sequence of `if` statements to test the conditions, as follows:

```
if (x == 2) {
    if (y != 2) {
       System.out.println("Both conditions are true.");
    }
}
```

This, however, is hard to write and harder to read. It only gets worse as you add more conditions. Fortunately, Java provides an easy way to handle multiple conditions: the logic operators.

	Operator	Result
1.	&	Logical AND
2.	|	Logical OR
3.	^	Logical XOR
4.	||	Short-circuit OR
5.	&&	Short-circuit AND
6.	!	Logical Unary NOT
7.	&=	AND Assignment
8.	|=	OR Assignment
9.	^=	XOR Assignment
10.	==	Equal to
11.	!=	Not Equal to
12.	?:	Ternary if-then-else

`&&` is logical and. `&&` combines two boolean values and returns a boolean which is true if and only if both of its operands are true. For instance

```
boolean b;
b = 3 > 2 && 5 < 7; // b is true
b = 2 > 3 && 5 < 7; // b is now false
```

`||` is logical or. `||` Combines two boolean variables or expressions and returns a result that is true if either or both of its operands are true. For instance

```
boolean b;
b = 3 > 2 || 5 < 7; // b is true
b = 2 > 3 || 5 < 7; // b is still true
b = 2 > 3 || 5 > 7; // now b is false
```

The last logic operator is `!` which means not. It reverses the value of a boolean expression. Thus if `b` is true `!b` is false. If `b` is false `!b` is true.

```
boolean b;
b = !(3 > 2); // b is false
b = !(2 > 3); // b is true
```

These operators allow you to test multiple conditions more easily. For instance the previous example can now be written as

The Order of Evaluation of Logic Operators

When Java sees a `&&` operator or a `||`, the expression on the left side of the operator is evaluated first. For example, consider the following:

```
boolean b, c, d;
b = !(3 > 2); // b is false
c = !(2 > 3); // c is true
d = b && c; // d is false
```

When Java evaluates the expression `d = b && c;`, it first checks whether `b` is true. Here `b` is false, so `b && c` must be false regardless of whether `c` is or is not true, so Java doesn't bother checking the value of `c`.

On the other hand when faced with an || Java short circuits the evaluation as soon as it encounters a true value since the resulting expression must be true. This short circuit evaluation is less important in Java than in C because in Java the operands of && and || must be boolean which are unlikely to have side effects that depend on whether or not they are evaluated. Still it's possible to force them. For instance consider this code.

```
boolean b = (n == 0) || (m/n > 2);
```

Even if n is zero this line will never cause a division by zero, because the left hand side is always evaluated first. If n is zero then the left hand side is true and there's no need to evaluate the right hand side. Mathematically this makes sense because m/0 is in some sense infinite which is greater than two.

This isn't a perfect solution though because m may be 0 or it may be negative. If m is negative and n is zero then m/n is negative infinity which is less than two. And if m is also zero, then m/n is very undefined.

The proper solution at this point depends on your problem. Since real world quantities aren't infinite, when infinities start popping up in your programs, nine times out of ten it's a sign that you've lost too much precision. The remaining times are generally signals that you've left out some small factor in your physical model that would remove the infinity.

Therefore if there's a real chance your program will have a divide by zero error think carefully about what it means and how you should respond to it. If, upon reflection, you decide that what you really want to know is whether m/n is finite and greater than zero you should use a line like this

```
boolean b = (n != 0) && (m/n > 0);
```

Java has a decision operator called Conditional operator. The Conditional operator is also known as TERNARY OPERATOR. Syntax for ternary operator is as follows.

Test Condition ? Expression 1 : Expression 2.

Example :

$a = 10$;

$b = 14$;

if $(a > b)$

MAX = 9 ;

else

MAX = b ;

The above code is written as

MAX = $(a > b)$? a ; b ;

The conditional expression can be assigned to another variable.

UNARY OPERATOR

Increment and Decrement Operators : The ++ and -- are increment and decrement operators. Increment operator increment operands by value one eq :

$x = 10$;
$x{++}$ // x will became //

or

$x = 10$
$x = x + 1$; // x will became //

Similarly the decrement operators.

$x = 10$;
$x = x - 1$ || x will become 9
or
$x = 10$
$x = -$; || x will become 9.

There operators are also called prefix and postfix operators eq⇒

$x = 10$;
$y = x{++}$;

In this care y is set to be 10 because assignment occur before incrementation of x. If

$x = 10$;
$y = {++}x$;

In this care y is set to be || because the increment occurs before x is assigned to y. Thus this y = ++ x is equivalent to the statement

$x = x + 1$;
$y = x$;

INSTANCE OF OPERATOR

This operator tests whether on instance derive from a particular class or interface. instance of is a reserved keyword in java. This return boolean value. Syntax for object instance of class ;

Example :

```
if (a instance of abc)
{
system.out. println ("Rose & Marry").
}
else
{
system.out. println ("Harish & Anu").
}
```

NEW ( ) OPERATOR

New operator dynamically allocates memory for an object. When you creak on object or instance of the class, we must allocate memory for it. It is in two way.

1. Classname object ; || memory deallocation. Object = new classname () || memory allocation

Example :

abc *a* ; || abc is *a* class, *a* is an instance of abc

a = new abc ( ) ; | | memory allocation.

2. Classname object = new classname ( ) ;

Example : abc *a* = new abc ( ); | | declare the object as well as allocation of memory.

EXERCISE

1. List all the java operators.
2. Explain Basic Arithmetic operators in detail.
3. Give the precedence and associativity of Java operators.
4. Write a program in java to reverse a number (e.g. 24 to 42) using modulus operator.
5. Explain the following
   - new() operator
   - instanceOf operator
   - Ternary operator
6. Write a program in java to check whether two strings are equal or not using equals() function.
7. What is the result of the following operations in java System.out.println (7 | 4).
8. What is the result of the following operation

```
int x = 10;
x >>= 1;
int y = x;
System.out.println(y);
```

CHAPTER 8

CONTROL STATEMENT AND KEYWORDS

INTRODUCTION

A programming languses controls statements to cause the flow of execution to advance and branch based on the changes to the state of program. Java supports several control flow statements including the following statements.

1. Decision Making
2. Loops.
3. Break, Continue, label, return.

DECISION MAKING STATEMENT

Decision making statements allows your program to choose different path of execution based on the output of an expression or the state of an identifies. Java supports two decision making statement.

(*a*) if statement

(*b*) switch statement

(*a*) **If statement :** The if statement is conditional branch statement. It can be used to route program execution through two different path. Syntax for it statement is if (condition) statement 1

if condition is true the statement 1 is executed else next statement will be executed.

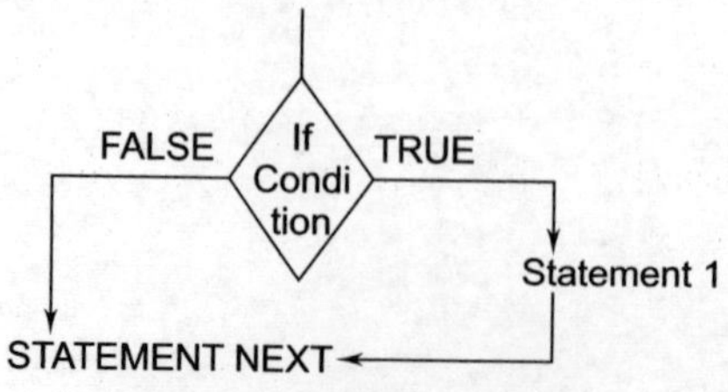

Flow chart for if condition

eg ⇒

```
        int a, b ;
    a = 10 ;
    b = 20 ;
        if (a < b)
        System.out.println ("A");
        System.out.println ("B");
```

Example :

```
class if condition
{
  public static void main (String args [ ])  {
  {
    if (args.length>0)
    {
      System.out.println (args[0]);
    }
      System.Out.Println ("My If program");
  }
}
```

If-else statement : The if-else construct executes different bits of code based on successful completion of a condition that returns only boolean values. If the execution is unsuccessful, the sets of instructions under else are executed.

Syntax :

```
If (condition)
  body of loop ;
else
  body of loop ;
```

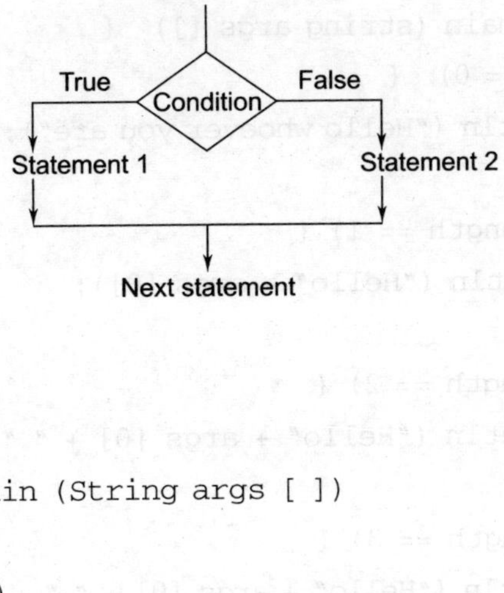

Example :

```
class Helloifelse
{
  public static void main (String args [ ])
  {
   if (args. Length >0)
   {
```

```
    system. Out println ("Hello" + args [ 0]);
   }
   else
    {
    system out println ("Hello, where are you");
   }
  }
}
```

Output

C:\ Javac Helloifelse.java

C:\ Java Helloifelse.

Hello where are you

OR

C:\ Java Helloifelse HARISH

Hello HARISH

Nesteol if statement :

ELSE IF

`If` statements are not limited to two cases. You can combine an `else` and an `if` to make an `else if` and test a whole range of mutually exclusive possibilities. For instance, here's a version of the Hello program that handles up to four names on the command line:

```
// This is the Hello program in Java
class Hello  {
    public static void main (string args [])  {
      if (args. Length == 0)  {
        System.out.println ("Hello whoever you are");
      }
      else if  (args. length == 1) {
        System .out println ("Hello" + args [0]);
      }
      else if (args. Length == 2) {
        System .out println ("Hello" + args [0] + " " + args [1]);
      }
      else if (args. Length == 3) {
        System .out println ("Hello" + args [0] + " " + args [1] + " " + args [2]);
      }
```

```
      else if (args. Length == 4) {
        System .out println ("Hello" + args [0] + " " + args [1] + " " + args [2])
+ " " + args [3]);
      }
      else {
        System.out.println ("Hello" + args [0] + " " + args [1] + " " + args [2])
+ " " + args [3]) + "and all the rest !");
      }
   }
}
```

You can see that this gets mighty complicated mighty quickly. No experienced Java programmer would write code like this. There is a better solution and you'll explore it in the next section.

Output : javac Hello. java

java Hello ↵

Hello whoever you are

or

java Hello HARISH KUMAR TALUJA

Hello HARISH KUMAR TALUJA

Switch statement : The switch statement dispatches control to the different parts of the code based on the value of single variable or expression. The values of expression is compared with each of literals value in case statements. If they matches, the following code sequence is executed. Otherwise the optional default statement is executed. It is a better alternative for if-else-if-ladder.

General Syntax :

```
switch (expression)
{
case<value one>:
            statement 1 ;
            break ;
case<value two>:
            statement 2 ;
            break ;
case<value three>:
            statement 3 ;
            break ;
default:
      default statement-block;
}
```

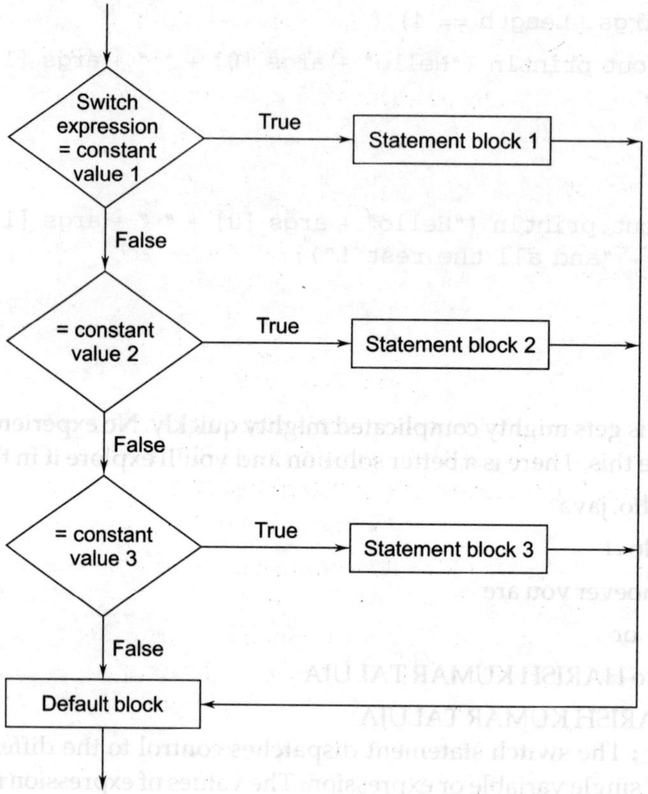

Example :

```
class switch 1
{
  public static void main (String args [ ])
  {
    char v;
    system.Out.println  ("Enter value for V");
    V =  (char) system.in.read ( );
    switch (V)
    {
               case 'a':
                          system.out.println ("a is vowel");
same for                  break;
'i','o','u'    case 'e':
                          system.out.println ("e is vowel")
                          break;
      :                   :
      :                   :
```

```
        default:
                system.out.println ("not a vowel character");
        }
    }
}
```

MULTIPLE INITIALIZERS AND INCREMENTERS

Some time it's necessary to initialize several variables before beginning a for loop.

Similarly you may want to increment more than one variable. Java lets you do this by placing a comma between the different initializers and incrementers like this:

```
for ( int i = 1, j = 100; i < 100; i = i + 1, j = j - 1)    {
   System.out .println (i + j);
}
```

you can't, however, include multiple test condition, at least not with commas. The following line is illegal and will generate a compiler error.

```
for (int i = 1, j = 100 ; i <= 100. j > 0;  i - 1, j = j - 1)  {
```

To include multiple tests you need to use the boolean logic operators && and // which will be discussed later

Looping Statement : Looping statement allows you to execute one or more lines of code repetitively.

Java support the following loops statement.

1. **While loop statement :**
2. **Do-while loop statement :**
3. **For loop statement :**

1. **While loop statement :** while loop in java is most fundamental looping statement. It repeat a statement of block while it controlling expression is true.

Syntax :

```
While (condition)
{
body of loop ;
}
```

the condition can be any boolean expression. The body of loop will be executed as long as the condition expression is true. When condition become false, control passes to the next line of code immediately following the loop.

```
{
            || are unnecessary if only a single statement is being executed.
}
```

Example :

```
class fibo
{
  public static void main (String args [])
  {
    int max = 25
    int prev = 0;
    int next = 1;
    int  sum ;
    while (next < = max)
    {
      System.out.println ("The fibonaci; series is" + next );
      Sum = prev + next;
      prev = next;
      next = sum;
    }
  }
}
```

Out put : The Fibonacci series is 1

```
        "      "      "    "1
        "      "      "    "2
        "      "      "    "3
        "      "      "    "5
        "      "      "    "8
        "      "      "    "13
        "      "      "    "21
```

Other example of while loop in java

```
// This is the Hello program in Java
class Hello {
  public static void main (String args [])   {
   System.out.print ("Hello");    // Say Hello
   int i = 0; // Declare and initialize loop counter
   while (i <args. length) { // Test and Loop
     System.out.print (args[i]);
     System.out.print(" ");
```

```
        i = i + 1;    // Increment Loop counter
      }
      System.out.println ( );    // Finish the line
    }
  }
```

2. **Do-while loop statement :** If the conditional expression controlling a while loop is initially false, then the body of loop will not be executed at all. Sometimes it is desirable to execute body of loop at least once. If the condition is false. To achieve this we can use do-while loop.

Syntax :

```
do
  {
    statement block;
  }
    while (condition);
```

Here the test expression is evaluated at the bottom of the loop. So no matter what the initial state at the test expression. The body is executed at least once.

If the test expression is true. The loop will repeat, otherwise the loop terminate. A Condition must be boolean expression.

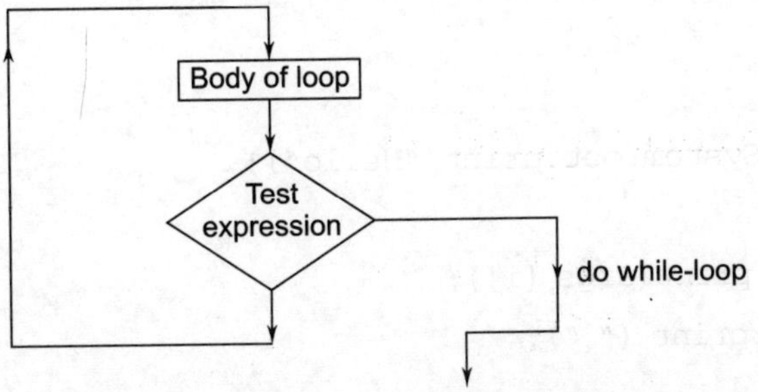

Example :

```
class dowhile
{
  public static void main (string args [])
  {
    int a, b, c, n, i
    n = Integers Parsc Int (args [ 0 ]);
          a = -1;
          b = 1 ;
          i = 1;
    System.out.println ("Fibonacci No");
    do
```

```
{
 c = b + a;
 System.out.println (c);
 a = b;
 b = c;
 i = i +1;
 } while (i< = n);
}
}
```

Output : javac dowhile. java

java dowhile

Fibonacci No 0 1 1 2 3 5 8

Another example of do while loop in java

```
// This is the Hello program in Java
class Hello   {
  public static void main (String args [])   {
    int i = -1;
    do   {
      if (i == -1) System.out.print("Hello");
      else  {
        System.out.print(args [i]);
        System.out.print (" ");
      }
      i = i + 1;
    }  while (i < args.length);
   System.out.println ( ) ;  // Finish the line
  }
}
```

3. **For statement :** The for loop repeats a set of statements a certain no. of times until a condition is matched. It is commonly used for simple iteration.

Syntax for the for loop :

```
for (initialization; termination condition; (iteration)
}
statement block;
}
```

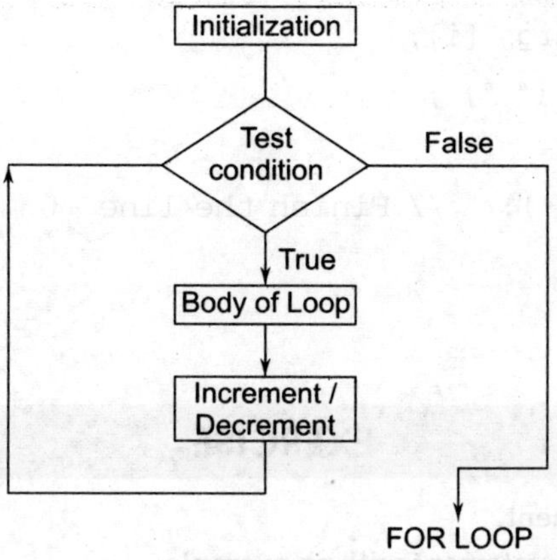

Example :

```
class forloop
{
public static void main (String args [ ] )
{
  int i ;
  for (i  = 0; i < 10; i = i +2)
  {
    if ((i % 2 ) = = 0)
    {
System. Out. println (i  + "is an Even No")
}
  }
}
```

Output: 0 is an Even No
2 " " " "
4 " " " "
6 " " " "
8 " " " "

THE FOR LOOP IN JAVA (<SYNTAX>)

```
// This is the Hello program in Java
class Hello {
  public static void main (string args [ ] ) {
    System.out.print ("Hello");     // Say Hello
    for (int i = 0; i<args.length; i = i + 1) {     // Test and Loop
```

```
      System.out.print(args [i];
      System.out.print  (" ") ;
    }
   System.out.println ( );    // Finish the line
  }
}
```

EXERCISE

1. Classify control flow statement.
2. Explain if-else and nested if statement with an example.
3. What is statement? What are different types of statements available in java?
4. What is the Input and output statements are available in java?
5. What is the difference between print and println command?
6. Explain if statement with an example.
7. Define relational expression.
8. Write a program that print and calculate the factorial value of a given number.
9. Write a program, get the input marks from the user through keyboard check the following condition
   - If marks <40 fail
   - >50 good
   - > 75–very good
   - >90–excellent
10. Write a for lop that display the even numbers from 1 to 100.
11. Compare and contrast the while and do-while lop.
12. What are the jump statements available in java? Give example.
13. What is type casting? What are the rules followed for type casting?
14. Write a program to display the following using for, while and do-while lops
   - 1
1 2
1 2 3
1 2 3 4
   - 1
2 2
3 3 3
4 4 4 4
15. Write a program to check the given number is prime or not.
16. Write a program for Fibonacci series.
   1 1 2 3 5 8 13.....................................

9 CHAPTER

CLASSES AND OBJECT

INTRODUCTION

In classic, procedural programming you try to make the real world problem you're attempting to solve fit a few, predetermined data types: integers, floats, Strings, and arrays perhaps. In object oriented programming you create a model for a real world system. Classes are programmer-defined types that model the parts of the system.

A *class* is a programmer defined type that serves as a blueprint for instances of the class. You can still have ints, floats, Strings, and arrays; but you can also have cars, motorcycles, people, buildings, clouds, dogs, angles, students, courses, bank accounts, and any other type that's important to your problem.

Classes specify the data and behavior possessed both by themselves and by the objects built from them. A class has two parts: the fields and the methods. Fields describe what the class is. Methods describe what the class does.

Using the blueprint provided by a class, you can create any number of objects, each of which is called an *instance* of the class. Different objects of the same class have the same fields and methods, but the values of the fields will in general differ. For example, all people have eye color; but the color of each person's eyes can be different from others.

On the other hand, objects have the same methods as all other objects in the class except in so far as the methods depend on the value of the fields and arguments to the method.

Every object has a separate block of memory to store its fields, but the bytes in the methods are shared between all objects in a class.

The data of an object can be accessed only by the functions associated with that object. However functions of one object can access the functions of other objects.

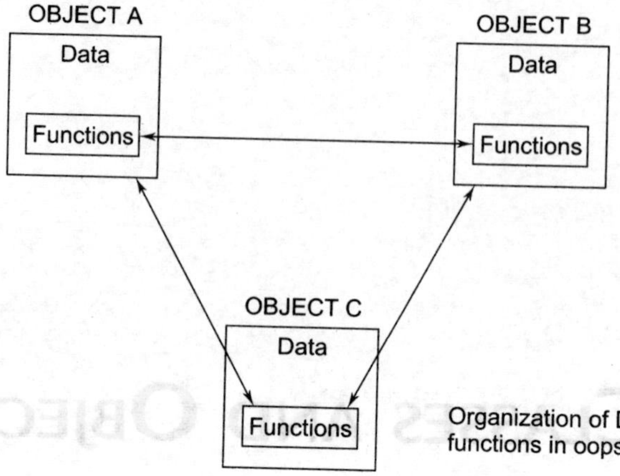

Organization of Data & functions in oops

CLASS FUNDAMENTALS

Classes have been used since the beginning of this moduk. However, until now, only the most rudimentary for a class has been used. A class is usually described as the blueprint or template from which the object is actually made. Its attributes and methods represent a class.

Declaring a class. When you define a class, you declare it exact form and nature, you do this by specifying the data that it contains and the code that operates on data. While very simple classes may contains only code or data, most real world classes may contains both. A class is described by use of the class keyword. The attributes and methods of a class are defined inside a class body. In jara braces { } marks the beginning and the end of a class or method.

Syntax

```
[access specifies] [modifies] class <class name>
{
datatype instance variable 1;
datatype instance variable 2;
datatype instance variable N;
datatype methodname 1 (Argument list)
{
 statement;
}
datatype methodname 2 (Argument list)
{
 statement;
}
datatype methodname N (Paraments list) or
{                           Argument list
 statement;
}
```

```
} || End of class.
```

The data or variable defined within a class are called instance variable. The code is contained within method. The methods and variable defined within a class is called member of the class. Variable defined within a class are called instance variable because each instance of a class contains its own copy of there variable. Thus the data for one object is separate and unique from the data for another.

Here class name is mandatory and must be given while declaring a class. The name is used to refer the class and to crack instance of a class. Example.

```
class can              // class is a keyword and can is the name of
                       class.
{
  spray licenseplate;  ) // are called member variable
  double speed;        } or Instance variable or fields of a class.
  Double max speed;    )
}
```

The optional part is access modifies and specifies these are covered later.

Rules for Naming class :

1. It can be began with a letter, an under score.
2. The name must contain embedded space or period (.).
3. A class name must not be a keyword in java.
4. They can be of any length.

Declaring object : An object is an instance of class. A software object maintains its states in variables and implements its behavior with methods. Declaring an object is similar to declaring a variable.

Syntax : `<class name> (object name>`

```
Example :   Car C1;
           Car C1, C2;
```

You can crack an object in two way.

1. You must declare a variable of class type. This variable not defines an object. It is simply an object that can refer to an object.
2. You must acquire an actual, physical copy of an object and assign it to that variable. You can do this by using the *new* operator.

```
Car C1; // declaring reference to object.                    - (i)
Car C1 = new car (); // declaring an allocating a car object  - (ii)
        OR
Car C1 ;
C1 = New Car (1);
```

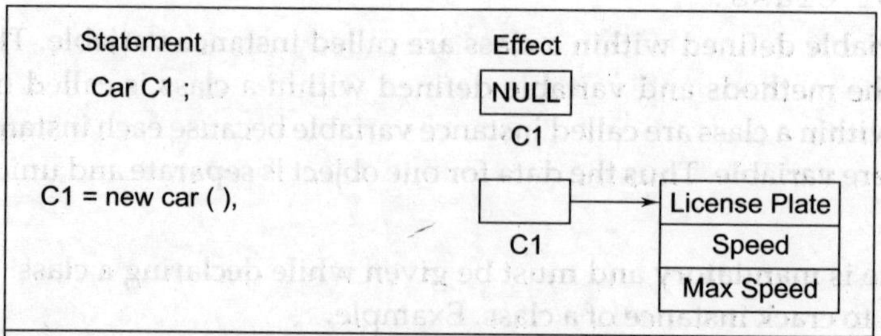

Declaring on object of Type car.

Any attempt to use car class object C1 at equation to will result in compile time error. The next equation (*ii*) allocates an actual object and assign a reference to it.

It is important to understand that new allocates memory for an object during run time. The advantage of this allocation is that your program can create as many as few objects as it needs during the execution of your program. However, since memory is finite, new will not able to allocate memory for an object became insufficient memory exists.

```
Car C = New Car ( )
```

In this example, ( ) parentheses tells you this a method and not a data type like can on left hand side of the assignment.

This is a constructor a method that create a new instance of class.

```
//Car class Example
class car
  {
      String licensePlate; // e.g. "New York 543 A23"
      double speed; // in kilometers per hour
      double maxSpeed; // in kilometers per hour
      public static void main(String args [])
      {
      car c = new car();
      c.licensePlate = "New York A45 636";
      c.speed = 70.0;
      c.maxSpeed = 123.45;
      System.out.println ( );(c.licensePlate + "\nis moving at " +
c.speed + "\nkilometers per hour.");
  }
  }
  Output:
```

USING A CAR OBJECT IN A DIFFERENT CLASS

```
class Car {
  String licensePlate; // e.g. "New York 543 A23"
  double speed;  // in kilometers per hour
  double maxSpeed;  // in kilometers per hour
}
```

The next program creates a new car, sets its fields, and prints the result:

```
Class CarTest {
  public static void main (String args[]) {
  Car c = new Car ( );
  c.licensePlate = "New York A45 636";
  c.speed = 70.0;
  c.maxSpeed = 123.45;
    System.out.println (c.licensePlate + " is moving at " + c.speed +
" kilometers per hour.");
   }
 }
```

This program requires not just the `CarTest` class but also the `Car` class. To make them work together put the `Car` class in a file called Car.java. Put the `CarTest` class in a file called CarTest.java. Put both these files in the same directory. Then compile both files in the usual way. Finally run `CarTest`. For example,

```
% javac Car.java
% javac CarTest.java
% java CarTest
New York A45 636 is moving at 70.0 kilometers per hour.
```

Note that `Car` does not have a `main ( )` method so you cannot run it. It can exist only when called by other programs that do have `main ( )` methods.

Many of the applications you write from now on will use multiple classes. It is customary in Java to put every class in its own file. Next week, you'll learn how to use packages to organize your commonly used classes in different directories. For now keep all your.java source code and.class byte code files in one directory

Initializing Fields

Fields can (and often should) be initialized when they're declared, just like local variables.

```
class Car {
  String licensePlate  = "";      // e.g. "New Delhi Dl-621"
  Double speed         = 0.0;     // in kilometers per hour
  Double maxSpeed      = 123.45;  // in kilometers per hour
}
```

The next program creates a new car and prints it:

```
class CarTest2 {
  public static void main (String [ ] args) {
    Car c = new Car ( );
    System.out.println (c.licensePlate + " is moving at " + c.speed +
      "kilometers per hour.");
  }
}
```

For example,

```
$ javac Car.java
$ javac CarTest2.java
$ java CarTest
  is moving at 0.0 kilometers per hour.
```

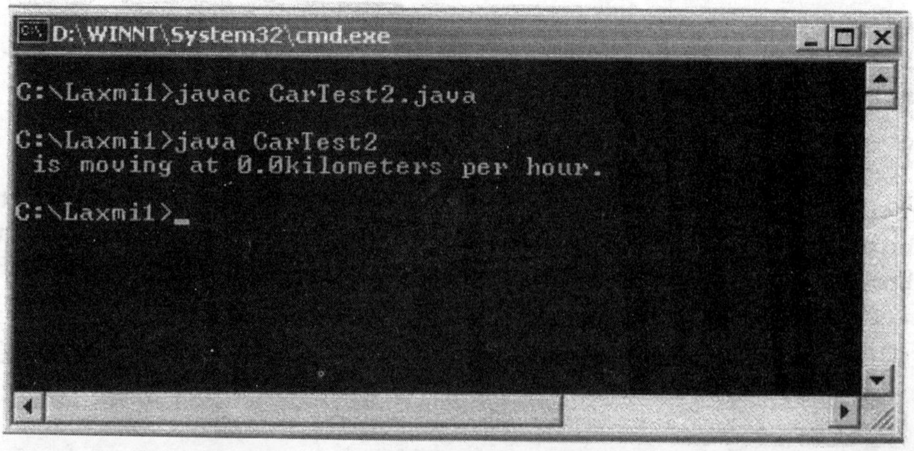

Methods

Classes usually consist of two things: instance variable and Methods. Data types aren't much use unless you can do things with them. For this purpose classes have methods. Fields say what a class *is*. Methods say what a class *does*. The fields and methods of a class are collectively referred to as the *members of the class.*

The classes you've encountered up till now have mostly had a single method, `main ( )`. However, in general classes can have many different methods that do many different things. For instance the `Car` class might have a method to make the `Car` go as fast as it can. For example,

```
class Car {
  String licensePlate    = "";     // e.g. "New Delhi D1-0621"
  double speed           = 0.0;    // in kilometers per hour
  double maxSpeed        = 123.45; // in kilometers per hour
  // accelerate to maximum speed
  // put the pedal to the metal
  void floorIt ( ) {
    this.speed = this.maxSpeed;
  }
}
```

The fields are the same as before, but now there's also a method called `floorIt ( )`. It begins with the Java keyword `void` which is the return type of the method. Every method must have a return type which will either be `void` or some data type like `int`, `byte`, `float`, or `String`. The return type says what kind of the value will be sent back to the calling method when all calculations inside the method are finished. If the return type is `int`, for example, you can use the method anywhere you use an `int` constant. If the return type is `void` then no value will be returned.

`floorIt ( )` is the name of this method. The name is followed by two empty parentheses. Any arguments passed to the method would be passed between the parentheses, but this method has no arguments. Finally an opening brace ({) begins the body of the method.

There is one statement inside the method

```
this.speed = this.maxSpeed;
```

Notice that within the `Car` class the field names are prefixed with the keyword `this` to indicate that I'm referring to fields in the current object.

Finally the `floorIt ( )` method is closed with a } and the class is closed with another }.

Invoking Methods

```
class Car {
  String licensePlate  = "";    // e.g. "New Delhi DL-0621"
  double speed         = 0.0;   // in kilometers per hour
  double maxSpeed      = 123.45; // in kilometers per hour
  // accelerate to maximum speed
  // put the pedal to the metal
  void floorIt ( ) {
    this.speed = this.maxSpeed;
  }
```

```
}
class CarTest3 {
  public static void main (String args [ ]) {
    Car c = new Car ( );
     c.licensePlate = " New Delhi DL=0621";
     c.maxSpeed = 123.45;
     System.out.println (c.licensePlate + " is moving at " + c.speed +
" kilometers per hour.");
     c.floorIt ( ) ;
     System.out.println (c.licensePlate + " is moving at " + c.speed +
" kilometers per hour.");
   }
 }
```

Outside the `Car` class, you call the `floorIt ( )` method just like you reference fields, using the name of the object you want to accelerate to maximum and the . separator as demonstrated below.

The output is:

```
New Delhi DL-0621is moving at 0.0 kilometers per hour.
New Delhi DL-0621is moving at 123.45 kilometers per hour.
```

The `floorIt ( )` method is completely enclosed within the `Car` class. Every method in a Java program must belong to a class. Unlike C++ programs, Java programs cannot have a method hanging around in global space that does everything you forgot to do inside your classes.

Implied this

```
class Car {
  String licensePlate  = "";      // e.g. "New York 543 A23"
  double speed         = 0.0;     // in kilometers per hour
  double maxSpeed      = 123.45;  // in kilometers per hour
  void floorIt ( ) {
    speed = maxSpeed;
  }
}
```

Within the `Car` class, you don't absolutely need to prefix the field names with `this.` like `this.licensePlate` or `this.speed`. Just `licensePlate` and `speed` are sufficient. The `this.` may be implied. That's because the `floorIt ( )` method must be called by a specific instance of the `Car` class, and this instance knows what its data is. Or, another way of looking at it, the every object has its own `floorIt ( )` method.

For clarity, I Will use an explicit `this` today, and I recommend you do so too, at least initially. As you become more comfortable with Java, classes, references, and OOP, you will be able to leave out the `this` without fear of confusion. Most real-world code does not use an explicit `this`.

Member Variables vs. Local Variables

```
class Car {
  String licensePlate  = "";     // member variable
  double speed;        = 0.0;    // member variable
  double maxSpeed;      = 123.45; // member variable
  boolean isSpeeding ( ) {
    double excess;     // local variable
    excess = this.maxSpeed - this.spped;
    if (excess < 0) return true;
    else return false;
  }
}
```

Until now all the programs you've seen quite simple in structure. Each had exactly one class. This class had a single method, `main( )`, which contained all the program logic and variables. The variables in those classes were all local to the `main( )` method. They could not be accessed by anything outside the `main( )` method. These are called *local variables.*

This sort of program is the amoeba of Java. Everything the program needs to live is contained inside a single cell. It's quite an efficient arrangement for small organisms, but it breaks down when you want to design something bigger or more complex.

The `licensePlate, speed` and `maxSpeed` variables of the `Car` class, however, belong to `a Car` object, not to any individual method. They are defined outside of any methods but inside the class and are used in different methods. They are called *member variables* or *fields.*

Member variable, instance variable, and *field* are different words that mean the same thing. Field is the preferred term in Java. *Member variable* is the preferred term in C++.

A *member* is not the same as a member variable or field. Members include both fields and methods.

Passing Arguments to Methods

It's generally considered bad form to access fields directly. Instead it is considered good object oriented practice to access the fields only through methods. This allows you to change the implementation of a class without changing its interface. This also allows you to enforce constraints on the values of the fields.

To do this you need to be able to send information into the `Car` class. This is done by passing arguments. For example, to allow other objects to change the value of the `speed` field in a `Car` object, the `Car` class could provide an `accelerate( )` method. This method does not allow the car to exceed its maximum speed, or to go slower than 0 kph.

```
void accelerate (double deltaV) {
  this.speed = this.speed + V;
  if (this.speed > this.maxSpeed) {
  this.speed = this maxSpeed;
  }
```

```
if (this.speed < 0.0) {
this.speed = 0.0;
}
}
```

The first line of the method is called its *signature*. The signature

```
void accelerate (double V)
```

indicates that `accelerate( )` returns no value and takes a single argument, a `double` which will be referred to as `V` inside the method.

`V` is a purely *formal* argument.

Java passes method arguments by value, not by reference.

Passing Arguments to Methods, An Example

```
class Car {
  String licensePlate  = "";   // e.g. "New York 543 A23"
  Double speed   = 0.0;   // in kilometers per hour
  Double maxSpeed = 123.45; // in kilometers per hour
  void floorIt ( ) {
     this.speed = this.maxSpeed;
  }
  void accelerate (double V) {
     this.speed = this.speed + V;
     if (this.speed > this.maxSpeed) {
     this.speed = this.maxSpeed;
     }
     if (this.speed < 0.0) {
     this.speed = 0.0;
     }  }}
class CarTest4 {
  public static void main (String [] args) {
   Car c = new Car ( ) ;
   c.licensePlate = "New Delhi DL-0621";
   c.maxSpeed = 123.45;
   System.out.println (c.licensePlate + " is moving at " + c.speed +
" kilometers per hour.");
   for (int i = 0; i < 10; i++) (
    c.accelerate (10.0);
    System.out.println (c.licensePlate + " is moving at " + c.speed
+ "kilometers per hour.");
  }  }}
```

Here's the output:

```
Command Prompt

C:\Laxmi1>javac CarTest4.java

C:\Laxmi1>java CarTest4
New York A45 636 is moving at 0.0 kilometers per hour.
New York A45 636 is moving at 10.0 kilometers per hour.
New York A45 636 is moving at 20.0 kilometers per hour.
New York A45 636 is moving at 30.0 kilometers per hour.
New York A45 636 is moving at 40.0 kilometers per hour.
New York A45 636 is moving at 50.0 kilometers per hour.
New York A45 636 is moving at 60.0 kilometers per hour.
New York A45 636 is moving at 70.0 kilometers per hour.
New York A45 636 is moving at 80.0 kilometers per hour.
New York A45 636 is moving at 90.0 kilometers per hour.
New York A45 636 is moving at 100.0 kilometers per hour.

C:\Laxmi1>_
```

Setter Methods

Setter methods, also known as mutator methods, merely set the value of a field to a value specified by the argument to the method. These methods almost always return `void`.

One common idiom in setter methods is to use `this.name` to refer to the field and give the argument the same name as the field. For example,

```
class Car {
  String licensePlate; // e.g. "New York A456 324"
  double speed;        // kilometers per hour
  double maxSpeed      // kilometers per hour
  // setter method for the license plate property
  void setLicensePlate (String licensePlate) {
   this.licensePlate = licensePlate;
  }
  // setter method for the maxSpeed property
  void setMaximumSpeed (double maxSpeed) {
     if (maxSpeed > 0) this.maxSpeed = maxSpeed;
     else this.maxSpeed = 0.0;
  }
  // accelerate to maximum speed
  // put the pedal to the metal
  void floorIt ( ) {
   this.speed = this.maxSpeed;
```

```
}
void accelerate (double deltaV) {
  this.speed = this.speed + deltaV;
  if (this.speed > this.maxSpeed) {
  this.speed = this.maxSpeed;
  }
  if (this.speed < 0.0) {
     this.speed = 0.0;
  }  }}
```

Using Setter Methods, An Example

```
class CarTest5 {
  public static void main (String arge[]) {
   Car c = new Car ( );
   c.setLicensePlate ("New York A45 636");
   c.setMaximumSpeed (123.45);
   System.out.println (c.licensePlate + " is moving at " + c.speed +
" kilometers per hour.");
   For (int i = 0; i < 15; i++) {
    c.accelerate (10.0);
    System.out.println (c.licensePlate + " is moving at " + c.speed
+ "kilometers per hour.");
   } }
}
```

Here's the output:

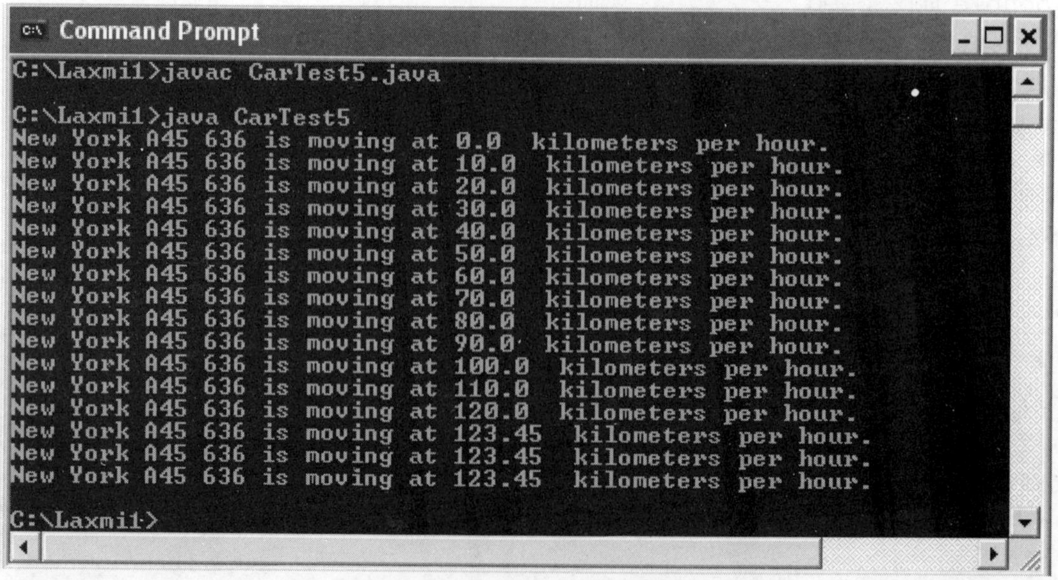

Returning Values from Methods

It's often useful to have a method return a value to the class that called it. this is accomplished by the `return` keyword at the end of a method and by declaring the data type that is returned by the method at the beginning of the method.

For example, the following `getLicensePlate( )` method returns the current value of the `licensePlate` field in the `Car` class.

```
String getLicensePlate ( ) {
   return this.licensePlate;
}
```

A method like this that merely returns the value of an object's field or property is called a *getter* or *accessor* method.

The signature `String getLicensePlate ( )` indicates that `getLicensePlate( )` returns a value of type `String` and takes no arguments. Inside the method the line

```
return this.licensePlate;
```

returns the `String` contained in the `licensePlate` field to whoever called this method. It is important that the type of value returned by the return statement match the type declared in the method signature. If it does not, the compiler will complain.

Returning Multiple Values From Methods

It is not possible to return more than one value from a method. You cannot, for example, return the `licensePlate`, `speed` and `maxSpeed` fields from a single method. You could combine them into an object of some kind and return the object. However this would be poor object oriented design.

The right way to solve this problem is to define three separate methods, `getSpeed ( )`, `getMaxSpeed ( )`, and `getLicensePlate ( )`, each of which returns its respective value. For example,

```
class Car {
 String licensePlate  = "";      // e.g. "New Delhi DL-0621"
 double speed         = 0.0;     // in kilometers per hour
 double maxSpeed      = 123.45;  // in kilometers per hour
 // getter (accessor) methods
 String getLicensePlate ( ) {
  return this.licensePlate;
 }
 double getMaxSpeed ( ) {
  return this.maxSpeed;
 }
 double getSpeed ( ) {
  return this.speed;
 }
 // setter method for the license plate property
```

```
  void setLicensePlate (String licensePlate){
    this.licensePlate = licensePlate;
  }
  // setter method for the maxSpeed property
  void setMaximumSpeed (double maxSpeed) {
    if (maxSpeed > 0) this.maxSpeed = maxSpeed;
    else this.maxSpeed = 0.0;
  }
  void accelerate (double V) {
    this.speed = this.speed + deltaV;
    if (this.speed > this.maxSpeed) {
      this.speed = this.maxSpeed;
    }
    if (this.speed < 0.0) {
      this.speed = 0.0;
    }
  }
}
```

Using Getter Methods, An Example

```
class CarTest6 {
  public static void main (String args [] ) {
    Car c = new Car ( );
    c.setLicensePlate ("New Delhi DL-0621");
    c.setMaximumSpeed (123.45);
    System.out.println(c.getLicensePlate ( ) + " is moving at " +
    c.getSpeed( ) +" kilometers per hour.");
    for (int i = 0; i < 15; i++) {
      c.accelerate (10.0);
      System.out.println (c.getLicensePlate ( ) + " is moving at"
     + c.getSpeed ( ) + " kilometers per hour.")'
    }
  }
}
```

There's no longer any direct access to fields!

Here's the output:

```
java CarTest6
New Delhi DL-0621is moving at 0.0 kilometers per hour.
New Delhi DL-0621is moving at 10.0 kilometers per hour.
New Delhi DL-0621is moving at 20.0 kilometers per hour.
```

```
New Delhi DL-0621is moving at 30.0 kilometers per hour.
New Delhi DL-0621is moving at 40.0 kilometers per hour.
New Delhi DL-0621is moving at 50.0 kilometers per hour.
New Delhi DL-0621is moving at 60.0 kilometers per hour.
New Delhi DL-0621is moving at 70.0 kilometers per hour.
New Delhi DL-0621is moving at 80.0 kilometers per hour.
New Delhi DL-0621is moving at 90.0 kilometers per hour.
New Delhi DL-0621is moving at 100.0 kilometers per hour.
New Delhi DL-0621is moving at 110.0 kilometers per hour.
New Delhi DL-0621is moving at 120.0 kilometers per hour.
New Delhi DL-0621is moving at 123.45 kilometers per hour.
New Delhi DL-0621is moving at 123.45 kilometers per hour.
New Delhi DL-0621is moving at 123.45 kilometers per hour.
another Example for
```

Returning a values: ⇒ are

```
class Box
{
    double width;
    double height;
    double depth;
  double volume ( )
  {
    return width * height * depth;
  }
}
class Boxdemo
{
public static void main (string args [])
{
  Box b1 = new Box ( );
  Box b2 = new Box ( );
  b1.width = 10;
  b1.height = 20;
  b1.depth = 30;
  b2.width = 20;
  b2.height = 30;
  b2.depth = 40;
  double vol1, vol2;
  Vol1 = b1.volume ( );
  Vol2 = b2. volume ( );
  System.out.println ("volume for Box1 is" + vol1)
```

```
        System.out.println ("volume for Box2 is" + vol2)
    }
}
```

As you can see, when volume ( ) is called, it is put on the right sick of an assignment statement. In this case vol1 & vol2 will receive the value returned by the funen volume.

The value of Vol1 is 6000

The value of Vol2 is 24000

There are two important things to understand about returning values.

1. The type of data returned by method must be compatible with the return type specified by method.
2. The variable receiving the value returned by a method must also be compatible with the return type specified for the method.

CONSTRUCTORS

A constructor is a number funer of a class. A constructor initializes an object immediately upon creation. Once defined the constructor is automatically called immediately after the object is created before the new completes. It initializes all the variables and does any work necessary to prepare the class to be used. Constructor do not have return type not even void. *e.g.*

```
Car C = new Car ( )
```

`Car( )` is a constructor. A constructor has the same name as the class. Constructors are of many type.

1. Default Constructor
2. Parameterized Constructor
3. Copy Constructor.

1. **Default Constructor :** Every class has a default constructor that does not take any argument and the body of it does not have any statement.
2. **Parameterized Constructor :** You create a constructor that accept argument but never return any value.

The following method is a constructor that initializes license plate to an empty string, speed to zero, and maximum speed to 120.0.

```
Car ( ) {
  this.licensePlate = "";
  this.speed = 0.0;
  this.maxSpeed = 120.0;
}
```

Better yet, you can create a constructor that accepts three arguments and use those to initialize the fields as below.

```
Car (String licensePlate, double speed, double maxSpeed) {
  this.licensePlate = licensePlate;
  this.speed = speed;
  if (maxSpeed > 0) this.maxSpeed = maxSpeed;
```

```
    else this.maxSpeed = 0.0;
    if (speed > this.maxSpeed) this.speed = this.maxSpeed;
    if (speed < 0) this.speed = 0.0;
    else this.speed = speed;
  }
```

Or perhaps you always want the initial speed to be zero, but require the maximum speed and license plate to be specified:

```
Car (String licensePlate, double maxSpeed) {
    this.licensePlate = licensePlate;
    this.speed = 0.0;
    if (maxSpeed > 0) this.maxSpeed = maxSpeed;
    else this.maxSpeed = 0.0;
  }
```

Calling another Constructor : A constructor can be called from another constructor. When a constructor is written, the functionalities of another defined constructor can be used. A call to the constructor can be made from the constructor currently being defined. *e.g.*

```
// Calling another Constructor
Class point
{
  int x, y;
  point (int x, int y)
  {
    this.x = x;
    this.y = y;
  }
  point ( )
  {
    this (.1,-1);
  }
  public static void main (string args [ ])
  {
    point p = new point ( ) ;
    System.out.println("x=") + p.x +",  y =" + P.y);
    p = new point (10.10);
    System.out.println("x=" + p.x +", y = " + P.y);
  }
}
output: x = -1,  y = -1
        x = 10, y = 10
```

Copy Constructor : A copy constructor is a constructor that replicates or duplicates an existing object. So it is called the copy constructor. It takes a parameter is a reference to an object of same class to which the constructor depend.

Syntax :

```
Class name (class name copy constructor name)
Car c = new car ( );
Car d = new car (C); // copy constructor.
```

Example:

```
class copy construct
{
  int a, b;
public copyconstruct(int a1, int b1)
{
  a = a1;
  b = b1;
}
public copyconstruct (copyconstruct C)
{
  a = c.a;
  b = c.b;
}
Void view ( )
{
  System.out.println("A=" + a + "B=" +b).
}
class test
{
public static void main (string args [ ] )
{
  copyconstruct cc = newcopyconstruct (10,15)
    cc.view;
  copyconstruct CC1 = new copyconstruct(cc),
    cc1.view;
}
}
```

```
Output: A = 10   B = 15
        A = 10 B = 15
```

Why Garbage Collection?

The name "garbage collection" implies that objects no longer needed by the program are "garbage" and can be thrown away. A more accurate and up-to-date metaphor might be "memory recycling."

When an object is no longer referenced by the program, the heap space it occupies can be recycled so that the space is made available for subsequent new objects. The garbage collector must somehow determine which objects are no longer referenced by the program and make available the heap space occupied by such unreferenced objects. In the process of freeing unreferenced objects, the garbage collector must run any finalizers of objects being free.

In addition to freeing unreferenced objects, a garbage collector may also combat heap fragmentation. Heap fragmentation occurs through the course of normal program execution. New objects are allocated, and un referenced objects are freed such that free portions of heap memory are left in between portions occupied by live objects. Requests to allocate new objects may have to be filled by extending the size of the heap even though there is enough total unused space in the existing heap. This will happen if there is not enough contiguous free heap space available into which the new object will fit. On a virtual memory system, the extra paging (or swapping) required to service an ever growing heap can degrade the performance of the executing program. On an embedded system with low memory, fragmentation could cause the virtual machine to "run out of memory" unnecessarily.

Garbage collection relieves you from the burden of freeing allocated memory. Knowing when the explicitly free allocated memory can be very tricky. Giving this job to the Java virtual machine has several advantages. First, it can make you more productive. When programming in non-garbage-collected languages you can spend many late hours (or days or weeks) chasing down an elusive memory problem. When programming in Java you can use that time more advantageously by getting ahead of schedule or simply going home to have a life.

A second advantage of garbage collection is that it helps ensure program integrity. Garbage collection is an important part of Java's security strategy. Java programmers are unable to accidentally (or purposely) crash the Java virtual machine by incorrectly freeing memory.

Potential disadvantage of a garbage-collected heap is that it adds an overhead that can affect program performance. The Java virtual machine has to keep track of which objects are being referenced by the executing program, and finalize and free unreferenced objects on the fly. This activity will likely require more CPU time than would have been required if the program explicitly freed unnecessary memory. In addition, programmers in a garbage-collected environment have less control over the scheduling of CPU time devoted to freeing objects that are no longer needed.

The finalize ( ) Method: Finalizes method functions in contradiction to the constructor method. Finalizes are called just before the object is garbage collected and its memory is reclaimed. The finalize method is represented by finalize ( ). Sometime an object will need to perform some action when it is destroyed. For example if an object is holding some non java resource such as file handle or window character font, then you might want to make sure there resources are freed before an object is destroyed. This can be handle by finalization method. To create a finizer method for a class, the finalize ( ) method can be overridden as shown below

```
Protected void finalize ( )
{
  // body of finalization method.
}
```

Here keyword protected is an access specifies that presents access to finalize ( ) by code defined outside its class. This method can be called at any point of time. Calling finalize ( ) need not trigger an object to be garbage collected. Removing reference to an object will cause it to be marked for deletion.

Finalizer methods are best used for optimizing the removal of an object.

Inner classes: It is possible to rest a class definition within another class and treat the rested class like any other method of that class. Such a class is called rested class. As a member of its enclosing class, a rested class has privileges to access all the members of class enclosing it. A rested class can either be static or non static. While static rested classes are just called as static rested classes, non static rested classes are called as inner class.

e.g.,

```
Class <enclosing class>
{
    class <inner class>
    {
    <Set of statements>
    }
}
```

The interesting feature about the relationship between there two classes is not that the Inner class is inside the Enclosing class and it has direct access to instance variable and methods of its enclosing instance.

ACCESS SPECIFIES

1. Public
2. Private
3. Protected.

The Public Access Specifier

Public means, it is accessible from all other classes. A class with in another class is called inner class. Inner class cannot have the public access specifier. All other class can have public access specifier. You can use a public access specifiers in a class, a data member, constructor, or a method from any object in any Java program.

e.g.:

```
public class Myclass //class with public
{
public Boolean flag;
public void test public() //method
{
}
public Myclass() //constructor
{
flag=true;
}
}
```

Note:

1. Public static void main (String args[ ]) the public is an access specifier. So the main method as unprotected and therefore making it accessible to all other class.
2. Only one public class can be defined in each source file. The name of the java source file is same name as the public class defined in the java file.

The Private Access Specifier

Only objects of the same class can access a private variable or method. You can declare variable, methods, constructor and inner class as private. If it is declared in constructor, it is accessible only from with in its own class and its subclass. This is also applied for ordinary methods and fields. This is the highest degree of protection. They cannot be inherited by subclass and also not accessible in subclass.

e.g.:

```
private int secure;
private void notaccess(){}
```

The Protected Access Specifier

Variable, methods and inner class are declared protected it is accessible only from within its own class and its subclass.

```
protected int protect-var;
protected_void finalize() throws Throwable{ }
```

Note:

1. The jdk1.0 release of the java language supports the private protected. This level is not supported in version of java higher than 1.0, so you should no longer be using it in your program. This modifier makes the field visible in all subclass regardless of what package they are in. Fields are not accessible by other class in the same package.
2. If none of these is specified (if left, unspecified) then the entity has package access. Which means that it can be accessed from any class in the same package. This scope is called as friendly (or) default. In java, friendly is not a keyword. It is a term that is used for the access level when no access specifier has been specified. Consider the following diagram.

Access protected

The above diagram shows the class B and C inherit (derived) from A. A is called supper class (or) base class. The package is nothing but collection of related classes. The class C is belong to the package p2. The class A and B belong to the package p1; method takeme() has been declared in the class A. The following situation arises your accessibility of the method takeme() from class B and C it is shown in the following table:

Access Specifier in Class A	Class B	Class C
protected takeme() takeme() [without an access specifier]	Accessible in sub-class B [same package]. Accessible it in the same package.	Accessible in C [even it is in other package p2]. Not accessible in different package (p2).

The following chart shows the access level permitted by each specifier.

Modifier	Meaning
private	It is accessible only from within own class.
protected	It is accessible only from within the class and its subclass.
public	It is accessible from all classes.

The other such modifiers are used to determine how the data members and methods are used in other class and objects.

Static

Every class has two parts. One is variable and the other one is method. The variables are called instance variable and methods are called instance methods. This is because every time the class is instantiated, a new copy of each of them is created. They are accessed with dot operator. The modifier static is used to specify that a method is a class method. A class method is a method that is invoked without being bound to any specific object of the class. These are associated with itself not an individual objects.

```
e.g.: public static void main (String args[ ])
```

Which means, this method as one that belong to the entire class and not a part of any object of the class. So interpreter uses this method before nay object is created.

If you also declare the variable as static, it make only one value of the variable exists for all instance of the class.

```
e.g.: static int I;
```

These variables are called class variable. This variable is used even if the class is never actually instantiated.

```
Example for class variable:
    public final static double PI
Example for class method:
    public static int abs(int a)
    public static int min(int a,int b)
```

The above are declared in java Math class library. These are used in mathematical operations in any program.

Program

```
class statictest
{
static double multiply(double a,double b)
```

Program

```
public class test
{
  int x;
  public static void main(String args[ ])
  {
  System.out.println(x);
  }
}
```

The above program will not compile and give error message Variable x may not have initialized to, avoid the error simply change

```
static int x;
```

It makes the variables with default value. The another way is create an instance of the class and then access the variable.

Program

```
public class test
{
  int x;
  public static void main(String args[ ])
  {
  test t = new test();
  System.out.println(t.x);
  }
}
```

Output: 0

The general form accessing class variable and method is

```
Classname.static variablename;
Classname.static method();
```

What will be the output of the following compilation unit?

Program

```
class wonder
{
static
{
System.out.println("I am first");
```

```
}
public static void main(String args[ ])
{
System.out.println("I am also first");
}
}
```

Output: Compile and see the result

```
{
return(a*b);
}
static double add(double a,double b)
{
return(a+b);
}
static double division(double a,double b)
{
return(a/b);
}
static double subtraction(double a,double b)
{
return(a-b);
}
}
public class mytest
{
public static void main(String args[ ])
{
double x=statictest.multiply(10.5);
double y=statictest.add(10.5);
double z=statictest.subtraction(10.5);
double w=statictest.division(10.5);
system.out.println("Simple Calculator");
system.out.println("Addition" +y);
system.out.println("Subtraction" +z);
system.out.println("Multiplication" +x);
system.out.println("Division" +w);
}
}
```

Output:

Simple Calculator

Addition 15.0

Subtraction 5.0

Multiplication 50.0

Division 2.0

In the above program statictest object is not created, but the method is called using classname.

Note:

1. Static method cannot use non-static methods and variable.
2. They cannot refer this or super. Consider the following segment.

EXERCISE

1. What is the most important features of Object oriented programming? How can we create the class?
2. What is a method? How can we access a method?
3. What is the difference between public member and private member of a class?
4. What are the various levels of access control? What is the difference between them?
5. Can an abstract method be declared as final or static? Try by your self.
6. Explain the use of this keyword.
7. When do we declare a member variable method or class final?
8. How do we pass argument to java programs and methods?
9. Describe the different level of access protection.
10. What are the constructors? How does it differ from a method? Can we overload constructors?
11. Can we call one constructor from other?
12. What is a finalizer? Explain we the suitable example.
13. When do we declare a method and class abstract?
14. Differentiate between concrete class and abstract class.
15. What is constructor? Write different type of constructor.
16. How do we invoke a constructor?
17. Does java support destructor?
18. Write a program using
    - Default Constructor
    - Argument Constructor
    - Copy Constructor
19. What is an object and class? Explain with the example.
20. Differentiate between class and instance variables.

10

CHAPTER

EXPLORING METHOD AND INHERITANCE

METHODS

The attributes (fields) and methods are backbone of the class. A method is a sequence of declaration and executable statements encapsulated together like an independent miniprogram. Once a method has written and debugged it can be used again and again. This is more import aspect. Reusability is a feature of java. Once a method has written and debugged, it can be used again and again. Methods are also called functions procedure, subroutine and subprograms.

Method is of two type

1. **Predefined Method :** These are library functions included alongwith the software.
2. **User-defined Method :** These functions are defined and coded by the user itself for a specific purpose.

Example :
```
class factorial
        {
         public static void main(String args[ ])
        {
         for (int i=0; i<S; i++)
         System.out.println("i=" + i + "factorial=" + fact(i));
        } // closing of main
        static int fact(int n)
        {
         int f = 1;
         while (n>1)
         f = n * fact (n - 1);
         return f;
```

```
    }
  }
```

In this case main is predefined method and fact is user defined method. The for loop which invoke println() to print the result. In fact() (user defined function) we just pass a single argument

(*a*) **Argument is of two types**

1. Formal argument
2. Actuals argument.

Example : ⇒

```
class addition
  {
    int a, b, c;
    a=10, b=20;
    public static void main (string args[ ])
    {
      c=add (a, b); // a & b are actual parameter.
    system.out.println ("Result after Addition = "+C);
    }
  static intc(int x, inty) // Here x & y are formal parameter
  {
    return x+y;
  }
  } // End of class.
```

X, y (formal argument or parameter) receive a single copy of actual parameter. In this x receive 10, & y receive 20;

Output: Result after Addition = 30

Argument Passing : There are two ways of passing functions to a method are :

1. Call by value
2. Call by reference.

1. Call by value : This method copies the value of an argument into the formal parameter of the subroutine. Therefore the changes made to the parameters of the subroutine hare no effect on argument.

Example :

```
class call_by_value
{
  void test (int i, intj)
  {
    j = i*2;
    j=j/2;
  }
}
```

```
class test call by value
{
public static void main (String args[ ])
{
  call by value ob = new call by value ( );
  int a = 25, b = 20;
  System.out.println("A & B before call "+ a +" "+ b);
  ob.test(a, b);
  System.out.println("A & B after call" + a + " " + b);
}
}
```

Output :

A and B before call 25 20

A and B after call 25 20

As you can see, we get the output is 25,20 in both case and their is no change in the value of A & B. The operation that occur inside test ( ) hare no effect on the values of *a* & *b* used in call. These value did not change to 50 and 10.

2. **Call by reference :** But in call by reference can the situation changes dramatically, object are passed by reference.

```
class Test
{
  int a,b;
Test(int i, int j)
{
  a = i;
  b = j;
}
void check(Test 0)
{
  o.a * = 2;
  o.b / = 2;
}
}
class reference
{
  public static void main(String args[ ])
   {
     Test ob = new Test (25, 20);
     System.out.println("value of A & B before check are " + ob.a +:
     "+ ob.b);
```

```
    Ob.check(ob);
    System.out.println("value of A & B after check are " + ob.a + "
    " + ob.b);
  }
}
```

Output:

Value of A & B before check are 25 20

Value of A & B after check are 50 10

Returning object : A method can return any type of data, including class type that you create.

```
class returntest
{
   int a;
  returntest(int x)
  {
   a = x;
  }
  returntest decrementbytwo( )
  {
    returntest temp = new returntest (a - 2);
    return temp;
  }
}
class output
 {
  public static void main(String args[ ])
  {
   returntest rt = new returntest (20);
   returntest rth;
   rth = rt.decrementbytwo( );
   System.out.println(" rt.a" + rt.a);
   System.out.println(" rth.a" + rth.a);
  }
 }
output :  rt.a = 20
          rt1.. = 18
```

Recursion : Recursion means when a function call itself. As it relates to java programming, recursion is the attributes that allows a method to call itself. **Example :** Factorial is an classic example of recursion. For Example :→ Factorial 6 is $6 \times 5 \times 4 \times 3 \times 2 \times 1$.

```
class factorial
{
```

```
    int fact (int n)
    {
      if (n = =1)
        return 1;
      else
        int result = fact (n - 1) * n;
        return rersult;
    }
}
class Recursion
{
  public static void main(String args[ ])
  {
    factorial f = new factorial( );
int K = f. fact (6);
      System.out.println( K );
  }
}
```

output: 720

The operation of fact() may seems a bit confusing. When fact() fune is called with an argument of to, the functions return to otherwise it returns n * fact (n – 1).

Static : It is possible to create a member that can be used by itself without reference to a specific instance. To create a such a member, start its declaration with keyword static. You can declared both methods and variable to be static. In java main () method is static because it must be called before any objects exist.

Method declared as static have several instructions

↳ They can only call other static methods.

↳ They must only access static data.

↳ They cannot refer to this or super in any way.

Example :

1. class static t {
2. static int a = 3;
3. static int b;
4. static void test (int K)
5. {
6. System.out.println("K=" + K);
7. System.out.println("A=" + a);
8. System.out.println("B=" + b);
9. }

```
static
{
System.out.println("USE OF STATIC");
b = a + 4;
}
public static void main (String args[ ])
{
test(10);
}
}
```

As soon as static class is loaded, all the static statement are run. First a is set to 3 then *b* is declared and static block is executed and initialized with 7. And finally main method is called, which calls test () by passing 10 to K.

Output :

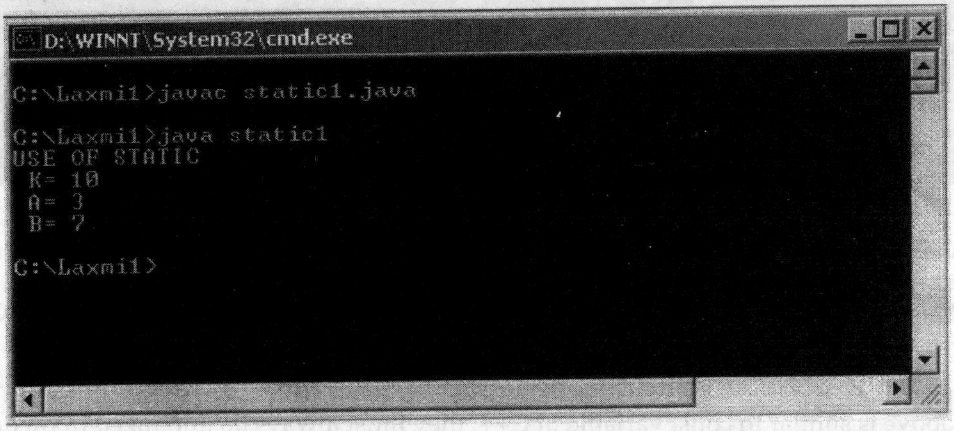

If you want to call a static method from outside its class you can call it by using following syntax

```
classname.method();
```

Example : ⇒

```
class static2
{
static int x = 92;
static int y = 10;
  static void value()
  {
    System.out.println("X=" + X);
    System.out.println("Y=" + Y);
    Int Z;
     Z = X + Y;
    System.out.println("Z=" + Z);
```

```
    }
   public static void main(String args[ ])
   {
     static 2. value ();
   }
 }
```

output:

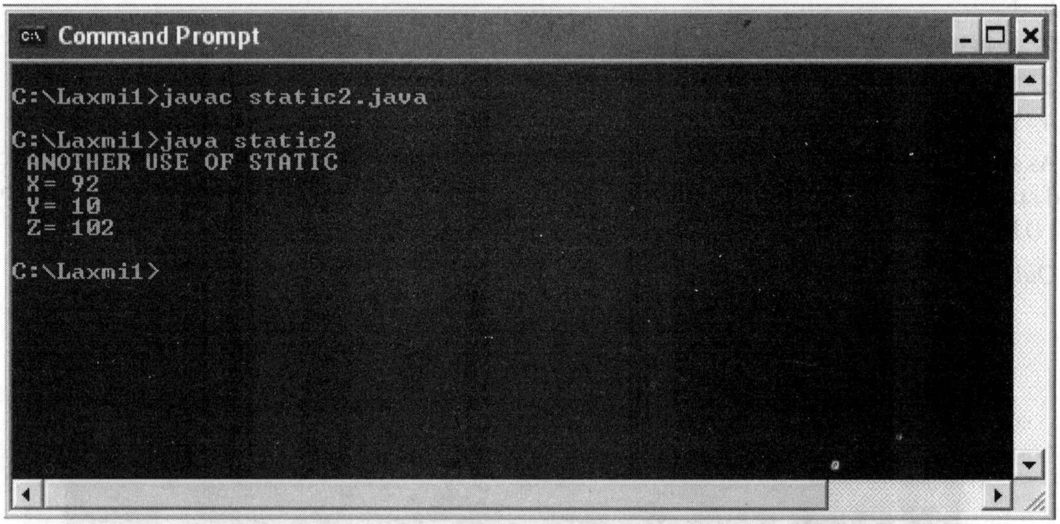

Final Modifier : Another useful modifiers in regard to controlling class member usage is the final modifier. The final modifier specifies that a variable as a constant value or that a method cannot be overridden in a subclass. The final modifier makes class member is the final version allowed for the class. For creating symbolic constant you can use final modifier.

```
final public int CENT=100; //constant
```

The above is similar to const variable in C++, they must always be initialized upon declaration and their value can't change any time afterward.

```
final boolean FLAG=true;
```

The three usage of final are

1. A final class cannot be inherited.
2. A final method cannot be changed by subclass (or) overriding.
3. A final data member cannot be changed after initialization (constant).

Example :

```
final void test() // cannot be overriding
{ }
final class test{ } // to prevent inheritance
```

OVERLOADING

Overloading is when the same method or operator can be used on many different types of data. For instance the + sign is used to add ints as well as concatenate strings. The plus sign behaves differently depending on the type of its arguments. Therefore the plus sign is inherently overloaded.

Methods can be overloaded as well. `System.out.println ( )` can print a `double`, a `float`, an `int`, a `long`, or a `String`. You don't do anything different depending on the type of number you want the value of. Overloading takes care of it.

Programmer-defined classes can overload methods as well. To do this simply write two methods with the same name but different argument lists. For instance last week you saw several different versions of the `car` constructor, one that took three arguments and one that took two arguments, and one that took no arguments. You can use all of these in a single class, though here I only use two because there really aren't any good default values for `licensePlate` and `maxSpeed`. On the other hand, 0 is a perfectly reasonable default value for `speed`.

```
public class Car {
  private String licensePlate;  // e.g. "New York A456 324"
  private double speed;    // kilometers per hour
  private double maxSpeed; // kilometers per hour
  // constructors
  public Car (String licensePlate, double maxSpeed) {
    this.licensePlate = licensePlate;
    this.speed = 0.0;
    if (maxSpeed >= 0.0) {
       this.maxSpeed = maxSpeed;
    }
    else {
      maxSpeed = 0.0;
    }
  }
  public Car (String licensePlate, double speed, double maxSpeed) {
    this.licensePlate = licensePlate;
    if (maxSpeed >= 0.0) {
       this.maxSpeed = maxSpeed;
    }
    else {
       maxSpeed = 0.0;
    }
    if (speed < 0.0) {
       speed = 0.0;
    }
    if (speed <= maxSpeed) {
       this.speed = speed;
    }
    else {
       this.speed = max.Speed;
```

```
    }
  }
  // other methods . . .
}
```

Normally a single identifier refers to exactly one method or constructor. When as above, one identifier refers to more than one method or constructor, the method is said to be *overloaded*. You could argue that this should be called identifier overloading rather than method overloading since it's the identifier that refers to more than one method, not the method that refers to more than one identifier. However in common usage this is called method overloading.

Which method an identifier refers to depends on the signature. The signature is the number, type, and order of the arguments passed to a method. The signature of the first constructor in the above program is `Car (String, double)`. The signature of the second method is `Car (String, double, double)`. Thus the first version of the `Car ( )` constructor is called when there is one String argument followed by one double argument and the second version is used when there is one String argument followed by two double arguments.

If there are no arguments to the constructor, or two or three arguments that aren't the right type in the right order, then the compiler generates an error because it doesn't have a method whose signature matches the requested method call. For example

```
Error: Method Car (double) not found in class Car.
Car.java line 17
```

This in Constructors

It is often the case that overloaded methods are essentially the same except that one supplies default values for some of the arguments. In this case, your code will be easier to read and maintain (though perhaps *marginally* slower) if you put all your logic in the method that takes the most arguments, and simply invoke that method from all its overloaded variants that merely fill in appropriate default values.

This technique should also be used when one method needs to convert from one type to another. For instance one variant can convert a `String` to an `int`, then invoke the variant that takes the int as an arguments.

This straight-forward for regular methods, but doesn't quite work for constructors because you can't simply write a method like this:

```
public Car (String licensePlate, double maxSpeed) {
  Car (licensePlate, 0.0, maxSpeed) ;
}
```

Instead, to invoke another constructor in the same class from a constructor you use the keyword `this` like so:

```
public Car (String licensePlate, double maxSpeed) {
  this (licensePlate, 0.0, maxSpeed) ;
}
```

Must this be the first line of the constructor?

For example,

```
public class Car {
  private String licensePlate;   // e.g. "New York A456 324"
  private double speed;          // kilometers per hour
  private double maxSpeed;       // kilometers per hour
  // constructors
  public Car (String licensePlate, double maxSpeed) {
   this (licensePlate, 0.0, maxSpeed) ;
  }
  public Car (String licensePlate, double speed, double maxSpeed) {
   this.licensePlate = licensePlate;
  if (maxSpeed >= 0.0) {
   this.maxSpeed = maxSpeed;
  }
  else {
   maxSpeed = 0.0;
  }
   if (speed < 0.0) {
      speed = 0.0;
  }
  if (speed <= maxSpeed) {
   this.speed = speed;
  }
  else {
   this.speed = maxSpeed;
  }
 }
 // other methods . . .
}
```

This approach saves several lines of code. In also means that if you later need to change the constraints or other aspects of construction of cars, you only need to modify one method rather than two. This is not only easier; it gives bugs fewer opportunities to be introduced either through inconsistent modification of multiple methods or by changing one method but not others.

OPERATOR OVERLOADING

Some object oriented languages, notably C++, allow you to not only overload methods but also operators like + or –. This is very useful when dealing with user defined mathematical classes like complex numbers where + and – have well-defined meanings.

However most non-mathematical classes do not have obvious meanings for operators like + and –. Experience has shown that operator overloading is a large contributor to making multi-person programming projects infeasible. Therefore Java does not support operator overloading.

```
class overloading
{
    void demo()
    {
    System.out.println("Without Argument ");
    }
    void demo(int x)
    {
    System.out.println("X ="+x);
    }
    void demo(int x,int y)
    {
    System.out.println("X ="+x);
    System.out.println("Y ="+y);
    }
    double demo(double x)
    {
    System.out.println("Double X ="+x);
    Return x*x;
    }
}
class overloaddemo
{
   public static void main(String args[])
   {
   overloading a=new overloading();
   double temp;
   a.demo();
   a.demo(10);
   a.demo(10,20);
   temp=a.demo(2.5);
   System.out.println("Temp=" +temp);
   }
}
```

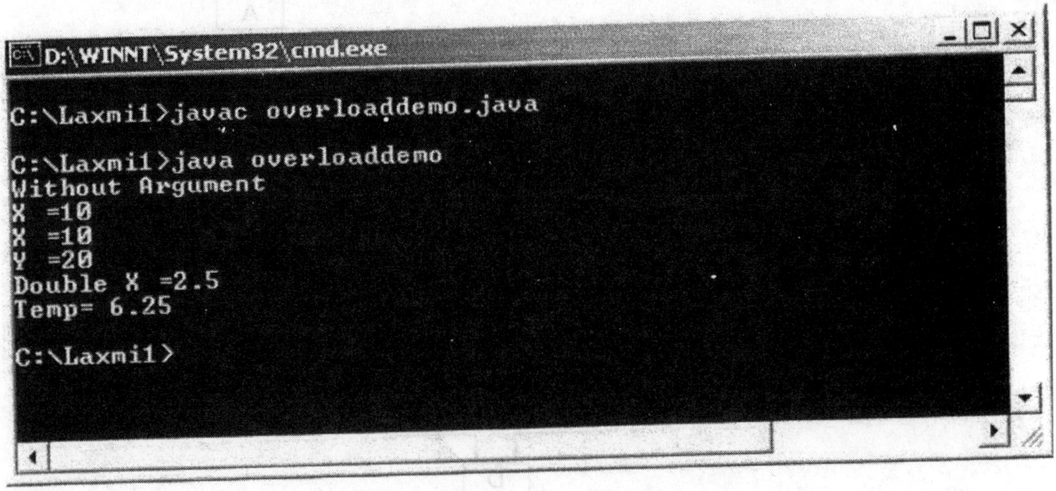

INTRODUCTION TO INHERITANCE

Reusability is yet another important feature of OOPs. It is always nice if we could reuse something that already exist rather than trying to create the same all over again using inheritance you can create a general class that defines traits common to a set of related items. This can then be inherited by other, more specific classes, those each adding there things that are unique to it.

INHERITANCE BASIC

You can inherit one class into another by using the extends keywords. "The mechanism of deriving a new class from an old one is called Inheritance or derivation". The old class is referred to as a Base class and new one is called the derived class. The derived class inherits some or all of the traits from the base class. A derived class with only one base class is called single level inheritance. Inheritance is of many type.

(*a*) Single Inheritance
(*b*) Multiple Inheritance
(*c*) Hierarchical Inheritance
(*d*) Multilevel Inheritance
(*e*) Hybrid Inheritance.

Single Inheritance

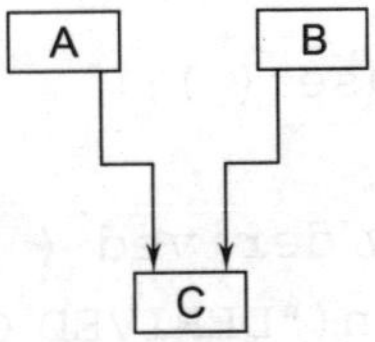

Multiple Inheritance

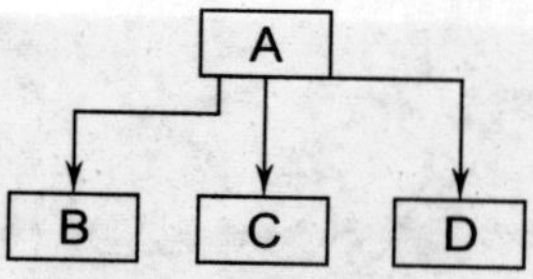

Hierarchical Inheritance

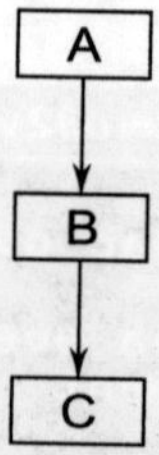

Multilevel Inheritance

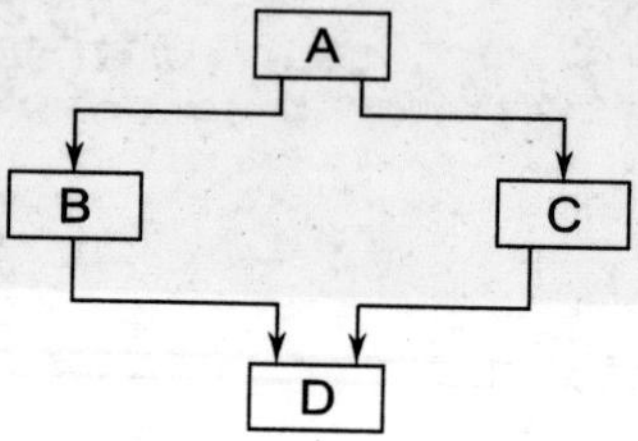

Hybrid Inheritance

```
class base
{
  void show( )
  {
   System.out.println("Base class");
  }
}
class derived extends base
{
 void show 1 ( )
 {
   System.out.println("Derived class");
 }
}
class Inheritance
{
  public static void main (String args[ ])
  {
   bare b1 = new base ( );
   b1.show ( );
   derived d1 = new derived ( );
  System.out.println("DERIVED CLASS SHOW METHOD"),.
   d1.show1( ),.
  System.out.println("BASE CLASS SHOW CALLED BY DERIVED CLASS"),.
   d1.show( );
```

```
    }
}
```

Output:

```
BASE CLASS
DERIVED CLASS SHOW METHOD
DERIVED CLASS
BASE CLASS SHOW CALLED BY DERIVED CLASS
BASE CLASS
```

MEMBER ACCESS AND INHERITANCE

Subclass access all the members of its superclass; it cannot access those members of the superclass or baseclass that have been declared private.

Example :

```
class base
{
  int i;
  private int j;
  i = 10;
  j = 20;
}
class derived extends base
{
  int total;
int sum ( )
  {
    total = i + j;
  }
}
class demo
{
public static void main(String args[ ])
{ int result;
  derived d = new derived ( );
result = d.sum( );
  System.out.println(result);
}
}
```

It will generate an error or it will not compile because reference to *i* & *j* in sum method causes an access violation.

Note : If a class member that has been declared as private will remain private to its class. It is not accessible by anycode outside its class including subclass.

USING SUPER KEYWORD

Whenever a subclass needs to refer to its immediate superclass. It can be do by use of super keyword. Super has two general forms. First call the super class constructor. The second is used to access a member of the superclass that has been hidden by a member of a subclass.

A subclass can call a constructor method defined by its superclass by use of the following form of super.

```
super (parameter list);
```

parameter list specifies may parameter needed by the constructor in the superclass.

1. super( ) must always be the first statements executed inside a subclass constructors.
2. super ( ) always refers to the super class immediately above the calling classes.

```
class superclass
{
  protected int a,b;
  superclass (int a1, int b1)
  {
    a = a1;
    b = b1;
  }
  int geta ( )
  {
    return a;
  }
  int getb ( )
  {
    return b;
  }
  }
class superclass1 extends superclass
{
  protected int c;
  superclass1 (int a1, int b1, int c1)
  {
    super (a1, b1);
    c = c1;
  }
  int getc ( )
  {
    return c;
  }
}
class test
{
  public static void main(String args[ ])
  {
```

```
superclass1 s1 = new superclass1 (10, 20, 30);
System.out.println("a =" + s1.geta( ));
System.out.println("b =" + s1.getb( ));
System.out.println("c =" + s1.getc( ));
}
}
```

In the above code super keyword is used access the base class constructor (supertest). It should be the first statement in the desired class constructor. We can also use the following syntax to access the base class variable and methods using the super keyword.

```
super.member of class.
```

Here member can be any method or an instance variable.

```
class x
{
 int i;
}
class y extends x
{
 int i // this i hides the i in x
 y (int a, int b)
 {
  super.i = a;  // i in x
  i = b;    // i in B
 }
 void show( )
 {
 System.out.println("i in superclass:" + super.i);
 System.out.println("i in subclass:" + i);
 }
}
class test subclass
{
 public static void main(String args[ ])
 {
  y yobj = now y (1, 2);
  yobj.show( );
 }
}
```

This program display the following

```
i in superclass : 1
i in subclass : 2
```

Multilevel Inheritance

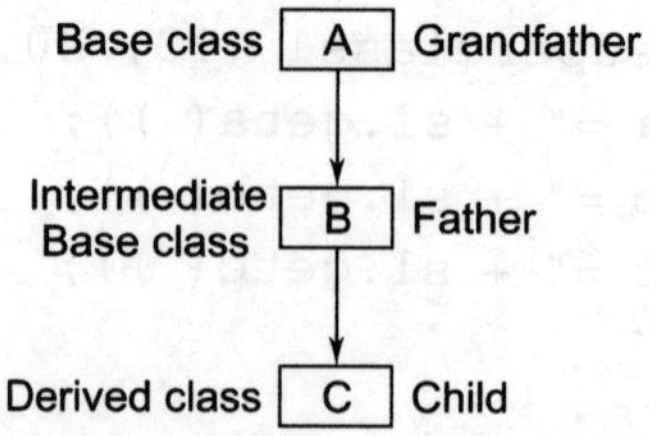

The class A serves as a base class for the derived class B which in turn serves as a base class for the derived class C. The class B is known as Intermediate base class since it provides a link for the inheritance between A & C. The chain ABC is known as inheritance path. General syntax:

```
class A
{
}
class B extends A
{
}
class C extends B
{
}
// Multilevel Inheritance
class A
{
   A()
   {
   System.out.println(" A is the Base Class\n");
   }
}
class B extends A
{
   B()
   {
   System.out.println(" B is the Intermediate Class\n");
   }
}
class C extends B
{
   C()
   {
   System.out.println(" C is the Derived class\n");
   }
}
```

```
class testmulti
{
public static void main(String args[])
{
System.out.println(" A class constructor");
A a1=new A();
System.out.println("B class constructor\n");
B b1=new B();
System.out.println("C class constructor\n");
C c1=new C();
}
}
```

Output:

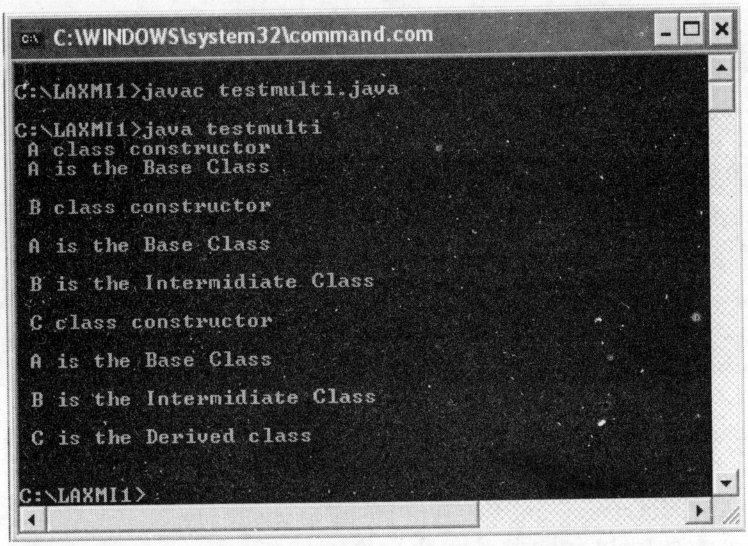


```
// Method Overriding
class base
{
    void methodoverride()
    {
    System.out.println(" Base class Method");
    }
}
class derived extends base
{
    void methodoverride()
    {
    System.out.println(" Derived class Method");
```

```
        }
}
class testoverride
{
        public static void main(String args[])
        {
        base b=new base();
        b.methodoverride();
        derived d=new derived();
        d.methodoverride();
        }
}
```

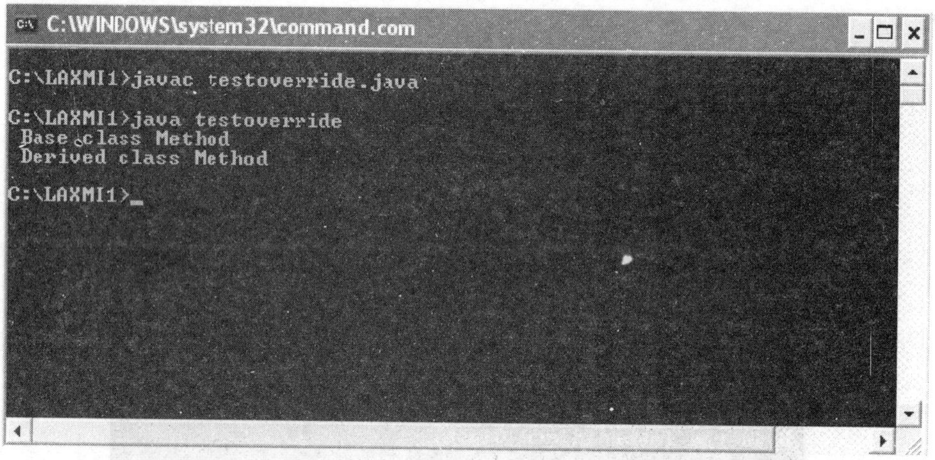

When a method in a subclass has the some name and type signature as a method in its superclass, then the method in the subclass is said to override the method in the superclass.

Abstract class : Abstract class is one that is not used to create object. An Abstract class is designed only to act as a base class (to be inherited by the other).

Rules for Abstract class :

1. An abstract methods is a method that is declared with only its signature it has no implementation.

   Abstract method name (parameter list)

2. An abstract class is a class that has at least one abstract method.

```
Abstract class classname
{
  abstract method name (parameterlist);
  ordinary methods;
}
```

3. You cannot declare any abstract constructor.
4. Abstract class has not include any abstract static method.

EXERCISE

1. Write a program that asks the user to enter a temperature in degrees Fahrenheit, and then prints out the equivalent temperature in degrees Celsius.
2. Write a function `twodigitreverse` that reverses the digits of a two-digit integer. For example, if the input is 24, the output would be 42.
3. Write the above program by using the concept of Inheritance.
4. Which of the following signature are valid for main() method in java
   - Public static void main (string args [])
   - public static void main (String args[])
   - public static void Main(string ags[])
5. Define recursion. Explain with the use of suitable example.
6. What is single level inheritance in java?
7. Write a program for Pascal triangle

   1

   1 1

   1 2 1

   1 3 3 1
8. What is the difference between overloading and overriding?
9. Assume that a class Derived is privately derived from class Base. Explain whether an object of derived class declared in main () can access the following members.

   The private members of derived class

   The protected members of derived class

   The public members of derived class

   The private members of base class

   The protected members of base class

   The Public members of base class
10. Create a class employee which have name, age, and address of employee. Include functions getdata() and showdata() getdata()1 takes the input from the user and insert it in a file person.dat and showdata() reads the same file to display the data of all the employees in that file in the following format.

    Name:

    Age:

    Address :

    Name:

    Age :

    Address :

    -
    -
    -
11. Implement the following class hierarchy where class person contains name and age of person and student class contains enroll.no. of student and the worker class contains social security number of worker.

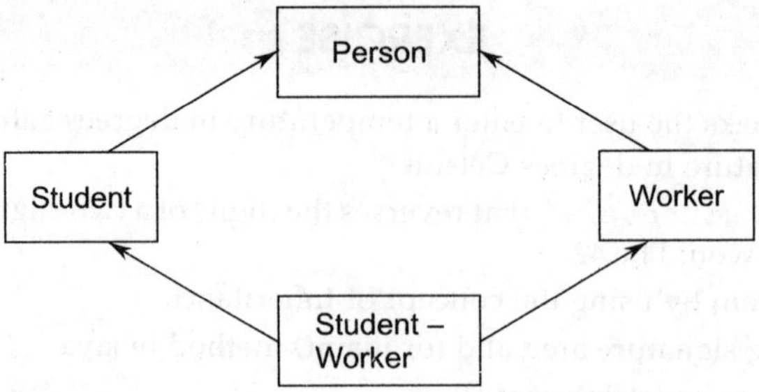

Try to implement in Java by yourself.

12. Write a class called CAccount which contains two private data elements, an integer accountNumber and a floating point accountBalance, and three member functions:
    (*i*) A constructor that allows the user to set initial values for accountNumber and accountBalance and a default constructor that prompts for the input of the values for the above data members.
    (*ii*) A function called inputTransaction, which reads a character value for transactionType ('D' for deposit and 'W' for withdrawal), and a floating point value for transactionAmount, which updates accountBalance.
    (*iii*) A function called printBalance, which prints on the screen the accountNumber and accountBalance.
13. What is the inheritance and what are the uses ?
14. What is the use of super keyword in java ?

CHAPTER 11

PACKAGES AND INTERFACES

PACKAGE INTRODUCTION

Packages are the collection of related classes. Packages are containers for classes that are used to keep the class. Java packages are defined into two ways.

1. Predefined Package or Built in Package or Java API
2. User–defined Package.

Example : A package allows you to create a class named employee which you can store in your own package without worry that it will be collide with some other class named employee stored elsewhere.

Example : Java API contains approximately 60 java.* package. For example. java.lang, java.util, java.io, java.awt, etc. are most commonly used package.

Why we need Package : Suppose you write a group of class that represent an employee record like calculate salary, employee details, department, etc.

You should boundle all there classes together and keep into a common place. You also need some way to be assured that the name you choose for a class will be reasonably unique and not collide with class name choosen by other programmes. Java provides a mechanism for partitioning the class name space into more manageable form. This mechanism is called package. You can define classes inside a package that are not accessible by code outside that package.

DEFINING A PACKAGE

To create a package is quite easy. The very first statement allowed in a java file is a package statement. This has the following syntax.

```
PEackage package.name;
```

Example :

```
Package mypackage;
```

Java uses file system directories to store packages. Class files for any classes you declare to be part of mypackage must be stored in a directory called mypackage.

Note : Directory name must match the package name exactly. Packages are also provides access protection and namespace management. For DOS create a directory using the following command.syntax.

```
        md directoryname;
eq : c:\> md mypackage ↵
```

Change the current position to particular directory use the following command.syntax.

```
    cd directory name;
```

Example : `c:\>cd mypackage ↵`

↓

```
    c : \ mypackage > -
```

More than one file can include the same package statement. The package statement simply specifies to which package the class defined in file belongs.

You can create hierarchy of package. Each package name must be different from other one.syntax.

```
    Package package1 [. Package 2 [. Package 3]];
```

Example : ⇒ User defined package.

```
    Package java.awt.image;
```

Example ⇒ Program :

```
package test;
public class abc
{
   public void show( )
   {
     System.out.println(" First Package Program");
   }
}.
```

You can create a class by the name of abc and stored into a folder test. Compile the program
C:\test\abc.java ↵

Program :

```
import test.*;
class testfinal
{
   public static void main(String args[ ])
   {
       abc a1 = new abc( );
       a1. show( );
   }
}
```

Output

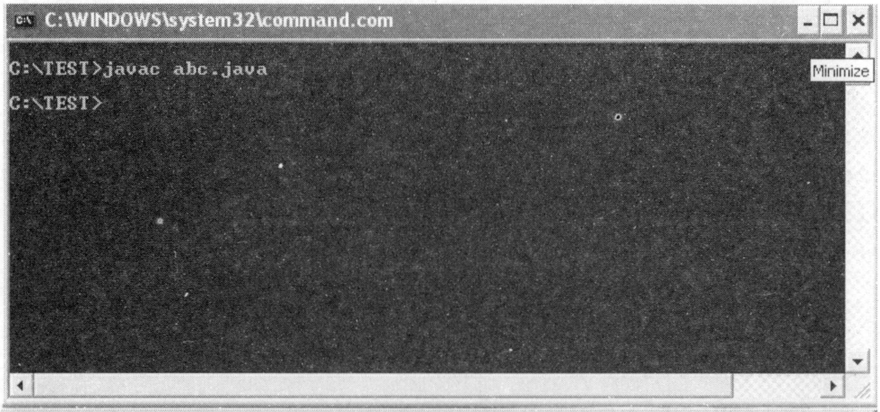

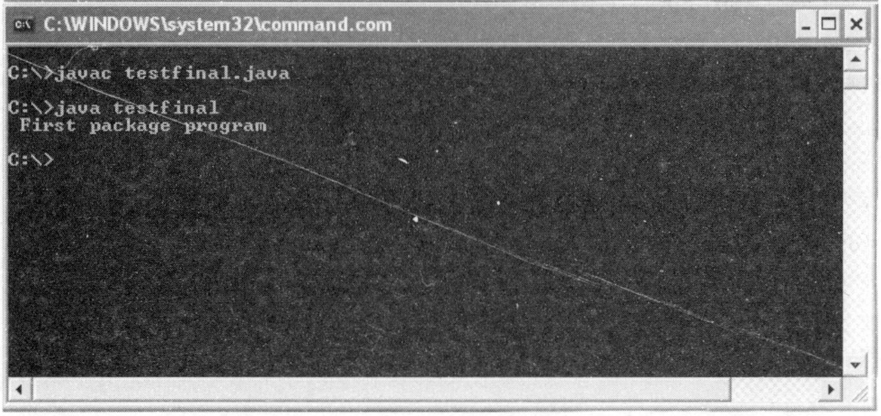

Access protection

Access Location	*Public*	*Protected*	*Private*	*No modifies (default)*
Same class	Y	Y	Y	Y
Same package subclass	Y	Y	N	Y
Same package non subclass	Y	Y	N	Y
Different package subclass	Y	Y	N	N
Different package non subclass	Y	N	N	N

In the preceding chapter you learned about access specifies (private public, protected). As you will know that access to a private member of a class is granted only to other member of class. Package add another dimension to access control. Anything declared **public** can be accessed from anywhere. Anything declared **private** cannot be seen outside of its class. If you want to allow an element to be seen outside your current package, but only to classes that subclass your directly, then declare that element **Protected.**

An Access Example :

```
Package mypack1;
public class abc
{
 int n = 1;
 private int n1 = 2;
 protected int n2 = 3;
 public int n3 = 4;
 abc( )
{
 System.out.println("Base Constructor");
 System.out.println("n =" + n);
 System.out.println("n1 =" + n1);
 System.out.println("n2 =" + n2);
 System.out.println("n3 =" + n3);
 }
}
```

Save it by the name abc.java

```
Package mypack1;
class xyz extends abc
{
 xyz( )
 {
 System.out.println("Derived Constructor");
 System.out.println("n =" +n);
 System.out.println("n1 =" + n1);
 System.out.println("n2 =" + n2);
 System.out.println("n3 =" + n3);
 }
}
```

Save it by the name xyz.java.

```
Package mypack1
class samepack
{
 samepack( )
 {
  abc a1 = new abc( );
  System.out.println("same package Constructor");
  System.out.println("n =" + a1.n);
  System.out.println("n1 =" + a1.n1);
  System.out.println("n2 =" + a1.n2);
```

```
     System.out.println("n3 =" +a1.n3);
    }
   }
   Package mypack2;
   Class abc 2 extends mypack1.abc
   {
      abc2( )
      {
      System.out.println("other package constructor");
      System.out.println("n =" + n); // generate error
      System.out.println("n1 =" + n1); // generate error  make them /
/ comment
      System.out.println("n2 =" + n2);
      S.o.p ("n3 =" + n3);
     }
   }
Save it by abc2.java.
    package mypack2;
    class xyz2
    {
     xyz2( )
     {
      mypack1.abc.a1 = new mypack1.abc( );
      System.out.println("other package constructor");
      System.out.println("n =" + n); // generate error
      System.out.println("n1 =" + n1); // generate error
      System.out.println("n2 =" + n2); // generate error make them //
 comment
      System.out.println("n3 =" + n3);
     }
    }
 Save it by xyz2.java
    package mypack1;
    public class test1
     {
      public static void main(String args[ ])
      {
       abc a1 = new abc( );
       xyz x1 = new xyz( );
       samepack s1 = new samepack( );
```

```
    }
  }
1) Save it by name test1.java
2) Compile it
3) Run it.
The test file for mypack2
   package mypack2;
   public class test2.
   {
     public static void main(String args[ ])
     {
       abc2 a2 = new abc2( );
       xyz2 x2 = new xyz2( );
     }
   }
1) Save it by name test2.java
2) Compile it
3) Run it.
```

INTERFACES

Interfaces are the next level of abstraction. An interface is like a class with nothing but `abstract` methods and `final`, `static` fields. All methods and fields of an interface must be public.

However, unlike a class, an interface can be added to a class that is already a subclass of another class. Furthermore an interface can apply to members of many different classes. For instance you can define an `Import` interface with the single method `calculateTariff( )`.

```
public interface Import {
   public double calculateTariff ( );
}
```

You might want to use this interface on many different classes, cars among them but also for clothes, food, electronic and more. It would be inconvenient to make all these objects derive from a single class. Furthermore, each different type of item is likely to have a different means of calculating the tariff. Therefore you define an `Import` interface and declare that each class implements `Import`.

The syntax is simple. `Import` is declared public so that it can be accessed from any class. It is also possible to declare that an interface is protected so that it can only be implemented by classes in a particular package. However this is very unusual. Almost all interfaces will be public. No interface may be private because the whole purpose of an Interface is to be inherited by other classes.

The `interface` keyword takes the place of the `class` keyword. Line 3 looks like a classic method definition. It's public (as it must be). It's abstract, also as it must be. And it returns a `double`. The method's name is `calculateTariff ( )` and it takes no arguments. The difference between this method and a method in a class is that there is no method body. That remains to be created in each class that implements the interface.

You can declare many different methods in an interface. These methods may be overloaded. An interface can also have fields, but if so they must be `final` and `static` (in other words constants).

IMPLEMENTING INTERFACES

To actually use this interface you create a class that includes a `public double calculateTariff ( )` method and declare that the class implements `Import`. For instance here's one such class:

```
public class Car extends MotorVehicle implements Import {
  int numWheels = 4;
  public double calculateTariff ( ) {
   return this.price * 0.1;
  }
}
```

One of the advantages of interfaces over classes is that a single class may implement more than one interface. For example, this `Car` class implements three interfaces: `Import`, `Serializable`, and `Cloneable`

```
import java.io.*;
public class Car extends MotorVehicle
  implements Import, Serializable, Cloneable {
  int numWheels = 4;
  public double calculateTariff ( ) {
   return this.price * 0.1;
  }
}
```

`Serializable` and `Cloneable` are marker interfaces from the class library that only add a type to a class, but do not declare any additional methods

IMPLEMENTING THE CLONEABLE INTERFACE

The `java.lang.Object` class contains a `clone ( )` method that returns a bitwise copy of the current object.

```
protected native Object clone ( ) throws CloneNotSupportedException
```

Not all objects are cloneable. It particular only instances of classes that implement the `Cloneable` interface can be cloned. Trying to clone an object that does not implement the `Cloneable` interface throws a `CloneNotSupportedException`.

For example, to make the `Car` class cloneable, you simply declare that it implements the `Cloneable` interface. Since this is only a *marker interface*, you do not need to add any methods to the class.

```
Public class Car extends MotorVehicle implements Cloneable {
  // . . .
}
```

For example

```
Car c1 = new Car("New York A12 345", 150.0};
```

```
Car c2 = (Car) cl.clone ( );
```

Most classes in the class library do not implement `Cloneable` so their instances are not cloneable.

Most of the time, clones are *shallow copies*. In other words if the object being cloned contains a reference to another object A, then the clone contains a reference to the same object A, not to a clone of A. If this isn't the behavior you want, you can override `clone ( )` yourself.

You may also override `clone ( )` if you want to make a subclass uncloneable, when one of its superclasses does implement `Cloneable`. In this case simply use a `clone ( )` method that throws a `CloneNotSupportedException`. For example,

```
public Object clone ( ) throws CloneNotSupportedException {
  throw new CloneNotSupportedException ("Can't clone a SlowCar");
}
```

You may also want to override `clone ( )` to make it `public` instead of `protected`. In this case, you can simply fall back on the superclass implementation. For example,

```
public Object clone ( ) throws CloneNotSupportedException {
  return super.clone ( ); }
```

INTERFACES CAN BE EXTENDED

An interface can inherit another interface by using the keyword **externals**. When a class implements an interface that inherits another interface, it must provide implementations for all methods defined within the interface inheritance. Example.

```
interface A
{
  void abc( );
  void xyz( );
}
interface B extends A
{
  void k/m ( );
}
class testinterface implements B
{
  public void abc ( )
  {
   System.out.println("HARISH");
  }
  public void xyz ( )
  {
   System.out.println("KUMAR");
  }
```

```
public void klm ( )
 {
  System.out.println("TALUJA");
 }
}
class test
{
  public static void main(String args[ ])
  {
  testinterface ti = new testinterface ( );
    ti.abc( );
    ti.xyz( );
    ti.klm( );
  }
}
```

As an experiment you might want to try removing the implementation for abc ( ) in testinterface. This will cause an compile time error. Any class that implements an interface must implement all methods defined by that interface, including any that are inhesited from others interfaces.

EXERCISE

1. What is the importance of using package in Java?
2. Differentiate between user defined package and built in package.
3. Give the steps involved in creating Package.
4. Explain implicit and explicit import statement.
5. What is the difference between public and default class?
6. What do you understand by implementing interface?
7. Differentiate between the following
   - Interface and class.
   - Interface and Abstract class
8. What is difference between abstract class and Interface?
9. How to extends one interface by other interface?
10. What is a package?
11. Write short note on Interface in Java.

CHAPTER 12

MANAGING ERRORS AND EXCEPTIONS

INTRODUCTION

- Errors are the wrongs that can make a program go wrong.
- An error may produce an incorrect output or may terminate the execution of the program abruptly or even may cause the system to crash.

TYPES OF ERRORS

Errors may broadly be classified into two categories :

1 Compile-time errors

2 Run-time errors

1. Compile-time Errors : All syntax errors will be detected and displayed by the java compiler and therefore these errors are known as compile-time errors. Whenever compiler displays an error, it will not create the class file.

```
/* This program contains an error*/
class Error1
{
  public static void main(String args[])
  {
    System.out.println("Hello Java") // Missing;
  }
}
```

Most of the compile-time errors are due to *typing mistake.* Typographical errors are hard to find. We may have to check the word by word, or even character by character. The most common problems are :-

- Missing semicolons
- Missing (or mismatch of) brackets in classes and methods
- Misspelling of identifiers and keywords
- Missing double quotes in strings
- Use of Undeclared variables
- Incompatible types in assignments / initialization.

2. Run-time Errors : Sometimes, a program may compile successfully creating the .class file but may not run properly such programs may produce wrong results due to wrong logic or may terminate due to errors such as stack over-flow. Most common run-time errors are:

- Dividing an integer by zero.
- Accessing an element that is out of the bounds of an array
- Trying to store a value into an array of an incompatible class or type
- Passing a parameter that is not in a valid range or value for a method. etc.

```
/* Illustration of run-time errors*/
class Error2
{
 public static void main(String args[])
 {
  int a = 10;
  int b = 5;
  int c = 5;
  int x = a/(b-c) // division by zero
  System.out.println("X=" +x);
  int y = a/(b+c);
  System.out.println("Y=" +y);
 }
}
```

EXCEPTION HANDLING

What is an Exception?

When an error is encountered during the execution of a Java program, an "Exception" is said to have occurred. Exceptions occur at run-time. This may be cause of certain conditions that arise at the time of execution, such as the following:

- Trying to access an out-of-bounds array elements.
- The file you try to open may not exist.
- The class file you want to load may be missing or in the wrong format.
- The other end of your network connection may be non-existent.

It is important to ensure that messages are flashed when errors are encountered. If this is not done the program could be terminated abruptly. *Exception handling is performed to identify errors and minimise the impact of errors on the program.*

The exception handling mechanism in Java minimise the chance of a system crash or abrupt termination of programs.

Due to this feature Java is a robust language.

The purpose of Exception Handling

A program should always have proper exception handling mechanism. Otherwise, an exception occurs and the program aborts. In such a situation all resources previously allocated by the system are left in the same state. This in turn will lead to a resource leak. To avoid the resource leak, all resources allocated by the system have to be returned to the system. For this, a proper exception handling mechanism is required.

Handling Exceptions

Checking for errors in Java is done with the help of an exception-handling model. The exception handling model is known as the 'catch and throw' model. According to this model, when an error occurs, an exception is *thrown* which is *caught* in a block.

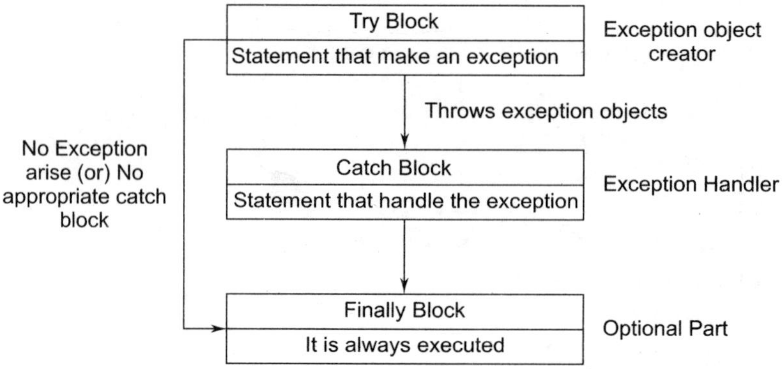

Exceptional conditions are treated as distinct from the normal flow of control in the program. Exceptions have to be caught or the program exits.

When an exception occurs, an object representing, that exception is created. The object is then passed to the method that handles the exception. This object contains detailed information about the exception. This information can be retrieved and processed.

Exceptions can be thrown by the run-time environment. They can also be manually generated by code. The class "Throwable" provided in Java is the super class of the class 'Exception'.

Advantages of the 'Catch and Throw' Model :

The catch and throw method of exception handling offers two advantages:

- An error condition has to be dealt with only where it is necessary. It need not be dealt with at every level.
- An error message can be provided in the exception handler.

The general form of an exception handling block :

```
try
{
  // Code for finding error
```

```
}
catch(ExceptionType1 ob)
{
  // exception handler for exceptiontype1
}
  catch(ExceptionType2 ob)
{
  // exception handler for exceptiontype2
}
. . . .
. . . .
finally
{
  // must be executed before return
}
```

Here exception type is the type of exception that has occurred.

By using exception to managing errors, Java programs have the following advantage over traditional error management techniques :

1. Separating Error Handling code from regular code.
2. Propagating error up the call stack.
3. Grouping error types and error differentiation.

The try Block. If we do not want the program to terminate by the exception we have to trap the exception using the try block. So we can place the statements that may cause an exception in the try block.

```
Syntax:
      try
        {
        // statements
        }
```

If an exception occurs within the try block, the appropriate exception handler that is associated with the try block handles the exception immediately following the try block, include a *catch* clause specifies the exception type that you wish to catch. A try block must have at least one catch block (or) finally that follows it immediately.

The catch Block : The catch block is used to process the exception raised. A try block can be one or more catch blocks can handle a try block. Catch handles are placed immediately after the try block.

```
Catch(Exceptiontype e)
  {
   // Error handle routine is placed
   // here for handling exception
  }
```

```
class trycatch
  {
    public static void main(String args[])
    {
      int [] no = {1,2,3};
      try {
        // out of bound
            System.out.println(no[3]);
        }
       catch(ArrayIndexOutofBoundsException e)
        {
        System.out.println("Out of the Range");
        }
       System.out.println("Quit");
       }
    }
```

This program generates the following output:
Out of the Range

Quit

Note : In the above the println() statement inside the try block is never executed. Exception occurs the control goes to the catch block.

Multiple Catch Statements. It is possible to have more than catch statement in the catch block as illustrated below:

```
  . . . . . .

  . . . . . .

  try
  {
    statement;  // generates an exception
  }
 catch(Exception-Type1 e)
  {
    statement;  // processes exceptiontype1
  }
 catch(Exception-Type 2 e)
  {
    statement;  // processes exceptiontype2
  }
  :
  :
```

```
catch(Exception-Type n e)
  {
    statement;  // processes exceptiontype n.
  }
. . . . . . . . . . . . . .
. . . . . . . . . . . . . .
```

When an exception in a try block is generated, the Java treats the multiple catch statements like cases in a switch statements.

The first statement whose parameter matches with the exception object will be executed, and the remaining statements will skipped.

Note that Java does not require any processing of the exception at all. We can simply have a catch statement with an empty block to avoid program abortion.

Example: catch(Exception e);

The catch statement simply ends with a semicolon, which does nothing. This statement will catch an exception and the n ignore it.

```
// Using multiple catch blocks
class Error3
  {
    public static void main(String args[])
      {
        int a[] = {S,10};
        int b = 5;
      try
        {
          int x = a[2]/b - a[1];
        }
      catch(ArithmeticException e)
        {
        System.out.println("Division by zero");
        }
      catch(ArrayIndexOutOfBounds e)
        {
        System.out.println("Array index error");
        }
      catch(ArrayStoreException e)
        {
        System.out.println("Wrong data type");
        }
        int y = a[1] / a[0];
```

```
        System.out.println("y=" + y);
    }
  }
```

Output:

```
Array index error
y = 2
```

Using finally statement : Java supports another statement known as *finally* statements. Finally block can be used to handle any exception generated within a try block. It may be added immediately after the try block or after the last catch block, shows as follows:

```
try                         try
  {                           {
  . . . . . . . . . .           . . . . . . . . . .
  . . . . . . . . . .           . . . . . . . . . .
   }                          }
finally                     catch(. . . . . . . . )
  {                           {
  . . . . . . . . . .           . . . . . . . . . .
  . . . . . . . . . .           . . . . . . . . . .
  }                           }
                            catch(. . . . . )
                              {
                                . . . . . . .
                                . . . . . . .
                              }
                            finally
                              {
                                . . . . . . .
                                . . . . . . .
                              }
```

When a *finally* block is defined, this is gauranteed to execute, regardless of whether or not an exception is thrown.

Throwing our Own Exceptions : There may be times when we would like to throw our own exceptions. We can do this by using the keyword *throw* as follows:

throw new Throwable_subclass;

Example:

throw new ArithmeticException();

throw new NumberFormatException();

Note that Exception is a subclass of Throwable and therefore MyException is a subclass of Throwable class. An object of a class that extends Throwable can be thrown and caught.

```
// Throwing our own exception.
import java.lang.Exception;
class MyException extends Exception
  {
      MyException(String message)
         {
           super(message);
         }
  }
class Test MyException
     {
       public static void main(String args[])
        {
          int x = 5, y = 1000;
          try
           {
            float z = (float) x / (float) y;
            if (z < 0.01)
            {
              throw new MyException("Number is toosmall");
            }
          }
      catch(MyException e)
        {
          System.out.println("Caught my exception");
          System.out.println(e.getMessage());
        }
     finally
        {
          System.out.println("I am always here");
        }
     }
  }
```

Java's Built-in Exceptions : Inside the standard package java.lang.java defines several exception classes.

The most general of these exceptions are subclass of the standard type *RuntimeException.* In the language of Java, these are called *unchecked exceptions* because the compiler does not check to see if a method handles or throws these exceptions. The unchecked exceptions defined in java.lang are listed in Table.

Exception	Meaning
ArithmeticException	Arithmetic error, such as divide-by-zero.
ArrayIndexOutOfBoundsException	Array index is out-of-bounds.
ArrayStoreException	Assignment to an array element of an array element of an incompatible type.
ClassCastException	Invalid Cast
IllegalArgumentException	Illegal argument used to invoke a method.
IllegalMonitorStateException	Illegal monitor operation, such as waiting or an unlocked thread.
IllegalStateException	Environment or application is in incorrect state.
IllegalThreadStateException	Requested operation not-compatible with current thread state.
IndexOutOfBoundsException	Some type of index is out-of-bounds.
NegativeArraySizeException	Array created with a negative size. etc.

Those exceptions defined by java.lang that must be included in a methods throws list if that method can generate one of these exceptions and does not handle it itself. These are called checked exceptions.

Checked Exceptions	Meaning
ClassNotFoundException	Class not found
IllegalAccessException	Access to a class is denied
InterruptedException	One thread has been interrupted by another thread.

EXERCISE

1. How do you define try and catch block?
2. What do you mean by exception? Explain the different type of exception.
3. Explain Finally block in Exception handling.
4. Write the short note on the following
   - throw
   - throws
   - finally
   - final
5. Is the code legal

```
try
{
}
finally
{
}
```

6. What exception types can be caught by the following handler?

```
Catch(Exception e)
{
}
```

What is wrong with using this type of exception handler?

7. Is there anything wrong with the following exception handler as written? Will this code compile?

```
try
{
}
Catch (Arithmetic Exception e)
{
}
```

8. Explain how exception-handling mechanism can be used in a program.
9. How many catch blocks and finally blocks can be use with a try blocks?

13

CHAPTER

STRING HANDLING

STRING CONSTRUCTOR

The string class supports the several string constructors Followings are the String constructors.

1. **public String() :** Initializes a newly created String object so that it represents an empty character sequence. Note that use of this constructor is unnecessary since Strings are immutable.
2. **public String(String original) :** Initializes a newly created String object so that it represents the same sequence of characters as the argument; in other words, the newly created string is a copy of the argument string. Unless an explicit copy of original is needed, use of this constructor is unnecessary since Strings are immutable.

   Parameters :

   original – a String.
3. **public String(char[] value) :** Allocates a new String so that it represents the sequence of characters currently contained in the character array argument. The contents of the character array are copied; subsequent modification of the character array does not affect the newly created string.

   Parameters:

   value – the initial value of the string.
4. **public String(char[] value, int offset, int count) :** Allocates a new String that contains characters from a subarray of the character array argument. The offset argument is the index of the first character of the subarray and the count argument specifies the length of the subarray. The contents of the subarray are copied; subsequent modification of the character array does not affect the newly created string.

   Parameters:

   value – array that is the source of characters.

   offset – the initial offset.

   count – the length.

Throws:

IndexOutOfBoundsException – if the offset and count arguments index characters outside the bounds of the value array.

5. **public String(byte[] ascii, int hibyte, int offset, int count) :** This method does not properly convert bytes into characters. As of JDK 1.1, the preferred way to do this is via the String constructors that take a charset name or that use the platform's default charset.

   Allocates a new String constructed from a subarray of an array of 8-bit integer values.

   The offset argument is the index of the first byte of the subarray, and the count argument specifies the length of the subarray.

   Each byte in the subarray is converted to a char as specified in the method above.

   Parameters:

   ascii – the bytes to be converted to characters.

   hibyte – the top 8 bits of each 16-bit Unicode character.

   offset – the initial offset.

   count – the length.

   Throws:

   IndexOutOfBoundsException – if the offset or count argument is invalid.

6. **public String(byte[] ascii, int hibyte) :** This method does not properly convert bytes into characters. As of JDK 1.1, the preferred way to do this is via the String constructors that take a charset name or that use the platform's default charset.

   Allocates a new String containing characters constructed from an array of 8-bit integer values. Each character *c* in the resulting string is constructed from the corresponding component *b* in the byte array such that:

   $$c == (char)(((hibyte \& 0xff) << 8) \mid (b \& 0xff))$$

   Parameters:

   ascii – the bytes to be converted to characters.

   hibyte – the top 8 bits of each 16-bit Unicode character.

7. **public String(byte[] bytes, int offset, int length, String charsetName):** Constructs a new **String** by decoding the specified subarray of bytes using the specified charset. The length of the new **String** is a function of the charset, and hence may not be equal to the length of the subarray.

   The behavior of this constructor when the given bytes are not valid in the given charset is unspecified.

   Parameters:

   Bytes – the bytes to be decoded into characters

   Offset – the index of the first byte to decode

   Length – the number of bytes to decode

   CharsetName – the name of a supported charset

   Throws:

   UnsupportedEncodingException – if the named charset is not supported

   IndexOutOfBoundsException – if the offset and length arguments index characters outside the bounds of the bytes array.

8. **public String(byte[] bytes, String charsetName) :** Constructs a new String by decoding the specified array of bytes using the specified charset. The length of the new String is a function

of the charset, and hence may not be equal to the length of the byte array.

The behavior of this constructor when the given bytes are not valid in the given charset is unspecified.

Parameters:

bytes – the bytes to be decoded into characters

charsetName – the name of a supported charset

Throws:

UnsupportedEncodingException – If the named charset is not supported

9. **public String(byte[] bytes, int offset, int length) :** Constructs a new String by decoding the specified subarray of bytes using the platform's default charset. The length of the new String is a function of the charset, and hence may not be equal to the length of the subarray.

   The behavior of this constructor when the given bytes are not valid in the default charset is unspecified.

   Parameters:

   bytes – the bytes to be decoded into characters

   offset – the index of the first byte to decode

   length – the number of bytes to decode

   Throws:

   IndexOutOfBoundsException – if the offset and the length arguments index characters outside the bounds of the bytes array.

10. **public String(byte[] bytes) :** Constructs a new String by decoding the specified array of bytes using the platform's default charset. The length of the new String is a function of the charset, and hence may not be equal to the length of the byte array.

    The behavior of this constructor when the given bytes are not valid in the default charset is unspecified.

    Parameters:

    bytes – the bytes to be decoded into characters.

11. **public String(StringBuffer buffer) :** Allocates a new string that contains the sequence of characters currently contained in the string buffer argument. The contents of the string buffer are copied; subsequent modification of the string buffer does not affect the newly created string.

    Parameters:

    buffer – a StringBuffer.

Example:

```
class firststring{
public static void main(String args[])
{
    char C[]={'H','A','R','I','S','H'};
    String s1=new String(C);
    String s2=new String(s1);
    System.out.println(s1);
    System.out.println(s2);
}}
```

Output:

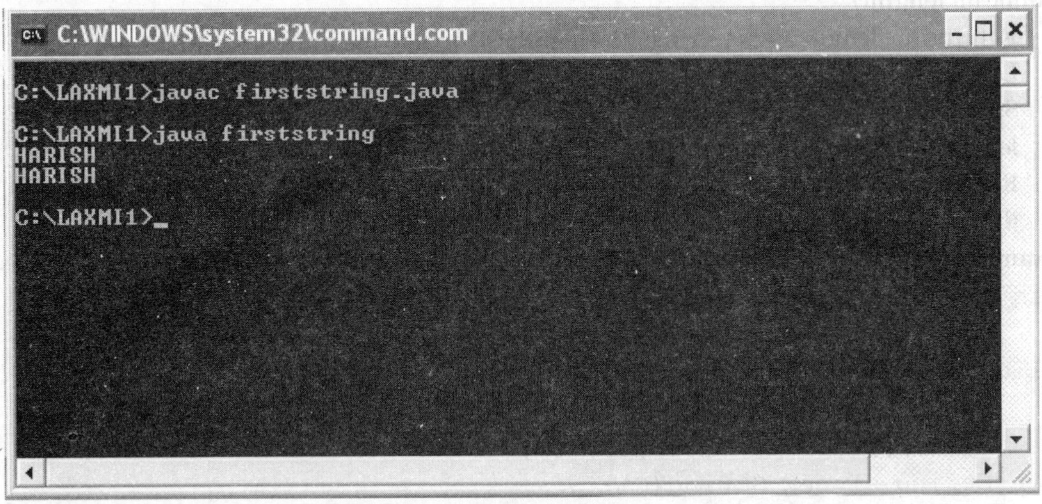

Example:

```
class firststring1{
public static void main(String args[])
                    { byte C[]={65,66,67,68,69,70};
                    String s1=new String(C);
                    String s2=new String(C,3,2);
                    System.out.println(s1);
                    System.out.println(s2);
}}
```

Output:

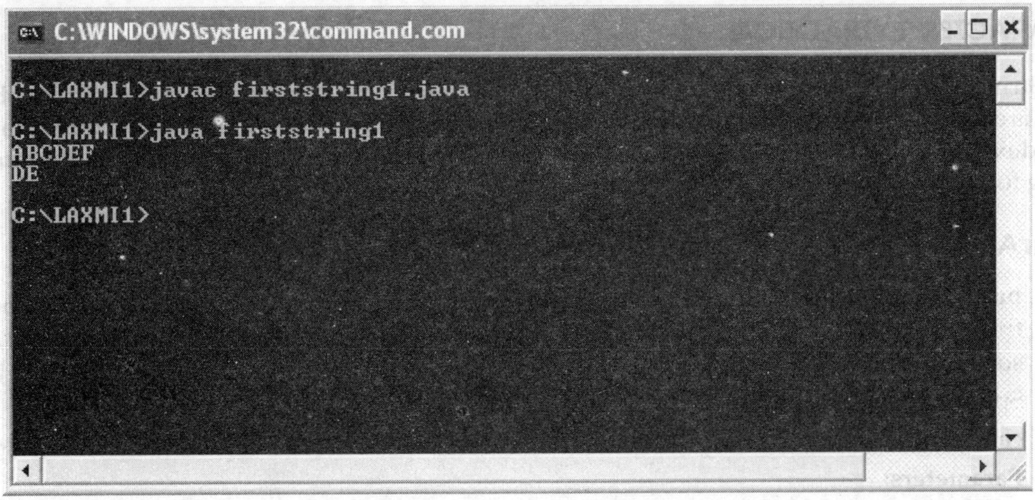

String Length

public int length()

Returns the length of this string. The length is equal to the number of 16-bit Unicode characters in the string.

Specified by:

length in interface CharSequence

Returns:

the length of the sequence of characters represented by this object.

Example:

```
class firststring1
{
public static void main(String args[])
{
        byte C[]={65,66,67,68,69,70};
        String s1=new String(C);
        String s2=new String(C,3,2);
        System.out.println(s1);
        System.out.println(s2);
        int length;
        length=s1.length();
        System.out.println(length);
}
}
```

Output:

ABCDEF

DE

6

CHARACTER EXTRACTION

The String class provides number of ways in which character can be extracted from a String object. Each is examined here. Although the character that comprise a string within a String object cannot be indexed as if they were a character array, many of the String methods employ an index into the string for their operations.

charAt

1. **public char charAt(int index) :** Returns the character at the specified index. An index ranges from 0 to length() – 1. The first character of the sequence is at index 0, the next at index 1, and so on, as for array indexing.

   Specified by:

   charAt in interface CharSequence

   Parameters:

   index – the index of the character.

Returns:

the character at the specified index of this string. The first character is at index 0.

Throws:

IndexOutOfBoundsException – if the index argument is negative or not less than the length of this string.

getChars

2. **public void getChars(int SourceBegin, int SourceEnd, char[] destination, int destinationBegin)** : Copies characters from this string into the destination character array. The first character to be copied is at index SourceBegin; the last character to be copied is at index SourceEnd–1 (thus the total number of characters to be copied is SourceEnd- SourceBegin). The characters are copied into the subarray of destination starting at index destinationBegin and ending at index:

   destinationBegin + (SourceEnd-SourceBegin) – 1

   Parameters:

   SourceBegin – index of the first character in the string to copy.

   SourceEnd – index after the last character in the string to copy.

   destination – the destination array.

   destinationBegin – the start offset in the destination array.

   Throws:

   IndexOutOfBoundsException – If any of the following is true :

   - sourceBegin is negative.
   - sourceBegin is greater than sourceEnd
   - sourceEnd is greater than the length of this string
   - destinationBegin is negative
   - destinationBegin +(sourceEnd-sourceBegin) is larger than destination.length

getBytes

3. **public void getBytes(int srcBegin, int srcEnd, byte[] dst, int dstBegin) :** This method does not properly convert characters into bytes. As of JDK 1.1, the preferred way to do this is via the getBytes() method, which uses the platform's default charset. Copies characters from this string into the destination byte array. Each byte receives the 8 low-order bits of the corresponding character. The eight high-order bits of each character are not copied and do not participate in the transfer in any way.

   The first character to be copied is at index srcBegin; the last character to be copied is at index srcEnd-1. The total number of characters to be copied is srcEnd-srcBegin. The characters, converted to bytes, are copied into the subarray of dst starting at index dstBegin and ending at index:

   dstbegin + (srcEnd-srcBegin) – 1

   Parameters:

   srcBegin – index of the first character in the string to copy.

   srcEnd – index after the last character in the string to copy.

   dst – the destination array.

dstBegin – the start offset in the destination array.

Throws:

IndexOutOfBoundsException – if any of the following is true:

- srcBegin is negative
- srcBegin is greater than srcEnd
- srcEnd is greater than the length of this String
- dstBegin is negative
- dstBegin+(srcEnd-srcBegin) is larger than dst.length

a. **public byte[] getBytes(String charsetName :** Encodes this String into a sequence of bytes using the named charset, storing the result into a new byte array. The behavior of this method when this string cannot be encoded in the given charset is unspecified. The CharsetEncoder class should be used when more control over the encoding process is required.

Parameters:

charsetName – the name of a supported charset

Returns:

The resultant byte array

Throws:

UnsupportedEncodingException – If the named charset is not supported

b. **public byte[] getBytes() :** Encodes this String into a sequence of bytes using the platform's default charset, storing the result into a new byte array.

The behavior of this method when this string cannot be encoded in the default charset is unspecified. The CharsetEncoder class should be used when more control over the encoding process is required.

Returns:

The resultant byte array

Example:

```
class getchardemo
{
    public static void main(String args[])
    {
    String s="Internet and Java Programming";
    int start=10;
    int end=18;
    int length;
    length=s.length();
    char buffer[]=new char[end-start];
    s.getChars(start,end,buffer,0);
    System.out.println(buffer);
    System.out.println("Length of String is ="+ length);
    }
}
```

Output:

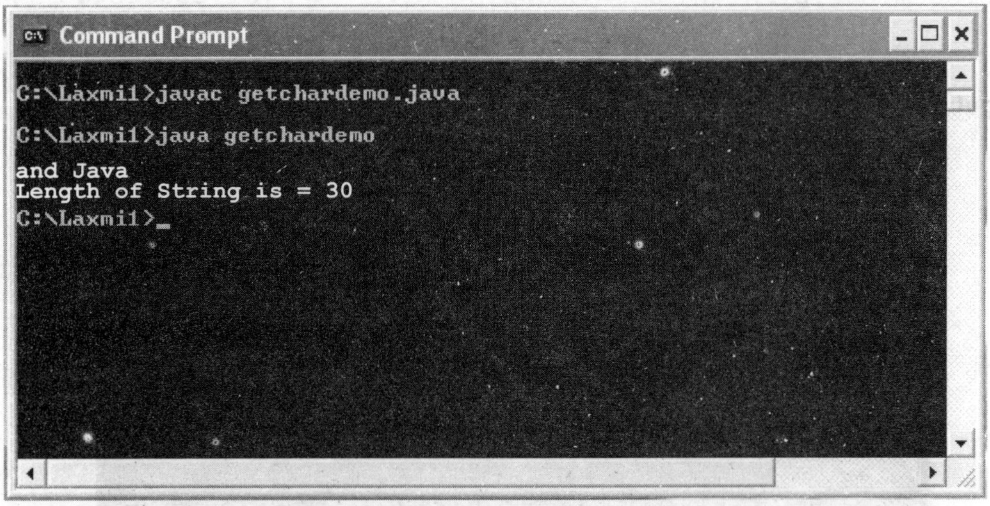

String Comparisons

equals

1. **public boolean equals(<u>Object</u> anObject) :** Compares this string to the specified object. The result is true if and only if the argument is not null and is a String object that represents the same sequence of characters as this object.

   Overrides:

   equals in class Object

   Parameters:

   anObject – the object to compare this String against.

   Returns:

   true if the String are equal; false otherwise.

```
// Equals and Equals Ignore case
class equals
{
public static void main(String args[])
{
     String a1=" harish ";
     String a2=" harish1";
     String a3=" Harish";
     String a4=" HARISH";
     String a5=" harish";
     System.out.println( a1 + "Equals" +a2+"->"+a1.equals(a2));
     System.out.println( a1 + "Equals" +a3+"->"+a1.equals(a2));
     System.out.println( a1 + "Equals" +a4+"->"+a1.equals(a2));
     System.out.println(a1 + "Equals Ignore Case" +a4+"->"
+a1.equalsIgnoreCase(a2));
```

```
    System.out.prentln( a1 + "Equals" +a5+" ->" +a1.equals(a5));
}
}
```

Output:

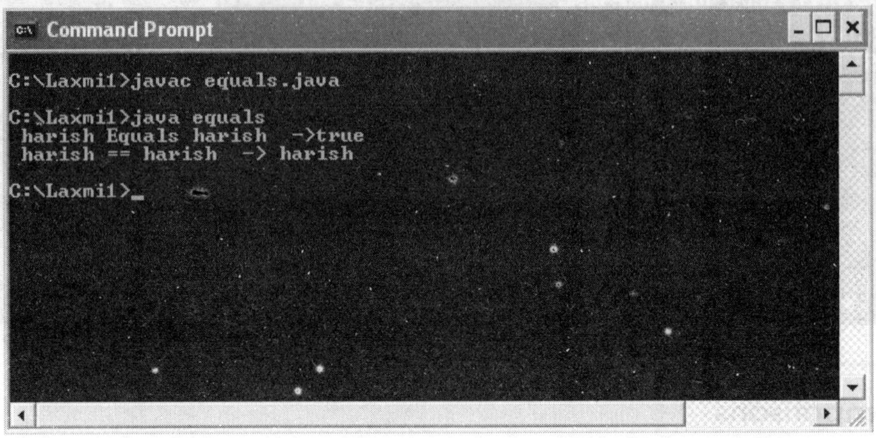


```
// Equal vs = =
class equalsvsequal
{
public static void main(String args[])
{
    String a1="harish";
    String a2=new String(a1);
    System.out.println( a1 + "Equals" +a2+"->"+a1.equals(a2));
    System.out.println( a1 + "==" +a2+"->"+(a1==a2));
}
}
```

Output:

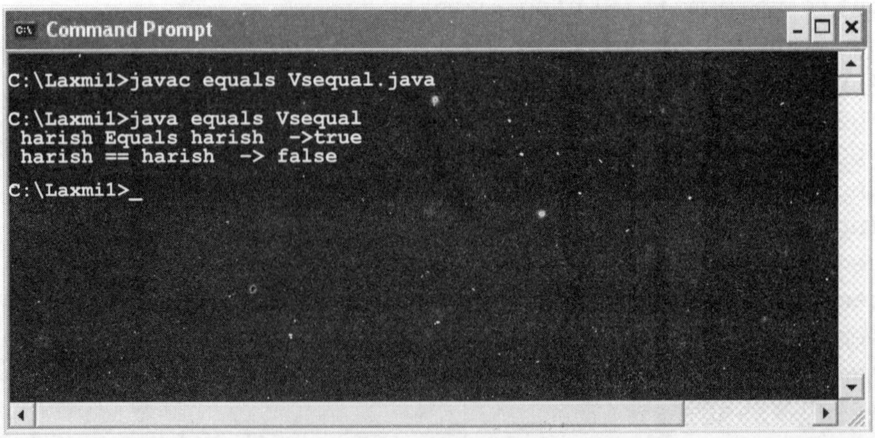

contentEquals

2. **public boolean contentEquals(StringBuffer sb) :** Returns true if and only if this String represents the same sequence of characters as the specified StringBuffer.

   Parameters:

   sb – the StringBuffer to compare to.

   Returns:

   true if and only if this String represents the same sequence of characters as the specified StringBuffer, otherwise false.

equalsIgnoreCase

3. **public boolean equalsIgnoreCase(String anotherString) :** Compares this String to another String, ignoring case considerations. Two strings are considered equal ignoring case if they are of the same length, and corresponding characters in the two strings are equal ignoring case.

   Two characters c1 and c2 are considered the same, ignoring case if at least one of the following is true:

   - The two characters are the same (as compared by the == operator).
   - Applying the method Character.toUpperCase(char) to each character produces the same result.
   - Applying the method Character.toLowerCase(char) to each character produces the same result.

   Parameters:-

   anotherString – the String to compare this String against.

   Returns:

   True if the argument is not null and the Strings are equal, ignoring case; false otherwise.

compareTo

4. **public int compareTo(String anotherString) :** Compares two strings lexicographically. The comparison is based on the Unicode value of each character in the strings. The character sequence represented by this String object is compared lexicographically to the character sequence represented by the argument string. The result is a negative integer if this String object lexicographically precedes the argument string. The result is a positive integer if this String object lexicographically follows the argument string. The result is zero if the strings are equal; compareTo returns 0 exactly when the equals(Object) method would return true.

   This is the definition of lexicographic ordering. If two strings are different, then either they have different characters at some index that is a valid index for both strings, or their lengths are different, or both. If they have different characters at one or more index positions, let *k* be the smallest such index; then the string whose character at position *k* has the smaller value, as determined by using the < operator, lexicographically precedes the other string. In this case, compareTo returns the difference of the two character values at position *k* in the two string – that is, the value:

   this.charAt(*k*)–anotherString.charAt(*k*)

If there is no index position at which they differ, then the shorter string lexicographically precedes the longer string. In this case, compareTo returns the difference of the lengths of the strings – that is, the value:

this.length()–anotherString.length()

Parameters:

anotherString – the String to be compared.

Returns:

The value 0 if the argument string is equal to this string; a value less than 0 if this string is lexicographically less than the string argument; and a value greater than 0 if this string is lexicographically greater than the string argument.

compareTo

5. **public int compareTo(Object o) :** Compares this String to another Object. If the Object is a String, this function behaves like compareTo(String). Otherwise, it throws a ClassCastException (as Strings are comparable only to other Strings).

   Specified by:

   compareTo in interface Comparable

   Parameters:

   o – the Object to be compared.

   Returns:

   The value 0 if the argument is a string lexicographically equal to this string; a value less than 0 if the argument is a string lexicographically greater than this string; and a value greater than 0 if the argument is a string lexicographically less than this string.

   Throws:

   ClassCastException – if the argument is not a String.

   compareToIgnoreCase

6. **public int compareToIgnoreCase(String str) :** Compares two strings lexicographically, ignoring case differences. This method returns an integer whose sign is that of calling compareTo with normalized versions of the strings where case differences have been eliminated by calling Character. toLowerCase(Character.toUpperCase(character)) on each character.

   Note that this method does *not* take locale into account, and will result in an unsatisfactory ordering for certain locales. The java.text package provides *collators* to allow locale-sensitive ordering.

   Parameters:

   str – the String to be compared.

   Returns:

   a negative integer, zero, or a positive integer as the specified String is greater than, equal to, or less than this String, ignoring case considerations.

regionMatches

7. **public boolean regionMatches(int toffset :** String other, int ooffset, int len) Tests if two string regions are equal.

A substring of this String object is compared to a substring of the argument other. The result is true if these substrings represent identical character sequences. The substring of this String object to be compared begins at index toffset and has length len. The substring of other to be compared begins at index ooffset and has length len. The result is false if and only if at least one of the following is true:

- toffset is negative.
- ooffset is negative.
- toffset+len is greater than the length of this String object.
- ooffset+len is greater than the length of the other argument.
- There is some nonnegative integer K less than len such that:

  this.charAt(toffset+K) != other.charAt(ooffset+K)

Parameters:

toffset – the starting offset of the subregion in this string.

other – the string argument.

ooffset – the starting offset of the subregion in the string argument.

len – the number of characters to compare.

Returns:

true if the specified subregion of this string exactly matches the specified subregion of the string argument; false otherwise.

regionMatches

8. **public boolean regionMatches(boolean ignoreCase, int toffset, String other, int ooffset, int len)**

   Tests if two string regions are equal. A substring of this String object is compared to a substring of the argument other. The result is true if these substrings represent character sequences that are the same, ignoring case if and only if ignoreCase is true. The substring of this String object to be compared begins at index toffset and has length len. The substring of other to be compared begins at index ooffset and has length len. The result is false if and only if at least one of the following is true:

   - toffset is negative.
   - ooffset is negative.
   - toffset+len is greater than the length of this String object.
   - ooffset+len is greater than the length of the other argument.
   - ignoreCase is false and there is some nonnegative integer K less than len such that:
     - this.charAt(toffset+K) != other.charAt(ooffset+K)
   - ignoreCase is true and there is some nonnegative integer K less than len such that:
     - Character.toLowerCase(this.charAt(toffset+K)) !=
     - Character.toLowerCase(other.charAt(ooffset+K))

     And:

     - Character.toUpperCase(this.charAt(toffset+K) !=
     - Character.toUpperCase(other.charAt(ooffset+K))

Parameters:

ignoreCase – if true, ignore case when comparing characters.

toffset – the starting offset of the subregion in this string.

other – the string argument.

ooffset – the starting offset of the subregion in the string argument.

len – the number of characters to compare.

Returns:

True if the specified subregion of this string matches the specified subregion of the string argument; false otherwise. Whether the matching is exact or case insensitive depends on the ignoreCase argument.

startsWith

9. **public boolean startsWith(String prefix, int toffset)** : Tests if this string Starts with the specified prefix beginning a specified index.

   Parameters:

   prefix – the prefix.

   toffset – where to begin looking in the string.

   Returns:

   true if the character sequence represented by the argument is a prefix of the substring of this object starting at index toffset; false otherwise. The result is false if toffset is negative or greater than the length of this String object; otherwise the result is the same as the result of the expression

   this.subString(toffset).startsWith(prefix)

startsWith

10. **public boolean startsWith(String prefix)** : Tests if this string starts with the specified prefix.

    Parameters:

    Prefix – the prefix.

    Returns:

    True if the character sequence represented by the argument is a prefix of the character sequence represented by this string; false otherwise. Note also that true will be returned if the argument is an empty string or is equal to this String object as determined by the equals(Object) method.

endsWith

11. **public boolean endsWith(String suffix)** : Tests if this string endswith the specified suffix.

    Parameters:

    suffix – the suffix.

    Returns:

    True if the character sequence represented by the argument is a suffix of the character sequence represented by this object; false otherwise. Note that the result will be true if the argument is the empty string or is equal to this String object as determined by the equals(Object) method.

hashCode

12. **public int hashCode() :** Returns a hash code for this string. The hashcode for a String object is computed as

$$s[0]*31^\wedge(n-1) + s[1]*31^\wedge(n-2) + \ldots + s[n-1]$$

using int arithmetic, where s[i] is the *i*th character of the string, n is the length of the string, and ^ indicates exponentiation. (The hash value of the empty string is zero.)

Overrides:

hashCode in class Object

Returns:

a hashcode value for this object.

SEARCHING STRINGS

The String class provides two methods that allow you to search a string for a specified character or substring.

indexOf

1. **Public int indexOf(int ch) :** Returns the index within this string of the first occurrence of the specified character. If a character with value ch occurs in the character sequence represented by this String object, then the index of the first such occurrence is returned – that is, the smallest value **K** such that:

this.charAt(**K**) = = *ch*

is true. If no such character occurs in this string, then –1 is returned.

Parameters:

ch – *a* character.

Returns:

the index of the first occurrence of the character in the character sequence represented by this object, or – 1 if the character does not occur.

indexOf

2. **public int indexOf(int ch, int fromIndex) :** Returns the index within this string of the first occurrence of the specified character, starting the search at the specified index.

If a character with value ch occurs in the character sequence represented by this String object at an index no smaller than fromIndex, then the index of the first such occurrence is returned- this is, the smallest value *k* such that:

(this.charAt(**K**) = = *ch*) && (**K**>= fromIndex)

is true. If no such character occurs in this string at or after position fromIndex, then – 1 is returned.

There is no restriction on the value of fromIndex. If it is negative, it has the same effect as if it were zero: this entire string may be searched. If it is greater than the length of this string, it has the same effect as if it were equal to the length of this string: – 1 is returned.

Parameters:

ch – a character.

fromIndex – the index to start the search from.

Returns:

the index of the first occurrence of the character in the character sequence represented by this object that is greater than or equal to fromIndex, or – 1 if the character does not occur.

lastIndexOf

3. **public int lastIndexOf(int ch) :** Returns the index within this string of the last occurrence of the specified character. That is, the index returned is the largest value **K** such that:

   this.charAt(**K**) = = *ch*

   is true. The String is searched backwards starting at the last character.

   Parameters:

   ch – *a* character.

   Returns:

   The index of the last occurrence of the character in the character sequence represented by this object, or – 1 if the character does not occur.

lastIndexOf

4. **public int lastIndexOf(int ch, int fromIndex) :** Returns the index within this string of the last occurrence of the specified character, searching backward starting at the specified index. That is, the index returned is the largest value **K** such that:

   this.charAt(*k*) = = *ch*) && (**K** <= fromIndex)

   is true.

   Parameters:

   ch – *a* character.

   fromIndex – the index to start the search from. There is no restriction on the value of fromIndex. If it is greater than or equal to the length of this string, it has the same effect as if it were equal to one less than the length of this string: this entire string may be searched. If it is negative, it has the same effect as if it were – 1: – 1 is returned.

   Returns:

   the index of the last occurrence of the character in the character sequence represented by this object that is less than or equal to fromIndex, or – 1 if the character does not occur before that point.

indexOf

5. **public int indexOf(String str) :** Returns the index within this string of the first occurrence of the specified substring. The integer returned is the smallest value *k* such that:

   this.startsWith(str, *k*)

   is true.

   Parameters:

   str – any string.

   Returns:

   if the string argument occurs as a substring within this object, then the index of the first character of the first such substring is returned; if it does not occur as a substring, – 1 is returned.

indexOf

6. **public int indexOf(String str, int fromIndex) :** Returns the index within this string of the first occurrence of the specified substring, starting at the specified index. The integer returned is the smallest value *k* for which:

   k >= Math.min(fromIndex, str.length()) && this.startsWith(str, *k*)

   If no such value of *k* exists, then – 1 is returned.

   Parameters:

   str – the substring for which to search.

   fromIndex – the index from which to start the search.

   Returns:

```
// Demonstration of indexOf
class startindex
{
public static void main(String args[])
{
String s="startindex specifies the index at which"+
    " point the search begins";
System.out.println(s);
System.out.println("indexOf(a)="+s.indexOf('a');
System.out.println("LastindexOf(a)="+s.lastIndexOf('a'));
System.out.println("indexOf(a.20)="+s.indexOf('a',20));
System.out.println("LastindexOf(a,15)="+s.lastIndexOf('a',15));
}
}
```

Output:

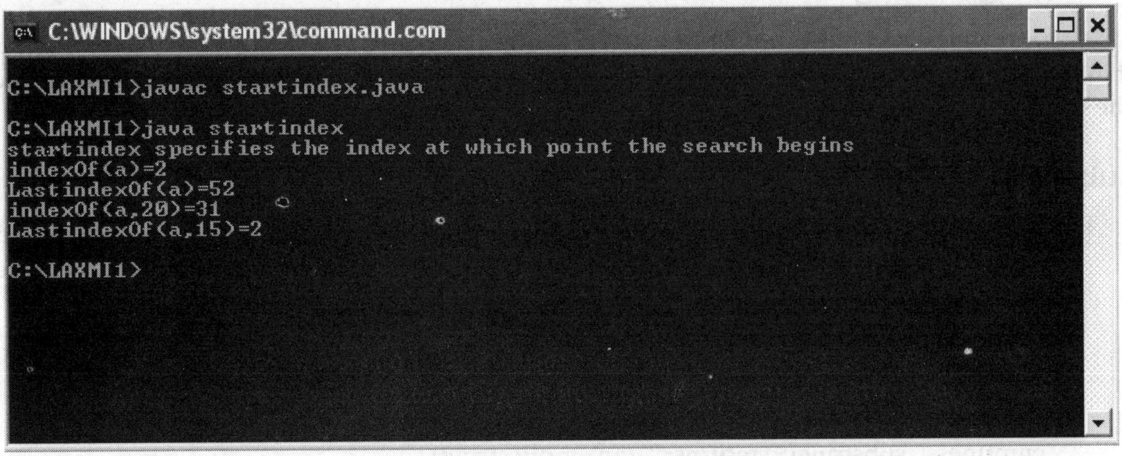

the index within this string of the first occurrence of the specified substring, starting at the specified index.

lastIndexOf

7. **public int lastIndexOf(String str) :** Returns the index within this string of the rightmost occurrence of the specified substring. The rightmost empty string "" is considered to occur at the index value this.length(). The returned index is the largest value *k* such that

   this.startsWith(str, *k*)

   is true.

   Parameters:

   str – the substring to search for.

   Returns:

   if the string argument occurs one or more times as a substring within this object, then the index of the first character of the last such substring is returned. If it does not occur as a substring, –1 is returned.

lastIndexOf

8. **public int lastIndexOf(String str, int fromIndex) :** Returns the index within this string of the last occurrence of the specified substring, searching backward starting at the specified index. The integer returned is the largest value *k* such that:

   k <= Math.min(fromIndex, str.length()) && this.startsWith(str, *k*)

   If no such value of *k* exists, then – 1 is returned.

   Parameters:

   str – the substring to search for.

   fromIndex – the index to start the search from.

   Returns:

   the index within this string of the last occurrence of the specified substring.

Modifying a String

Because String objects are immutable, wherever you want to modify a String. You must either copy it into a StringBuffer or use one of the following String methods, which will construct a new copy of the string with your modification complete.

substring

1. **public String substring(int beginIndex) :** Returns a new string that is a substring of this string. The substring begins with the character at the specified index and extends to the end of this string.

   Examples:

   "unhappy".substring(2) returns "happy"

   "Harbison".substring(3) returns "bison"

   "emptiness".substring(9) returns "" (an empty string)

   Parameters:

   beginIndex – the beginning index, inclusive.

Returns:

the specified substring.

Throws:

IndexOutOfBoundsException – if beginIndex is negative or larger than the length of this String object.

substring

2. **public String substring(int beginIndex, int endIndex) :** Returns a new string that is a substring of this string. The substring begins at the specified beginIndex and extends to the character at index endIndex –1. Thus the length of the substring is endIndex-beginIndex.

   Examples:

   "hamburger".substring(4, 8) returns "urge"

   "smiles".substring(1, 5) returns "mile"

   Parameters:

   beginIndex – the beginning index, inclusive.

   endIndex – the ending index, exclusive.

   Returns:

   the specified substring.

   Throws:

   IndexOutOfBoundsException – if the beginIndex is negative, or endIndex is larger than the length of this String object, or beginIndex is larger than endIndex.

subSequence

3. **public CharSequence subSequence(int beginIndex, int endIndex) :** Returns a new character sequence that is a subsequence of this sequence.

   An invocation of this method of the form

   str.subSequence(begin, end)

   behaves in exactly the same way as the invocation

   str.substring(begin, end)

   This method is defined so that the String class can implement the CharSequence interface.

   Specified by:

   subSequence in interface CharSequence

   Parameters:

   beginIndex – the begin index, inclusive.

   endIndex – the end index, exclusive.

   Returns:

   the specified subsequence.

   Throws:

   IndexOutOfBoundsException – if beginIndex or endIndex are negative, if endIndex is greater than length(), or if beginIndex is greater than startIndex

concat

4. **public String concat(String str) :** Concatenates the specified string to the end of this string. If the length of the argument string is 0, then this String object is returned. Otherwise, a new String object is created, representing a character sequence that is the concatenation of the character sequence represented by this String object and the character sequence represented by the argument string.

   Examples:

   "cares".concat("s") returns "caress"

   "to".concat("get").concat("her") returns "together"

   Parameters:

   str – the String that is concatenated to the end of this String.

   Returns:

   a string that represents the concatenation of this object's characters followed by the string argument's characters.

   replace

5. **public String replace(char oldChar, char newChar) :** Returns a new string resulting from replacing all occurrences of oldChar in this string with newChar.

   If the character oldChar does not occur in the character sequence represented by this String object, then a reference to this String object is returned. Otherwise, a new String object is created that represents a character sequence identical to the character sequence represented by this String object, except that every occurrence of oldChar is replaced by an occurrence of newChar.

   Parameters:

   oldChar – the old character.

   newChar – the new character.

   Returns:

   a string derived from this string by replacing every occurrence of oldChar with newChar.

matches

6. **public boolean matches(String regex) :** Tells whether or not this string matches the given regular expression.

   An invocation of this method of the form *str*.matches(*regex*) yields exactly the same result as the expression

   Pattern.matches(*regex*, *str*)

   Parameters:

   regex – the regular expression to which this string is to be matched

   Returns:

   true if, and only if, this string matches the given regular expression

   Throws:

   PatternSyntaxException – if the regular expression's syntax is invalid

   Since:

   1.4

   See Also:

   Pattern

replaceFirst

7. **public String replaceFirst(String regex, String replacement) :** Replaces the first substring of this string that matches the given regular expression with the given replacement.

   An invocation of this method of the form *str*.replaceFirst(*regex*, *repl*) yields exactly the same result as the expression

```
// Insert()
class insert1
{
public static void main(String args[])
{
StringBuffer sb=new StringBuffer(" Harish Taluja");
Sb.insert(2," Kumar");
System.out.println(sb);
}
}
```

Output:

The insert( ) methods inserts one string into another. It is overload d to accepts value of all the simple type plus string and object, it calls string.valueof( ) to obtain the string representation of the value it is called with.Syntax

String Buffer insert(int index, string str)

String Buffer insert(int index, char ch)

String Buffer insert(int index, object obj)

Reverse( ): you can reverse the character within a string Buffer object using reverse.syntax

String Buffer reverse( );

```
// Reverse String
class reverse
{
public static void main(String args[])
{
StringBuffer sb=new StringBuffer("ABCDEF");
```

```
System.out.println(" Original String " +sb);
sb.reverse();
System.out.println(" Reverse String "+sb);
}
}
```

Output:

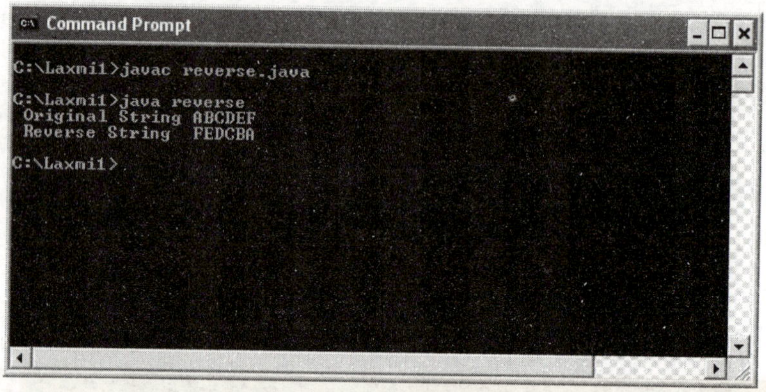

Pattern.compile(*regex*).matcher(*str.*)replaceFirst(*repl*)

Parameters:

regex – the regular expression to which this string is to be matched

Returns:

The resulting String

Throws:

PatternSyntaxException – if the regular expression's syntax is invalid

replaceAll

8. **public String replaceAll(String regex, String replacement) :** Replaces each substring of this string that matches the given regular expression with the given replacement.

   An invocation of this method of the form *str*.replaceAll(*regex, repl*) yields exactly the same result as the expression

   Pattern.compile(regex).matcher(*str*).replaceAll(*rpl*)

   Parameters:

   regex – the regular expression to which this string is to be matched

   Returns:

   The resulting String

   Throws:

   PatternSyntaxException – if the regular expression's syntax is invalid

split

9. **public String[] split(String regex, int limit) :** Splits this string around matches of the given regular expression.

The array returned by this method contains each substring of this string that is terminated by another substring that matches the given expression or is terminated by the end of the string. The substrings in the array are in the order in which they occur in this string. If the expression does not match any part of the input then the resulting array has just one element, namely this string.

The limit parameter controls the number of times the pattern is applied and therefore affects the length of the resulting array. If the limit *n* is greater than zero then the pattern will be applied at most *n* – 1 times, the array's length will be no greater than *n*, and the array's last entry will contain all input beyond the last matched delimiter. If *n* is non-positive then the pattern will be applied as many times as possible and the array can have any length. If *n* is zero then the pattern will be applied as many times as possible, the array can have any length, and trailing empty strings will be discarded.

The string "boo:and:foo", for example, yields the following results with these parameters:

Regex	Limit	Result
:	2	{ "boo", "and:foo" }
:	5	{ "boo", "and", "foo" }
:	– 2	{ "boo", "and", "foo" }
o	5	{ "b", "", ":and:f", "", "" }
o	– 2	{ "b", "", ":and:f", "", "" }
o	0	{ "b", "", ":and:f" }

An invocation of this method of the form *str*.split(*regex, n*) yields the same result as the expression

Pattern.compile(*regex*).split(*str, n*)

Parameters:

regex – the delimiting regular expression

limit – the result threshold, as described above

Returns:

the array of strings computed by splitting this string around matches of the given regular expression

Throws:

PatternSyntaxException – if the regular expression's syntax is invalid

split

10. **public String[] split(String regex)** : Splits this string around matches of the given regular expression.

This method works as if by invoking the two-argument split method with the given expression and a limit argument of zero. Trailing empty strings are therefore not included in the resulting array.

The string "boo:and:foo", for example, yields the following results with these expressions:

Regex	Result
:	{ "boo", "and", "foo" }
o	{ "b", "", ":and:f" }

Parameters:

regex – the delimiting regular expression

Returns:

the array of strings computed by splitting this string around matches of the given regular expression

Throws:

PatternSyntaxException – if the regular expression's syntax is invalid

toLowerCase

11. **public String toLowerCase(Locale locale) :** Converts all of the characters in this String to lower case using the rules of the given Locale. Case mappings rely heavily on the Unicode specification's character data. Since case mappings are not always 1:1 char mappings, the resulting String may be a different length than the original String.

    Parameters:

    locale – use the case transformation rules for this locale

    Returns:

    the String, converted to lowercase.

toLowerCase

12. **public String toLowerCase() :** Converts all of the characters in this String to lower case using the rules of the default locale. This is equivalent to calling toLowerCase(Locale.getDefault()).

    Returns:

    the String, converted to lowercase.

toUpperCase

13. **public String toUpperCase(Locale locale) :** Converts all of the characters in this String to upper case using the rules of the given Locale. Case mappings rely heavily on the Unicode specification's character data. Since case mappings are not always 1:1 char mappings, the resulting String may be a different length than the original String.

    Examples of locale-sensitive and 1:M case mappings are in the following table.

    Parameters:

    locale – use the case transformation rules for this locale

    Returns:

    the String, converted to uppercase.

```
// Change case
class changecase
{
public static void main(String args[])
{
    String s="CHangeCAse";
    System.out.println(" Original String "+s);
```

```
        String upper= s.toUpperCase();
        String lower= s.toUpperCase();
        System.out.println(" Upper Case "+upper);
        System.out.println(" Lower Case "+lower);
    }
}
```

Output:

toUpperCase

14. **public String toUpperCase() :** Converts all of the characters in this String to upper case using the rules of the default locale. This method is equivalent to toUpperCase(Loale.getDefault()).

    Returns:

    The String, converted to uppercase.

trim

15. **public String trim()** : Returns a copy of the string, with leading and trailing whitespace omitted.

    If this String object represents an empty character sequence, or the first and last characters of character sequence represented by this String object both have codes greater than '\u0020' (the space character), then a reference to this String object is returned.

    Otherwise, if there is no character with a code greater than '\u0020' in the string, then a new String object representing an empty string is created and returned.

    Otherwise, let *k* be the index of the first character in the string whose code is greater than '\u0020', and let *m* be the index of the last character in the string whose code is greater than '\u0020'. A new String object is created, representing the substring of this string that begins with the character at index *k* and ends with the character at index *m*-that is, the result of this.substring(*k*, *m*+1).

    This method may be used to trim whitespace from the beginning and end of a string; in fact, it trims all ASCII control characters as well.

    Returns:

    A copy of this string with leading and trailing white space removed, or this string if it has no leading or trailing white space.

toString

16. **public String toString()** : This object (which is already a string!) is itself returned.

    Specified by:

    toString in interface CharSequence

    Overrides:

    toString in class Object

    Returns:

    the string itself.

    toCharArray

17. **public char[] toCharArray()**

    Converts this string to a new character array.

    Returns :

    a newly allocated character array whose length is the length of this string and whose contents are initialized to contain the character sequence represented by this string.

    Data conversion using Valueof

ValueOf

1. **public static String valueOf(Object obj)** : Returns the string representation of the Object argument.

   Parameters:

   Obj – an Object.

   Returns:

   If the argument is null, then a string equal to "null"; otherwise, the value of obj.toString() is returned.

valueOf

2. **public static String valueOf(char[] data)** : Returns the string representation of the char array argument. The contents of the character array are copied; subsequent modification of the character array does not affect the newly created string.

   Parameters:

   data – a char array.

   Returns:

   a newly allocated string representing the same sequence of characters contained in the character array argument.

valueOf

3. **public static String valueOf(char[] data, int offset, int count)** : Returns the string representation of a specific subarray of the char array argument.

   The offset argument is the index of the first character of the subarray. The count argument specifies the length of the subarray. The contents of the subarray are copied; subsequent modification of the character array does not affect the newly created string.

Parameters:

data – the character array.

offset – the initial offset into the value of the String.

count – the length of the value of the String.

Returns:

a string representing the sequence of characters contained in the subarray of the character array argument.

Throws:

IndexOutOfBoundsException – if offset is negative, or count is negative, or offset+count is larger than data.length.

copyValueOf

4. **public static String copyValueOf(char[] data, int offset, int count) :**

   Returns a String that represents the character sequence in the array specified.

   Parameters:

   Data – the character array.

   Offset – initial offset of the subarray.

   Count – length of the subarray.

   Returns:

   a String that contains the characters of the specified subarray of the character array.

copyValueOf

5. **public static String copyValueOf(char[] data) :** Returns a String that represents the character sequence in the array specified.

   Parameters:

   data – the character array.

   Returns:

   a String that contains the characters of the character array.

valueOf

6. **public static String valueOf(boolean b) :** Returns the string representation of the boolean argument.

   Parameters:

   b – a boolean.

   Returns:

   if the argument is true, a string equal to "true" is returned; otherwise, a string equal to "false" is returned.

valueOf

7. **public static String valueOf(char c) :** Returns the string representation of the char argument.

Parameters:

c – a char.

Returns:

a string of length 1 containing as its single character the argument c.

valueOf

8. **public static String valueOf(int i) :** Returns the string representation of the int argument. The representation is exactly the one returned by the Integer.toString method of one argument.

   Parameters:

   i – an int.

   Returns:

   a string representation of the int argument.

valueOf

9. **public static String valueOf(long l) :** Returns the string representation of the long argument. The representation is exactly the one returned by the Long.toString method of one argument.

   Parameters:

   l – a long.

   Returns:

   a string representation of the long argument.

valueOf

10. **public static String valueOf(float f) :** Returns the string representation of the float argument. The representation is exactly the one returned by the Float.toString method of one argument.

    Parameters:

    f – a float.

    Returns:

    a string representation of the float argument.

valueOf

11. **public static String valueOf(double d) :** Returns the string representation of the double argument.

    The representation is exactly the one returned by the Double.toString method of one argument.

    Parameters:

    d – a double.

    Returns:

    a string representation of the double argument.

EXERCISE

1. Distinguish between the following terms:
   - String and StringBuffer
   - length and length()
   - equals and ==
2. Write a program to check whether a string is Palindrome or not.
3. Write a method called remove (String s1, int n) that returns the input string with nth element removed.
4. What will be the output of the following code
   - Class test

```
{
static String b;
public static void main(String args[])
{
String a=new String();
System.out.println(" A="+a);
System.out.println(" B="+b);
}
}
```

5. Explain the following character extraction function
   - charAt()
   - getChars()
   - getBytes()
6. What will be the output of the following code

```
class startindex
{
public static void main(String args[])
{
String s="startindex specifies the index at which"+
" point the search begins";
System.out.println(s);
System.out.println("indexOf(a)="+s.indexOf('I'));
System.out.println("LastindexOf(a)="+s.lastIndexOf('s'));
System.out.println("indexOf(a,20)="+s.indexOf('a',10));
System.out.println("LastindexOf(a,15)="+s.lastIndexOf('a',5));
}
}
```

7. Write a program to calculate the length of string.
8. Write a program to reverse a String.

CHAPTER 14

MULTITHREADING

INTRODUCTION

Those who are familiar with the modern operating system such as windows XP may recognize that they can execute several programs simultaneously. This ability is known as multitasking. In system's terminology it is called multithreading.

(Multithreading enables you to write very efficient programs that make - maximum use of CPU because ideal time can be kept minimum.)

Multitasking is of two type :

1. process based
2. thread based

In process based multitasking your system run two or more program concurrently. In thread based multitasking environment, thread is the smallest unit of dispatchable code. This means that a single program can perform two or more tasks simultaneously. Multitasking threads require less overhead than multitasking process. Process are heavy weight tasks that requires their own separate address spaces. Interprocess communication is expensive and limited. Context switching from one process to another is also costly. Threads on the other hand light in weight. They show the same address space Interthread communication is in expensive.

Multithreading enables you to write very efficient programs that makes maximum use of the CPU, because ideal time can be kept to a minimum

1. Thread is a single flow of control within a prog. It is some time called the execution context because each thread must have its own resource. A thread is similar to a program that has a single flow of control. It has a beginning, a body and an end and execute command sequentially. A Program that contains multiple flows of control is known as Multithreading program.

Thread exist in several states.

1. Running
2. Ready
3. Suspended
4. Blocked
5. Terminate

Java assigns to each thread a priority that determines how that thread should be treated with respect to the others. Higher priority thread does not run any foots than a lower-priority thread if it is the only thread running.

THREAD CLASS AND RUNNABLE INTERFACE

Java's multithreading system is built upon the Thread class and its companion interfaces. Runnable thread class defines the several methods.

Methods	Meaning
get Name	obtain a thread Name
get Priority	obtain a thread Priority
is Alive	if thread is Alive or running
join	wait for thread to terminate
run	entry point for thread
sleep	suspended a thread for a period of time.
start	start a new thread.

The main thread : The main thread is created automatically when your program is started it can be controlled through a thread object. **CurrentThread()** method return a reference to the thread in which it is called syntax of currentThread( ) is static thread currentThread( );

Example ⇒

```
// Thread Demo
class threaddemo
{
public static void main(String args[])
{
        Thread t=new Thread();
        t=Thread.currentThread();
        System.out.println(" Thread Name" +t);
        t.setName(" My Thread");
        System.out.println(" Changed Thread Name" +t);
        try
        {
        for(int i=0;i<5;i++)
        {
        System.out.println(i+" " +t);
        t.sleep(1000);
```

```
            }
            }
            catch(InterruptedException ae)
            {
            System.out.println(" Thread Stopped" );
            }
    }
    }
```

Output:

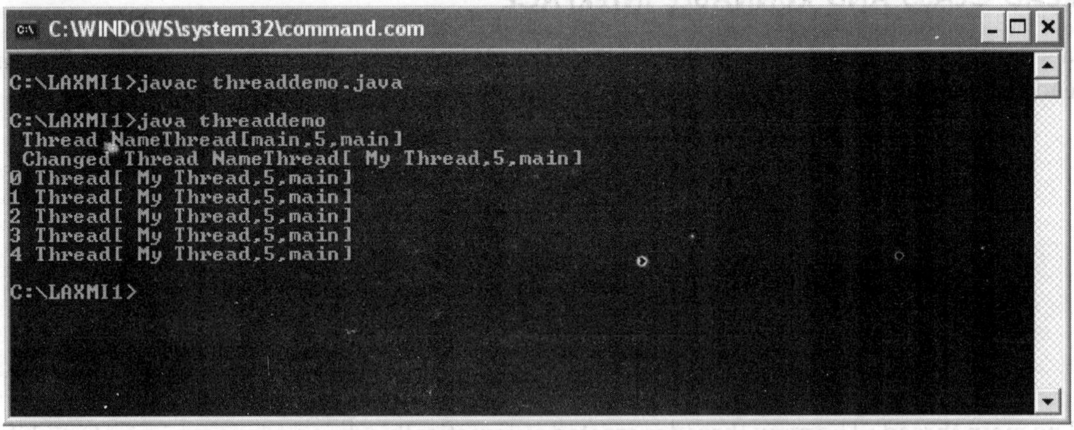

The sleep( ) method cause the thread from which it is called to suspend execution for the specified period of milliseconds. Syntax for sleep( ) thread is :

Static void sleep(long milliseconds)throws Interrupt Exception

Life cycle of Thread : During the life time of a thread, there are many states it can enter. They includes

1. Newborn state
2. Runnable state
3. Running state
4. Blocked state
5. Dead state.

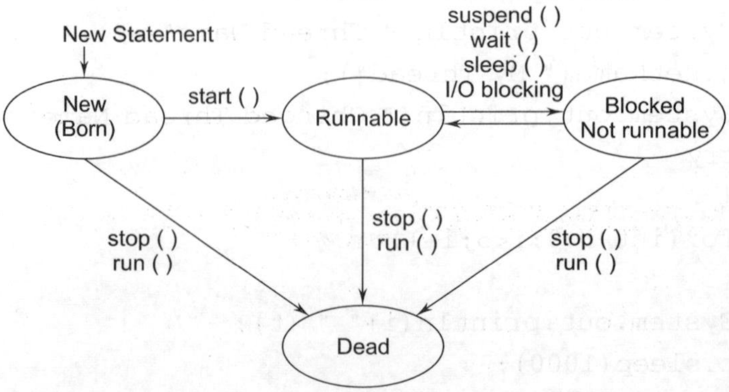

A thread is always in one of these five states. It can more from one state to another via a variety of ways.

1. **Newborn state :** When we create a thread object, the thread is born and is said to be is newborn state. The thread is not yet scheduled for running. At this state, we can do only one of the following things with it.
   (*a*) Schedule it for running using start( ) method
   (*b*) Kill it using stop( ) method.

   If scheduled it moves to the runnable state.

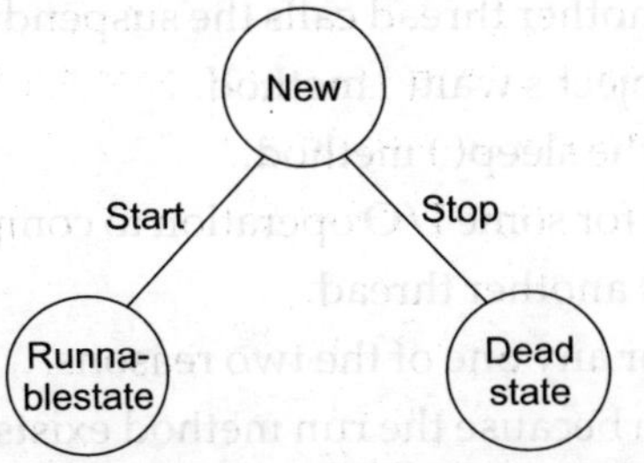

2. **Runnable state :** Once you invoke the start( ) method, the thread is runnable. It is subdivided into two statesd. Running and queued states. When the thread is running state. It is assigned by CPU cycles and is actually running. When it is in queued state, it is waiting in the queue and competing for its turn to spend CPU cycles. It is controlled by virtual machine controller. When you use the yield( ) method it makes sure other thread of the same priority have chance to run. This method causes voluntary move itself to the queued state from the running state.

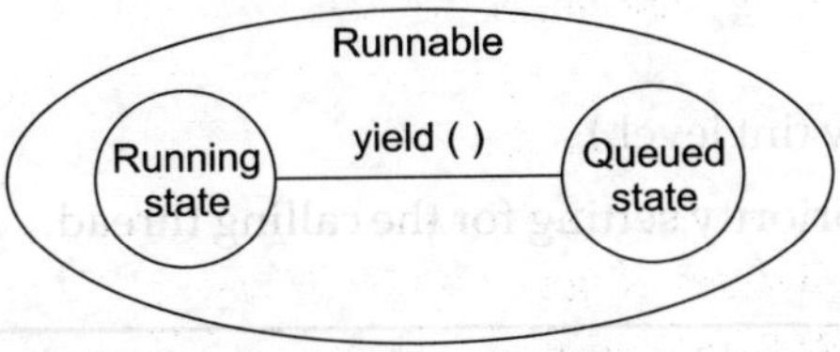

   (*a*) It has been suspended using suspend( ) method. A suspended thread can be revived by using the resume( ) method.

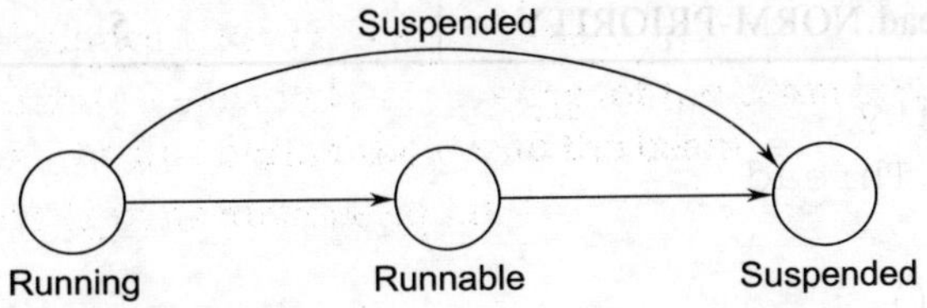

Relinquishing control using suspend ( ) method

   (*b*) It has been made to sleep. We can put a thread to sleep for a specified time period using the method sleep (time) where time is in millisecond.

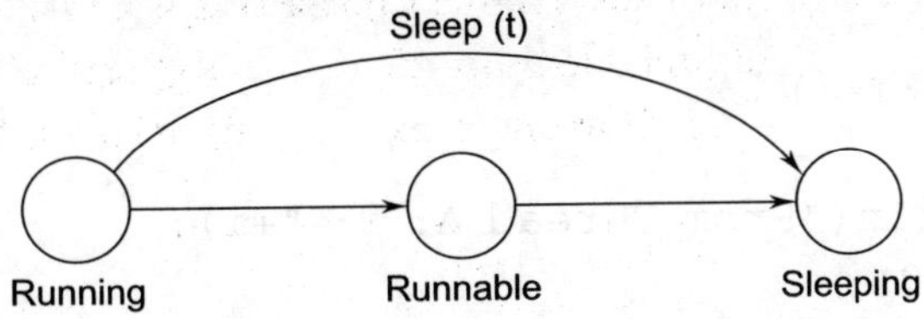

(c) It has been told to wait until some event occurs. This is done using the wait( ) method.

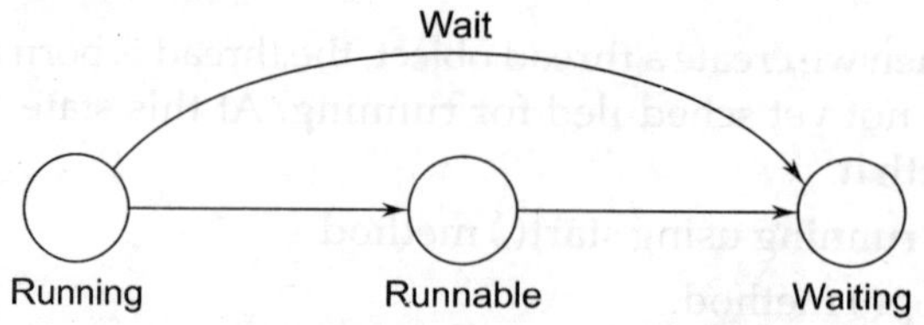

3. **Blocked :** The blocked state is entered when one of the following events occurs.
   (a) The thread itself or another thread calls the suspend( ) method.
   (b) The thread calls an object's wait( ) method.
   (c) The thread itself call the sleep( ) method.
   (d) The thread is waiting for some I/O operation to complete.
   (e) The thread will join( ) another thread.
4. **Dead :** A thread is dead for any one of the two reasons.
   (a) It dies a natural death because the run method exists normally.
   (b) It dies abruptly because an uncaught exception terminates the run method.

In particular the stop( ) method is used to kill the thread.

Thread Priorities : Thread priorities are used by the thread schedules to decide when each thread should be allowed to run. Higher – priority threads get more CPU time than lower priority threads. The amount of CPU time that a threads get often depends on several factors besides its priority. To set the thread's use the setPriority( ) method, which is a member of Thread.

Syntax for

final void setPriority (int level.)

level → specifies the new priority setting for the calling thread.

Constants	Integer value
Thread.MIN-PRIORITY	1
Thread.MAX-PRIORITY	10
Thread.NORM-PRIORITY	5

```
// Thread Priority
class A extends Thread
{
public void run()
{
System.out.println("A Thread Started\n");
try
{
for(int i=1;i<=5;i++)
{
System.out.println("From Thread A: i= "+i);
Thread.sleep(1000);
```

```
}
}
catch(InterruptedException ae)
{
System.out.println("A");
}
System.out.println("A Thread Ended");
}
}
class B extends Thread
{
public void run()
{
System.out.println("B Thread Started\n");
try
{
for(int j=1;j<=5;j++)
{
System.out.println("From Thread B: j="+j);
Thread.sleep(700);
}
}
catch(InterruptedException ae)
{
System.out.println("B");
}
System.out.println("B Thread Ended");
}
}
class C extends Thread
{
public void run()
{
System.out.println("C Thread Started\n");
try
{
for(int k=1;k<=5;k++)
{
System.out.println("From Thread C: k= "+k);
Thread.sleep(600);
}
}
```

```
catch(InterruptedException ae)
{
System.out.println("C");
}
System.out.println("C Thread Ended");
}
}
class ThreadPriority
{
public static void main(String args[])
{
A a1=new A();
B a2=new B();
C a3=new C();
a1.setPriority(Thread.MAX_PRIORITY);
a2.setPriority(4);
a3.setPriority(Thread.MIN_PRIORITY);
a1.start();
a2.start();
a3.start();
}
}
```

Output:

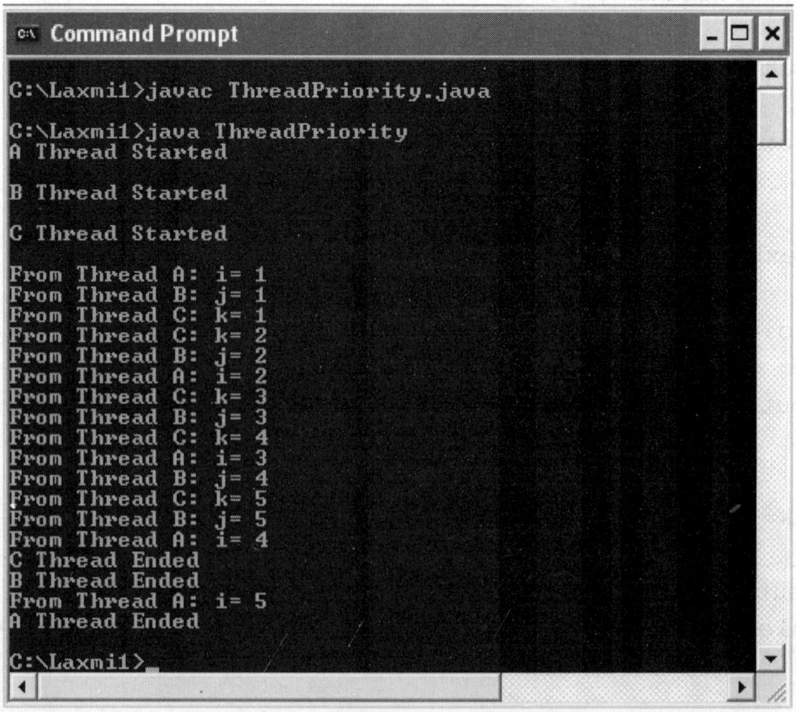

Creating thread : A new thread can be created in two ways.

1. **By creating a thread class.** Define a class that extends Thread class and override run( ) method.
2. **Define a class that implements Runnable interface.** The Runnable interface has only one method, run( ) that is to be defined in the method with the code to be executed by the thread.

   1. Extending the thread class :

It includes the following steps.

1. Declare the class, extends the Thread class.

Example ⇒

```
class MyThread extends Thread
{
. . . . . . . . . . .
. . . . . . . . . . .
}
```

2. Implement the run( ) method : The run( ) method has been inherited by the class MyThread.

```
public void run( )
{
}
```

3. Starting the new Thread :
   Thread. start( );

To actually create and run an instance of your thread class, you must call Thread.start( ) method.

```
// Extend a Thread Class
class MyThread extends Thread
{
public void run()
{
for(int i=0;i<5;i++)
{
System.out.println(" MyThread : i = " +i);
}
System.out.println(" Exit from MyThread ");
}
}
class MyThread1 extends MyThread
{
public void run()
{
for(int j=0;j<5;j++)
{
System.out.println(" MyThread 1 : j =" +j);
}
```

```
System.out.println(" Exit from MyThread1 ");
}
}
class ThreadTest
{
public static void main(String args[])
{
MyThread a=new MyThread();
a.start();
MyThread b=new MyThread();
b.start();
}
}
```

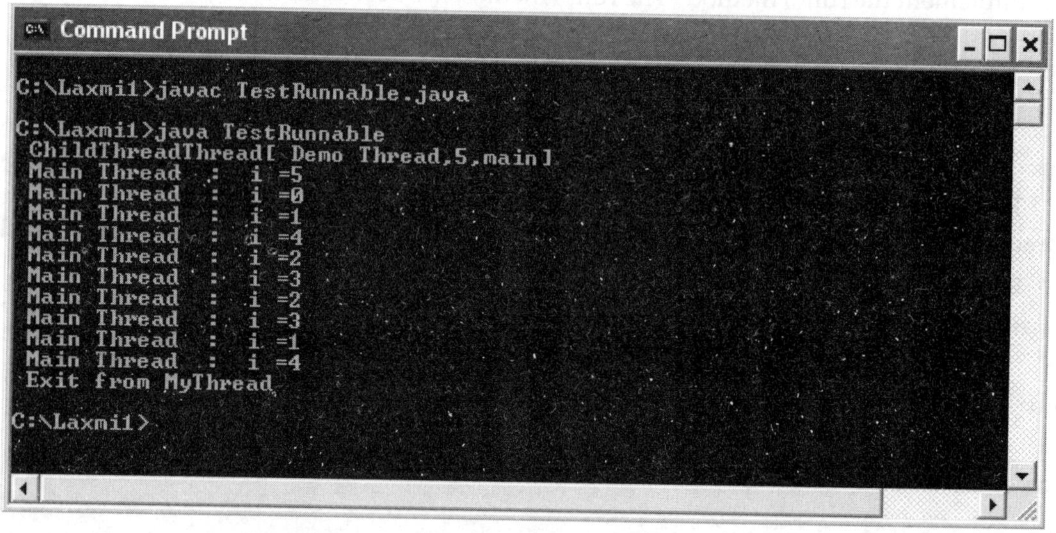

Implementing the Runnable Interface

We can create a thread in two ways : Extended a Thread and Runnable Interface. The Runnable Interface declare the run ( ) method that is required for implementing, threads in our program.

1. Declare the class implementing the Runnable Interface.
2. Implement the run ( ) method.
3. Create a thread by defining an object that is instantiated from this "Runnable" class as the target of the thread.
4. Call the thread's start( ) method to run the thread.

```
// Runnable Method
class NewThread implements Runnable
{
        Thread t;
        NewThread()
```

```
{
t=new Thread(this," Demo Thread");
System.out.println(" ChildThread" +t);
t.start();
}
public void run()
{
try
{
for(int i=0;i<5;i++)
{
System.out.println(" Main Thread : i =" +i);
Thread.sleep(500);
}
}
catch(InterruptedException ie)
{
System.out.println(" Child Interrupted");
}
System.out.println(" Exit from MyThread ");
}
}
class TestRunnable
{
public static void main(String args[])
{
new NewThread();
try
{
for(int i=5;i>0;i--)
{
System.out.println(" Main Thread : i =" +i);
Thread.sleep(500);
}
}
catch(InterruptedException ie)
{
System.out.println(" Main Interrupted");
}
}
}
```

Output:

```
Command Prompt

C:\Laxmi1>javac TestRunnable.java

C:\Laxmi1>java TestRunnable
 ChildThreadThread[ Demo Thread,5,main]
 Main Thread  :  i =5
 Main Thread  :  i =0
 Main Thread  :  i =1
 Main Thread  :  i =4
 Main Thread  :  i =2
 Main Thread  :  i =3
 Main Thread  :  i =2
 Main Thread  :  i =3
 Main Thread  :  i =1
 Main Thread  :  i =4
 Exit from MyThread

C:\Laxmi1>
```

(is Alive( ), join( ), yield, stop( ), sleep Methods : Two ways exist to determine whether a thread has finished First call is Alive ( ) method on thread.

```
final boolean is Alive ( )
```

The is Alive ( ) method return true if the thread upon which it is called is still running. It return false if thread is not Alive.

```
final void join ( )
```

This method waits until the thread on which it is called terminates. It names comes from the concept of the calling. Thread waiting until the specified thread joins it. yield( ), stop( ), sleep( ) methods force a thread to move from one state to another.

```
// yield(),stop(),sleep() methods
class A extends Thread
{
public void run()
{
System.out.println("A Thread Started\n");
for(int i=1;i<=5;i++)
{
if(i==1)
yield();
System.out.println("From Thread A: i= "+i);
}
System.out.println("A Thread Ended");
}
}
class B extends Thread
```

```
{
public void run()
{
System.out.prinln("B Thread Started\n");
for(int j=1;j<=5;j++)
{
System.out.println("From Thread B: j= "+j);
If(j==3)
Stop();
}
System.out.println("B Thread Ended");
}
}
class C extends Thread
{
public void run()
{
System.out.println("C Thread Started\n");
For(int k=1;k<=5;k++)
{
System.out.println("From Thread C: k= "+k);
If(k==1)
try
{
Thread.sleep(1000);
}
catch(InterrupedException e)
{
System.out.println(" C ");
}
System.out.println("C Thread Ended");
}
}
}
class demo1
{
public static void main(String args[])
{
A a1=new A();
B a2=new B();
```

```
C a3=new C();
a1.setPriority(Thread.MAX_PRIORITY);
a2.setPriority(4);
a3.setPriority(Thread.MIN_PRIORITY);
a1.start();
a2.start();
a3.start();
}
}
```

SYNCHRONIZATION

Problems may occur when multiple threads are accessing the same data concurrently. Synchronization is the way to avoid data corruption caused by simultaneous access to the same data.

A synchronized method is a method that must acquire a lock on object or on a class before it can be executed.

There are two ways to make the code as synchronized:

1. Synchronization an entire method by putting the **synchronized** modifier in the methods declaration.
2. Synchronize a subset of a method by surrounding the desired lines of code with curly brackets and inserting the synchronized keyword before the curly brace. The general form is synchronized (objectnarne){ }.

The following program illustrate the synchronized keyword

```
class syncTest extends Thread
{
    static int n =5;
    public syncTest(String s1)
    {
    super(s1);
    }
    public void run()
    {
    syncClass.view(getName(),n);
    }
    void pleasewait()
    {
    try
    {
    sleep(1000);
    }
```

```
catch(InterruptedException e)
{
System.out.println("Interrupted Exception arised");
    }
  }
}
class syncClass
    {
    public static synchronized void view(String tname,int n1)
    {
    for(int i=1;i<=n1;i++)
    {
     syncTest s=(syncTest)Thread.currentThread();
     s.pleasewait();
    System.out.println(tname+" "+);
  }
 }
}
class test
 {
 public static void main(String args[ ])
 {
 syncTest s1=new syncTest("First");
 syncTest s2=new syncTest("Second");
 s1.start();
 s2.start();
 }
 }
```

Output

```
First 1
First 2
First 3
First 4
First 5
Second 1
Second 2
Second 3
Second 4
Second 5
```

From the output we understand the First thread is completed, then the next thread get chance. So only one Thread will access any object at any point in time.

In the above program remove the keyword synchronized and compile the program, run and observe the result. The output will be like this

```
First 1
Second 1
First 2
Second 2
First 3
Second 3
First 4
Second 4
Second 5
```

EXERCISE

1. Explain the fundamental of thread.
2. Explain the life cycle of thread.
3. What are the advantages of using methods using threads over process?
4. What is the importance of thread synchronization in multithreading?
5. Is it necessary to synchronized single thread application?
6. Write a program to create multiple thread? The main method sleep for about 10 seconds at the end of which all the threads should be terminated.
7. Write a program to create two threads, use a Button to set the priorities of two thread levels above and below. Display the changed priority.
8. Is it necessary to synchronized Single thread applications?
9. What is multithreading?
10. What is synchronization?

15 CHAPTER

MANAGING INPUT AND OUTPUT FILES IN JAVA

INTRODUCTION

This chapter explores java.io, which provides support for Input out operations.

We have used variable and arrays for storing data inside the program. But these variable cause the following problem.

1. The data is lost either when a variable goes out of scope or when the prog. is terminated.
2. if the data is too large, it is difficult to handle. We can overcome these problems by storing data on secondary storage device such as floppy disks or hard disks. The data is stored in these device using the concept of file. A file is a collection of related record stored in a particular area of disk.

   Stream : Java programs performs I/O through streams. A streams is an abstraction that either produces or consumes information. A stream is linked to a physical device by the java I/O stream. All stream behaves in the same manner even the actual physical devices to which they are linked differ. A stream in java is a path along which data flows. It has a source and a destination. Both the source and the destination may be physical devices or programs or other stream in the same program.

   Java streams are classified into two basic types.

   1. Input stream
   2. Output stream

   An input stream extracts data from the source and send it to the program. An output stream takes data from the program and sends it to the destination.

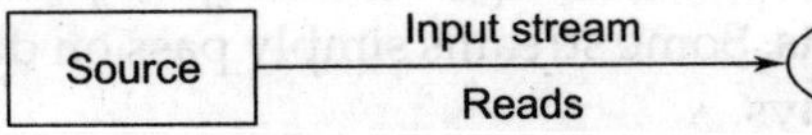

(a) Reading data into a program

(b) Writing data to a destination

Stream classes :

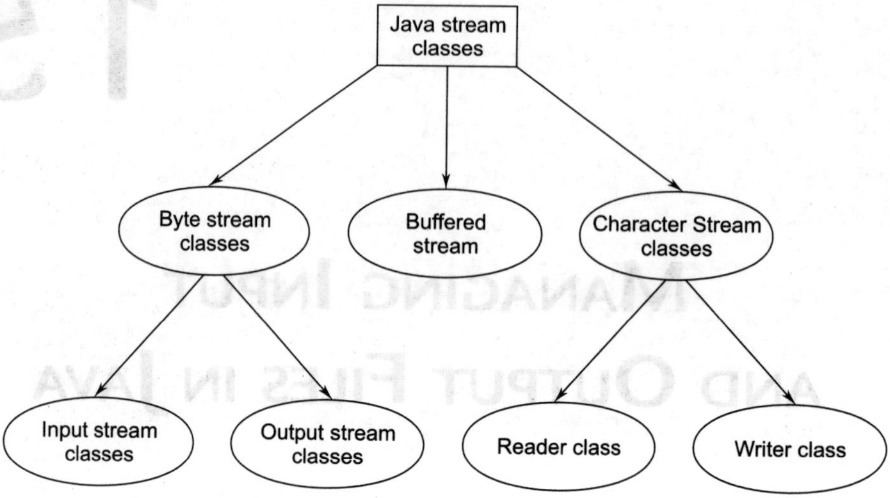

I/O STREAMS

- Byte Streams handle I/O of raw binary data.
- Character Streams handle I/O of character data, automatically handling translation to and from the local character set.
- Buffered Streams optimize input and output by reducing the number of calls to the native API.
- Scanning and Formatting allows a program to read and write formatted text.
- I/O from the Command Line describes the Standard Streams and the Console object.
- Data Streams handle binary I/O of primitive data type and String values.
- Object Streams handle binary I/O of objects.

File I/O

- File Objects help you to write platform-independent code that examines and manipulates files.
- Random Access Files handle non-sequential file access.

I/O Streams

An I/O *Stream* represents an input source or an output destination. A stream can represent many different kinds of sources and destinations, including disk files, devices, other programs, and memory arrays.

Streams support many different kinds of data, including simple bytes, primitive data types, localized characters, and objects. Some streams simply pass on data; others manipulate and transform the data in useful ways.

No matter how they work internally, all streams present the same simple model to programs that use them: A stream is a sequence of data. A program uses an *input stream* to read data from a source, one item at a time:

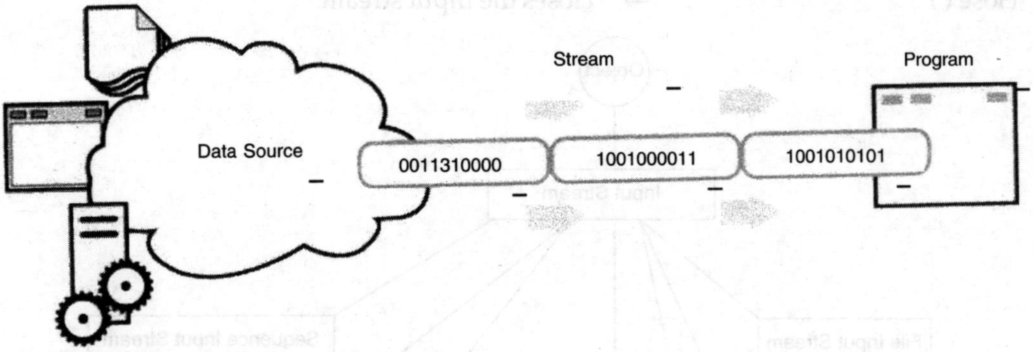

Reading information into a program.

A Program uses an *output stream* to write data to a destination, one item at time :

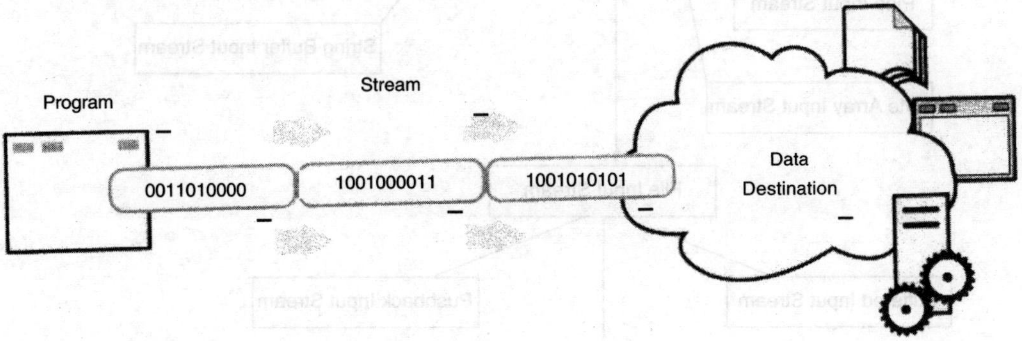

Writing information from a program.

In this lesson, we'll see streams that can handle all kinds of data, from primitive values to advanced objects.

The data source and data destination pictured above can be anything that holds, generates, or consumes data. Obviously this includes disk files, but a source or destination can also be another program, a peripheral device, a network socket, or an array.

Input Stream class : Inputstream is an abstract class therefore we cannot create instance (object) of this class. The Inputstream class defines methods for performing Input functions as

1) Reading
2) Closing
3) Making positions in streams
4) Finding the no. of byte in a stream

Method		Description
read ()	→	Reads a byte from an Input stream
read (byte b[])	→	Reads an array of byte into b
read (byte b[], int n, int m)	→	Reads m bytes into b starting from n^{th} byte.
available ()	→	Gives no. of byte available in the Input.
skip (n)	→	skip over n bytes from the Input stream.
reset ()	→	goes back to the beginning of the stream.

close ( ) → closes the Input stream.

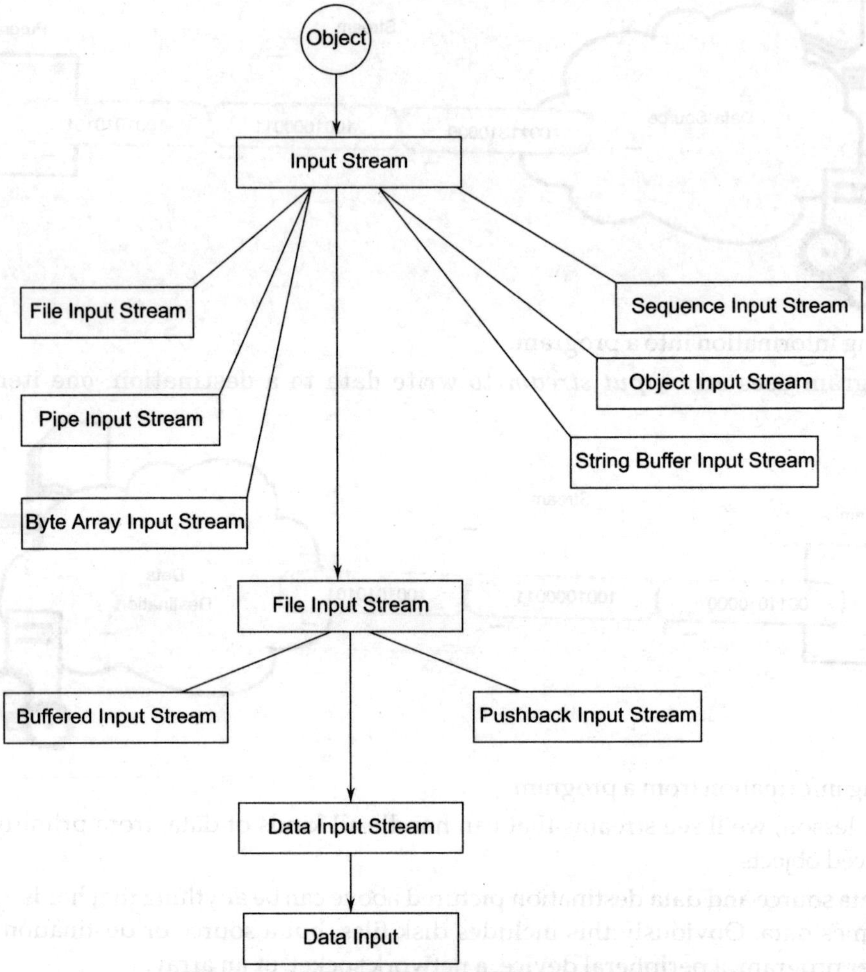

Input Stream Hierarchy

Output Stream class : The output stream includes methods that are designed to perform the following tasks.

1. Writing bytes
2. Closing streams
3. *Flushing* streams

Method		Description
Write	→	Write a byte to the output stream.
Write(byte [] b)	→	Write all byte in the array b to the output stream.
Write(byte [] b, int n, int m)	→	Writes all byte from array b starting from n^{th} byte.
Close( )	→	Closes the output stream.
Flush( )	→	Flushes the output stream.

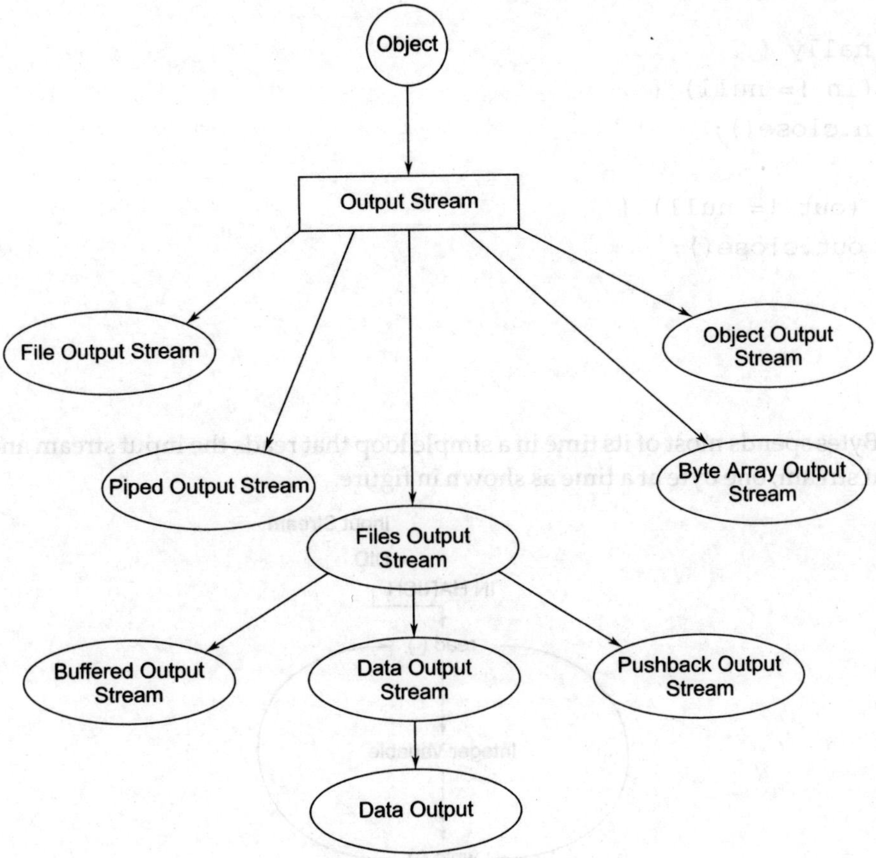

Output Stream Hierarchy

Using Byte Streams

We'll explore FileInputStream and FileOutputStream by examining an example program named CopyBytes, which uses byte streams to copy harish, one byte at a time.

```
import java.io.FileInputStream;
import java.io.FileOutputStream;
import java.io.IOException;
public class CopyBytes {
public static void main(String[] args) throws IOException {
FileInputStream in = null;
  FileOutputStream out = null;
  try {
    in = new FileInputStream("harish.txt");
    Out = new FileOutputStream("Outagain.txt");
    int c;
    while ((c = in.read()) != -1) {
      out.write(c);
```

```
        }
      } finally {
        if(in != null) {
          in.close();
        }
        if (out != null) {
           out.close();
        }
      }
    }
  }
```

CopyBytes spends most of its time in a simple loop that reads the input stream and writes the output stream, one byte at a time as shown in figure.

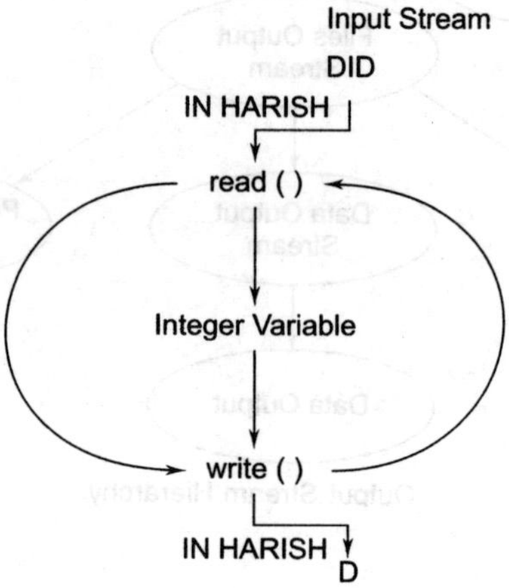

Simply byte stream I/O.
read( ) return an int value.

Always Close Streams : Closing a stream when it is no longer needed is very important so important that CopyBytes uses a finally block to guarantee that both stream will be closed even if an error occurs. This practice helps avoid serious resource leaks. One possible error is that CopyBytes was unable to open one or both files when that happens, the stream variable corresponding to the file never changes from its initial null values.

CHARACTER STREAMS

The Java platform stores character values using Unicode conventions Character stream I/O automatically translates this internal format to and from the local character set. In Western locales, the local character set is usually an 8-bit superset of ASCII.

For most applications, I/O with character streams is no more complicated than I/O with byte streams. Input and output done with stream classes automatically translates to and from the local character set. A program that uses character streams in place of byte streams automatically adapts to the local character set and is ready for internationalization — all without extra effort by the programmer.

If internationalization isn't a priority, you can simply use the character stream classes without paying much attention to character set issues. Later, if internationalization becomes a priority, your program can be adapted without extensive recoding. See the internationalization trail for more information.

Using Character Streams

All character stream classes are descended from Reader and Writer. As with byte streams, there are character stream classes that specialize in file I/O: FileReader and FileWriter. The CopyCharacters example illustrates these classes.

```
import java.io.FileReader;
import java.io.FileWriter;
import java.io.IOException;
public class CopyCharacters {
  public static void main(String[] args) throws IOException {
    FileReader inputStream = null;
    FileWriter outputStream = null;
    try {
      inputStream = new FileReader("harish.txt");
      outputStream = new FileWriter("characteroutput.txt");
      int c;
      while ((c = inputStream.read()) != -1) {
        outputStream.write(c);
      }
    } finally {
      if (inputStream != null) {
        inputStream.close();
      }
      if (outputStream != null) {
        outputStream.close();
        }
      }
    }
  }
```

CopyCharacters is very similar to CopyBytes. The most important difference is that CopyCharacters uses FileReader and FileWriter for input and output in place of FileInputStream and FileOutputStream. Notice that both CopyBytes and CopyCharacters use an int variable to read to and write from. However, in CopyCharacters, the int variable holds a character value in its last 16 bits; in CopyBytes, the int variable holds a byte value in its last 8 bits.

Character Streams that use Byte Streams

Character streams are often "wrappers" for byte streams. The character stream uses the byte stream to perform the physical I/O, while the character stream handles translation between characters and bytes. FileReader, for example, uses FileInputStream, while FileWriter uses FileOutputStream.

There are two general-purpose byte-to-character "bridge" streams: InputStreamReader and OutputStreamWriter. Use them to create character streams when there are no prepackaged character stream classes that meet your needs.

LINE-ORIENTED I/O

Character I/O usually occurs in bigger units than single characters. One common unit is the line: a string of characters with a line terminator at the end. A line terminator can be a carriage-return/line-feed sequence ("\r\n"), a single carriage-return ("\r"), or a single line-feed ("\n"). Supporting all possible line terminators allows programs to read text files created on any of the widely used operating systems.

Let's modify the CopyCharacters example to use line-oriented I/O. To do this, we have to use two classes we haven't seen before, BufferedReader and PrintWriter. We'll explore these classes in greater depth in Buffered I/O and Formatting. Right now, we're just interested in their support for line-oriented I/O.

The CopyLines example invokes BufferedReader.readLine and PrintWriter. println to do input and output one line at a time.

```
import java.io.FileReader;
import java.io.FileWriter;
import java.io.BufferedReader;
import java.io.PrintWriter;
import java.io.IOException;
public class CopyLines {
    public static void main(String[] args) throws IOException {
      BufferedReader inputStream = null;
      PrintWriter outputStream = null;
      try {
        inputStream =
          new BufferedReader(new FileReader("harish.txt"));
        outputStream =
          new PrintWriter(new FileWriter("characteroutput.txt"));
        String l;
        while ((l = inputStream.readLine()) != null) {
          outputStream.println(l);
        }
      } finally {
        if (inputStream != null) {
```

```
            inputStream.close();
        }
        if (outputStream != null) {
            outputStream.close();
        }
    }
  }
}
```

Invoking readLine returns a line of text with the line CopyLines outputs each line using println, which appends the line terminator for the current operating system. This might not be the same line terminator that was used in the input file.

BUFFERED STREAMS

Most of the examples we've seen so far use *unbuffered* I/O. This means each read or write request is handled directly by the underlying OS. This can make a program much less efficient, since each such request often triggers disk access, network activity, or some other operation that is relatively expensive.

To reduce this kind of overhead, the Java platform implements *buffered* I/O streams. Buffered input streams read data from a memory area known as a *buffer*; the native input API is called only when the buffer is empty. Similarly, buffered output streams write data to a buffer, and the native output API is called only when the buffer is full.

A program can convert a unbuffered stream into a buffered stream using the wrapping idiom we've used several times now, where the unbuffered stream object is passed to the constructor for a buffered stream class. Here's how you might modify the constructor invocations in the CopyCharacters example to use buffered I/O:

```
inputStream =
    new BufferedReader(new FileReader("harish.txt"));
outputStream =
    new BufferedWriter(new FileWriter("characteroutput.txt"));
```

There are four buffered stream classes used to wrap unbuffered streams: BufferedInputStream and BufferedOutputStream create buffered byte streams, while BufferedReader and BufferedWriter create buffered character streams.

Flushing Buffered Streams

It often makes sense to write out a buffer at critical points, without waiting for it to fill. This is known as *flushing* the buffer.

Some buffered output classes support *autoflush*, specified by an optional constructor argument. When autoflush is enabled, certain key events cause the buffer to be flushed. For example, an autoflush PrintWriter object flushes the buffer on every invocation of println or format.

To flush a stream manually, invoke its flush method. The flush method is valid on any output stream, but has no effect unless the stream is buffered.

Scanning and Formatting

Programming I/O often involves translating to and from the neatly formatted data humans like to work with. To assist you with these chores, the Java platform provides two APIs. The scanner API breaks input into individual tokens associated with bits of data. The formatting API assembles data into nicely formatted, human-readable form.

Scanning

Objects of type Scanner are useful for breaking down formatted input into tokens and translating individual tokens according to their data type.

Breaking Input into Tokens

By default, a scanner uses white space to separate tokens. (White space characters include blanks, tabs, and line terminators. For the full list, refer to the documentation for Character.isWhitespace.) To see how scanning works, let's look at Scan, a program that reads the individual words in xanadu.txt and prints them out, one per line.

Example ⇒

```
import java.io.*;
import java.until.Scanner;
public class Scan {
  public static void main(String[] args) throws IOException {
    Scanner s = null;
    try {
      s = new Scanner(new BufferedReader(new
FileReader("harish.txt")));
      while (s.hasNext()) {
        System.out.println(s.next());
      }
    } finally {
      if (s != null) {
        s.close();
      }
    }
  }
}
```

Notice that Scan invokes Scanner's close method when it is done with the scanner object. Even though a scanner is not a stream, you need to close it to indicate that you're done with its underlying stream.

The output of Scan looks like this:

In
Harish

did

Sameer

Khanna

A

stately

pleasure-dome

...

To use a different token separator, invoke useDelimiter(), specifying a regular expression. For example, suppose you wanted the token separator to be a comma, optionally followed by white space. You would invoke,

s.useDelimiter(",\\s*");

Translating Individual Tokens

The Scan example treats all input tokens as simple String values. Scanner also supports tokens for all of the Java language's primitive types (except for char), as well as BigInteger and BigDecimal. Also, numeric values can use thousands separators. Thus, in a US locale, Scanner correctly reads the string "32,767" as representing an integer value.

We have to mention the locale, because thousands separators and decimal symbols are locale specific. So, the following example would not work correctly in all locales if we didn't specify that the scanner should use the US locale. That's not something you usually have to worry about, because your input data usually comes from sources that use the same locale as you do. But this example is part of the Java Tutorial and gets distributed all over the world.

The ScanSum example reads a list of double values and adds them up. Here's the source:

Example ⇒

```
import java.io.FileReader;
import java.io.BufferedReader;
import java.io.IOException;
import java.util.Scanner;
import java.util.Locale;
public class ScanSum {
  public static void main(String[] args) throws IOException {
    Scanner s = null;
    double sum = 0;
    try {
      s = new Scanner(
        new BufferedReader(new FileReader("usnumbers.txt")));
      s.useLocale(Locale.US);
    while (s.hasNext()) {
      if (s.hasNextDouble()) {
        sum += s.nextDouble();
      } else {
        s.next();
```

```
      }
    }
  } finally {
    s.close();
  }
  System.out.println(sum);
}}
```

And here's the sample input file, usnumbers.txt

8.5

32,767

3.14159

1,000,000.1

The output string is "1032778.74159". The period will be a different character in some locales, because System.out is a PrintStream object, and that class doesn't provide a way to override the default locale.

Formatting

Stream objects that implement formatting are instances of either PrintWriter, a character stream class, and PrintStream, a byte stream class.

Note: The only PrintStream objects you are likely to need are System.out and System.err. (See I/O from the Command Line for more on these objects.) When you need to create a formatted output stream, instantiate PrintWriter, not PrintStream.

Like all byte and character stream objects, instances of PrintStream and PrintWriter implement a standard set of write methods for simple byte and character output. In addition, both PrintStream and PrintWriter implement the same set of methods for converting internal data into formatted output. Two levels of formatting are provided:

- print and println format individual values in a standard way.
- format formats almost any number of values based on a format string, with many options for precise formatting.

The print and println Methods

Invoking print or println outputs a single value after converting the value using the appropriate toString method. We can see this in the Root example:

```
public class Root {
  public static void main(String[] args) {
    int i = 2;
    double r = Math.sqrt(i);
    System.out.print("The square root of ");
    System.out.print(i);
    System.out.print(" is ");
    System.out.print (r);
    System.out.println(".");
```

```
    i = 5;
    r = Math.sqrt(i);
    System.out.println("The square root of" + i + " is " + r + ".");
  }
}
```

Here is the output of Root:

The square root of 2 is 1.4142135623730951.

The square root of 5 is 2.23606797749979.

The i and r variables are formatted twice: the first time using code in an overload of print, the second time by conversion code automatically generated by the Java compiler, which also utilizes toString. You can format any value this way, but you don't have much control over the results.

The format Method

The format method formats multiple arguments based on a *format string*. The format string consists of static text embedded with *format specifiers*; except for the format specifiers, the format string is output unchanged.

Format strings support many features. In this tutorial, we'll just cover some basics. For a complete description, see format string syntax in the API specification.

The Root2 example formats two values with a single format invocation:

```
public class Root2 {
   public static void main(String[] args) {
    in i = 2;
    double r = Math.sqrt(i);
    System.out.format("The square root of %d is %f.%n", i, r);
   }
}
```

Here is the output:

The square root of 2 is 1.414214.

Like the three used in this example, all format specifiers begin with a % and end with a 1- or 2-character *conversion* that specifies the kind of formatted output being generated. The three conversions used here are:

- d formats an integer value as a decimal value.
- f formats a floating point value as a decimal value.
- n outputs a platform-specific line terminator.

In the Java programming language, the \n escape always generates the linefeed character (\u000A). Don't use \n unless you specifically want a linefeed character. To get the correct line separator for the local platform, use %n.

In addition to the conversion, a format specifier can contain several additional elements that further customize the formatted output. Here's an example, Format, that uses every possible kind of element.

```
public class Format { public static void main(String[] args) {
```

```
System.out.format("%f, %1$+020.10f%n", Math.PI);
}}
```

Here's the output:

3.141593, +00000003, 1415926536

The additional elements are all optional. The following figure shows how the longer specifier breaks down into elements.

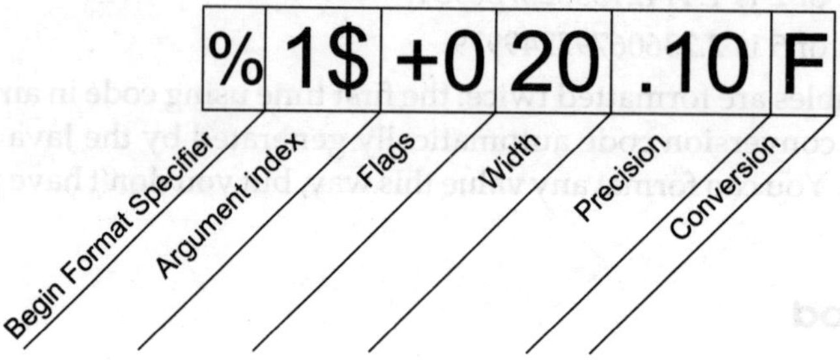

Elements of a Format Specifier.

The elements must appear in the order shown. Working from the right, the optional elements are:

1. **Precision.** For floating point values, this is the mathematical precision of the formatted value. For s and other general conversions, this is the maximum width of the formatted value; the value is right-truncated if necessary.
2. **Width.** The minimum width of the formatted value; the value is padded if necessary. By default the value is left-padded with blanks.
3. **Flags** specify additional formatting options. In the Format example, the + flag specifies that the number should always be formatted with a sign, and the 0 flag specifies that 0 is the padding character. Other flags include – (pad on the right) and, (format number with locale-specific thousands separators). Note that some flags cannot be used with certain other flags or with certain conversions.
4. **The Argument Index** allows you to explicitly match a designated argument. You can also specify < to match the same argument as the previous specifier. Thus the example could have said:

System.out.format("%f, %<+020.10f%n", Math.PI);

IO from the Command Line

A program is often run from the command line and interacts with the user in the command line environment. The Java platform supports this kind of interaction in two ways: through the Standard Streams and through the Console.

STANDARD STREAMS

Standard Streams are a feature of many operating systems. By default, they read input from the keyboard and write output to the display. They also support I/O on files and between programs, but that feature is controlled by the command line interpreter, not the program.

The Java platform supports three Standard Streams: *Standard Input*, accessed through System.in; *Standard Output*, accessed through System.out; and *Standard Error*, accessed through System.err. These objects are defined automatically and do not need to be opened. Standard Output and Standard Error are both for output; having error output separately allows the user to divert regular output to a file and still be able to read error messages. For more information, refer to the documentation for your command line interpreter.

You might expect the Standard Streams to be character streams, but, for historical reasons, they are byte streams. System.out and System.err are defined as PrintStream objects. Although it is technically a byte stream, PrintStream utilizes an internal character stream object to emulate many of the features of character Streams.

By contrast, System.in is a byte stream with no character stream features. To use Standard Input as a character stream, wrap System.in in InputStream Reader.

InputStreamReader cin = new InputStreamReader(System.in);

The Console

A more advanced alternative to the Standard Streams is the Console. This is a single, predefined object of type Console that has most of the features provided by the Standard Streams, and others besides. The Console is particularly useful for secure password entry. The Console object also provides input and output streams that are true character streams, through its reader and writer methods.

Before a program can use the Console, it must attempt to retrieve the Console object by invoking System.console(). If the Console object is available, this method returns it. If System.console returns NULL, then Console operations are not permitted, either because the OS doesn't support them or because the program was launched in a noninteractive environment.

The Console object supports secure password entry through its readPassword method. This method helps secure password entry in two ways. First, it suppresses echoing, so the password is not visible on the user's screen. Second, readPassword returns a character array, not a String, so the password can be overwritten, removing it from memory as soon as it is no longer needed.

The Password example is a prototype program for changing a user's password. It demonstrates several Console methods.

```
import java.io.Console;
import java.util.Arrays;
import java.io.IOException;
public class Password {
   public static void main (String args[]) throws IOException {
    Console c = System.console();
    If (c = = null) {
      System.err.println("No console.");
      System.exit(1);
    }
    String login = c.readLine("Enter your login: ");
```

```
Char [] oldPassword = c.readPassword("Enter your old password: ");
if (verify(login, oldPassword)) {
 boolean noMatch;
 do {
     char [] newPassword1 =
       c.readPassword("Enter your new password: ");
     char [] newPassword2 =
       c.readPassword("Enter new password again: ");
     noMatch = ! Arrays.equals(newPassword1, newPassword2);
     if (noMatch) {
       c.format("Passwords don't match. Try again.%n");
     } else {
       change(login, newPassword1);
       c.format("Password for %s changed.%n", login);
     }
     Arrays.fill(newPassword1, ' ');
     Arrays.fill(newPassword2, ' ');
   } while (noMatch);
  }
  Arrays.fill(oldPassword, ' ');
}
//Dummy verify method.
static boolean verify(String login, char[] password) {
 return true;
}
//Dummy change method.
static void change(String login, char[] password) {}
}
```

Password program follows these steps:

1. Attempt to retrieve the Console object. If the object is not available, abort.
2. Invoke Console.readLine to prompt for and read the user's login name.
3. Invoke Console.readPassword to prompt for and read the user's existing password.
4. Invoke verify to confirm that the user is authorized to change the password. (In this example, verify is a dummy method that always returns true.)
5. Repeat the following steps until the user enters the same password twice.
   a. Invoke Console.readPassword twice to prompt for and read a new password.
   b. If the user entered the same password both times, invoke change to change it. (Again, change is a dummy method.)
   c. Overwrite both passwords with blanks.
6. Overwrite the old password with blanks.

DATA STREAMS

Data streams support binary I/O of primitive data type values (boolean, char, byte, short, int, long, float, and double) as well as String values. All data streams implement either the DataInput interface or the DataOutput interface. This section focuses on the most widely-used implementations of these interfaces, DataInputStream and DataOutputStream.

The DataStreams example demonstrates data streams by writing out a set of data records, and then reading them in again. Each record consists of three values related to an item on an invoice, as shown in the following table:

Order in record	Data type	Data description	Output Method	Input Method	Sample Value
1	double	Item price	DataOutputStream.writeDouble	DataInputStream.readDouble	19.99
2	int	Unit count	DataOutputStream.writeInt	DataInputStream.readInt	12
3	String	Item description	DataOutputStream.writeUTF	DataInputStream.readUTF	"Java magic

Let's examine crucial code in DataStreams. First, the program defines some constants containing the name of the data file and the data that will be written to it:

```
static final String dataFile = "invoicedata";
static final double[] prices = { 19.99, 9.99, 15.99, 3.99, 4.99 };
static final int[] units = { 12, 8, 13, 29, 50 };
static final String[] descs = { "Java magic",
    "Java Mug",
    "Duke Juggling Dolls",
    "Java Pin",
    "Java Key Chain" };
```

Then DataStreams opens an output stream. Since a DataOutputStream can only be created as a wrapper for an existing byte stream object, DataStreams provides a buffered file output byte stream.

```
out = new DataOutputStream(new
    BufferedOutputStream(new FileOutputStream(dataFile)));
```

DataStreams writes out the records and closes the output stream.

```
for (int i = 0; i < prices.length; i ++) {
    out.writeDouble(prices[i]);
    out.writeInt(units[i]);
    out.writeUTF(descs[i]);
}
```

The writeUTF method writes out String values in a modified form of UTF-8. This is a variable-width character encoding that only needs a single byte for common Western characters.

Now DataStreams reads the data back in again. First it must provide an input stream, and variables to hold the input data. Like DataOutputStream, DataInputStream must be constructed as a wrapper for a byte stream.

```
in = new DataInputStream(new
```

```
BufferedInputStream(new FileInputStream(dataFile)));
double price;
int unit;
String desc;
double total = 0.0;
```

Now DataStreams can read each record in the stream, reporting on the data it encounters.

```
try {
    while (true) {
     price = in.readDouble();
     unit = in.readInt();
     desc = in.readUTF();
     System.out.format("You ordered %d units of %s at $%.2f%n",
        unit, desc, price);
        total += unit * price;
     }
    } catch (EOFException e) {
    }
```

Notice that DataStreams detects an end-of-file condition by catching EOFExce-ption, instead of testing for an invalid return value. All implementations of DataInput methods use EOFException instead of return values.

Also notice that each specialized write in DataStreams is exactly matched by the corresponding specialized read. It is up to the programmer to make sure that output types and input types are matched in this way: The input stream consists of simple binary data, with nothing to indicate the type of individual values, or where they begin in the stream.

DataStreams uses one very bad programming technique: it uses floating point numbers to represent monetary values. In general, floating point is bad for precise values. It's particularly bad for decimal fractions, because common values (such as 0.1) do not have a binary representation.

OBJECT STREAMS

Just as data streams support I/O of primitive data types, object streams support I/O of objects. Most, but not all, standard classes support serialization of their objects. Those that do implement the marker interface Serializable.

The object stream classes are ObjectInputStream and ObjectOutputStream. These classes implement ObjectInput and ObjectOutput, which are subinterfaces of DataInput and DataOutput. That means that all the primitive data I/O methods covered in Data Streams are also implemented in object streams. So an object stream can contain a mixture of primitive and object values. The ObjectStreams example illustrates this. ObjectStreams creates the same application as DataStreams, with a couple of changes. First, prices are now BigDecimalobjects, to better represent fractional values. Second, a Calendar object is written to the data file, indicating an invoice date.

If readObject() doesn't return the object type expected, attempting to cast it to the correct type may throw a ClassNotFoundException. In this simple example, that can't happen, so we don't try to catch the exception. Instead, we notify the compiler that we're aware of the issue by adding ClassNotFound-Exception to the main method's throws clause.

Output and Input of Complex Objects

The writeObject and readObject methods are simple to use, but they contain some very sophisticated object management logic. This isn't important for a class like Calendar, which just encapsulates primitive values. But many objects contain references to other objects. If readObject is to reconstitute an object from a stream, it has to be able to reconstitute all of the objects the original object referred to. These additional objects might have their own references, and so on. In this situation, writeObject traverses the entire web of object references and writes all objects in that web onto the stream. Thus a single invocation of writeObject can cause a large number of objects to be written to the stream.

This is demonstrated in the following figure, where writeObject is invoked to write a single object named **a**. This object contains references to objects **b** and **c**, while **b** contains references to **d** and **e**. Invoking writeobject(a) writes not just **a**, but all the objects necessary to reconstitute **a**, so the other four objects in this web are written also. When **a** is read back by readObject, the other four objects are read back as well, and all the original object references are preserved.

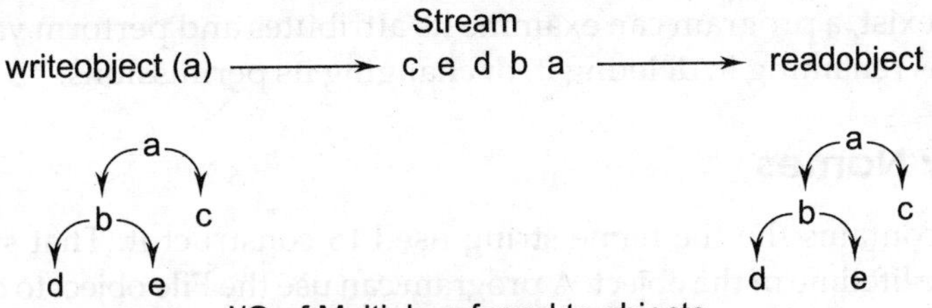

I/O of Multiple referred to objects

You might wonder what happens if two objects on the same stream both contain references to a single object. Will they both refer to a single object when they're read back? The answer is "yes." A stream can only contain one copy of an object, though it can contain any number of references to it. Thus if you explicitly write an object to a stream twice, you're really writing only the reference twice. For example, if the following code writes an object ob twice to a stream:

```
Object ob = new Object();
out.writeObject(ob);
out.writeObject(ob);
```

Each writeObject has to be matched by a readObject, so the code that reads the stream back will look something like this:

```
Object ob1 = in.readObject();
Object ob2 = in.readObject();
```

This results in two variables, ob1 and ob2, that are references to a single object.

However, if a single object is written to two different streams, it is effectively duplicated – a single program reading both streams back will see two distinct objects.

File I/O

So far, this lesson has *focused* on streams, which provide a simple model for reading and writing data. Streams work with a large variety of data sources and destinations, including disk files. However, streams don't support all the operations that are common with disk files. In this part of the lesson, we'll focus on non-stream file I/O. There are two topics:

1. File is a class that helps you write platform-independent code that examines and manipulates files and directories.
2. Random access files support nonsequential access to disk file data.

File Objects

The File class makes it easier to write platform-independent code that examines and manipulates files. The name of this class is misleading: File instances represent file names, not files. The file corresponding to the file name might not even exist.

Why create a File object for a file that doesn't exist? A program can use the object to parse a file name. Also, the file can be created by passing the File object to the constructor of some classes, such as FileWriter.

If the file *does* exist, a program can examine its attributes and perform various operations on the file, such as renaming it, deleting it, or changing its permissions.

A File has Many Names

A File object contains the file name string used to construct it. That string never changes throughout the lifetime of the object. A program can use the File object to obtain other versions of the file name, some of which may or may not be the same as the original file name string passed to the constructor.

Suppose a program creates a File object with the constructor invocation

File a = new File("harish.txt");

The program invokes a number of methods to obtain different versions of the file name. The program is then run both on a Microsoft Windows system (in directory c:\java\examples) and a Solaris system (in directory /home/cafe/java/examples). Here is what the methods would return:

Method Invoked	Returns on Microsoft Windows	Returns on Solaris
a.toString()	harish.txt	harish.txt
a.getName()	harish.txt	harish.txt
b.getParent()	NULL	NULL
a.getAbsolutePath()	c:\Laxmi1\harish.txt	\home\Laxmi1\harish.txt
a.getCanonicalPath()	c:\Laxmi1\harish.(txt)	\home\Laxmi1\harish.txt

Then the same program constructs a File object from a more complicated file name, using File.separator to specify the file name in a platform-independent way.

File b = new File(".." + File.separator + "examples" + File.separator + "harish.txt");

Although b refers to the same file as a, the methods return slightly different values:

Method Invoked	Returns on Microsoft Windows	Returns on Solaris
b.toString()	..\Laxmi1\harish.txt	..\Laxmi1\harish.txt
b.getName()	harish.txt	harish.txt
b.getParent()	..\Laxmi1	..\Laxmi1
b.getAbsolutePath()	c:\Laxmi1\harish.txt	\home\Laxmi1\harish.txt
b.getCanonicalPath()	c:\Laxmi1\harish.txt	\home\Laxmi1\harish.txt

Running the same program on a Linux system would give results similar to those on the Solaris system.

It's worth mentioning that File.compareTo()would not consider a and b to be the same. Even though they refer to the same file, the names used to construct them are different.

The FileStuff example creates File objects from names passed from the command line and exercises various information methods on them. You'll find it instructive to run FileStuff on a variety of file names. Be sure to include directory names as well as the names of files that don't actually exist. Try passing FileStuff a variety of relative and absolute path names.

Manipulating Files

If a File object names an actual file, a program can use it to perform a number of useful operations on the file. These include passing the object to the constructor for a stream to open the file for reading or writing.

The delete method deletes the file immediately, while the deleteOnExit method deletes the file when the virtual machine terminates.

The setLastModified sets the modification date/time for the file. For example, to set the modification time of harish.txt to the current time, a program could do

```
new File("harish.txt").setLastModified(new Date().getTime());
```

The renameTo() method renames the file. Note that the file name string behind the File object remains unchanged, so the File object will not refer to the renamed file.

Working with Directories

File has some useful methods for working with directories.

The mkdir method creates a directory. The mkdirs method does the same thing, after first creating any parent directories that don't yet exist.

The list and listFiles methods list the contents of a directory. The list method returns an array of String file names, while listFiles returns an array of File objects.

Static Methods

File contains some useful static methods.

The createTempFile method creates a new file with a unique name and returns a File object referring to it

Random Access Files

Random access files permit nonsequential, or random, access to a file's contents.

Consider the archive format known as ZIP. A ZIP archive contains files and is typically compressed to save space. It also contain a directory entry at the end that indicates where the various files contained within the ZIP archive begin, as shown in the following figure.

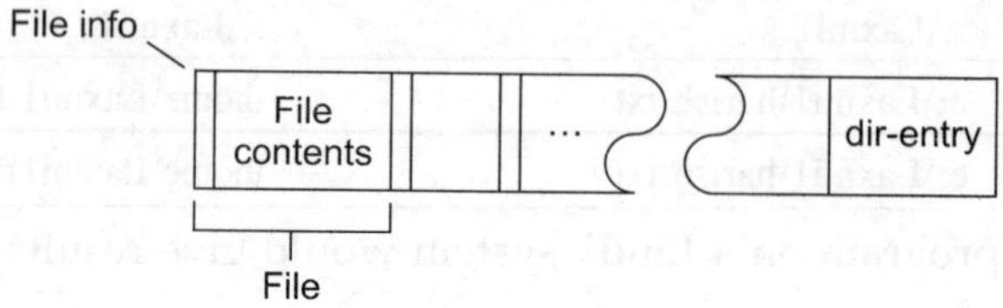

ZIP Archive

Suppose that you want to extract a specific file from a ZIP archive. If you use a sequential access stream, you have to:

1. Open the ZIP archive.
2. Search through the ZIP archive until you locate the file you want to extract.
3. Extract the file.
4. Close the ZIP archive.

Using this procedure, on average, you'd have to read half the ZIP archive before finding the file that you want to extract. You can extract the same file from the ZIP archive more efficiently by using the seek feature of a random access file and following these steps:

- Open the ZIP archive.
- Seek to the directory entry and locate the entry for the file you want to extract from the ZIP archive.
- Seek (backward) within the ZIP archive to the position of the file to extract.
- Extract the file.
- Close the ZIP archive.

This algorithm is more efficient because you read only the directory entry and the file that you want to extract.

The java.io.RandomAccessFile class implements both the DataInput and DataOutput interfaces and therefore can be used for both reading and writing. RandomAccessFile is similar to FileInputStream and FileOutputStream in that you specify a file on the native file system to open when you create it. When you create a RandomAccessFile, you must indicate whether you will be just reading the file or also writing to it. (You have to be able to read a file in order to write it.) The following code creates a RandomAccessFile to read the file named farrago.txt:

new RandomAccessFile("harish.txt", "r");

And this one opens the same file for both reading and writing:

new RandomAccessFile("harish.txt", "rw");

After the file has been opened, you can use the common read or write methods defined in the DataInput and DataOutput interfaces to perform I/O on the file.

RandomAccessFile supports the notion of a file pointer. The file pointer indicates the current location in the file. When the file is first created, the file pointer is set to 0, indicating the beginning of the file. Calls to the read and write methods adjust the file pointer by the number of bytes read or written.

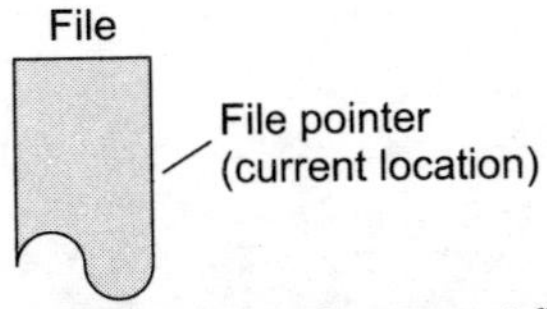

A ZIP file has the notion of a current file pointer.

In addition to the normal file I/O methods that implicitly move the file pointer when the operation occurs, RandomAccessFile contains three methods for explicitly manipulating the file pointer.

1. int skipBytes(int) – Moves the file pointer forward the specified number of bytes
2. void seek(long) – Positions the file pointer just before the specified byte
3. long getFilePointer()–Returns the current byte location of the file pointer

EXERCISE

1. Compare and contrast Byte Stream Class and Character stream class in java.
2. Explain the steps involved in creating File.
3. Explain the Input stream and output stream class in detail.
4. Write a program in java for Password and store all the data in a file.
5. While reading a file, how do you check whether you have reached at the end of a file?
6. What are the various modes available in Random Access file?
7. Distinguish between
   - FileInputStream and FileReader
   - FileOutputStream and FileWrite.
8. What is the SequenceInputStream? Explain with an example.
9. What is the file? Why we need file?
10. What is a Stream? What are the different types of streams available in java?

CHAPTER 16

APPLETS

INTRODUCTION

An applet is a special kind of Java prog that a browser enabled with Java technology can download from the Internet and run. An applet is typically embedded inside a web page and runs in the context of the browser. Lets begin with sample applet shown here

```
import java.awt.*;
import java.applet.*;
public class myapplet extends Applet
{
   public void paint (Graphics g)
   {
      g.drawString("Welcome to Applet", 30,30);
   }
}
```

This applet consist of two important statement.

1. First import the awt. because applet programs are GUI based not console based. The AWT supports the windows based graphical interface.
2. The second important statement import here Applet class.

   The Myapplet extends the class Applet because an applet must be subclass of java.applet. Applet

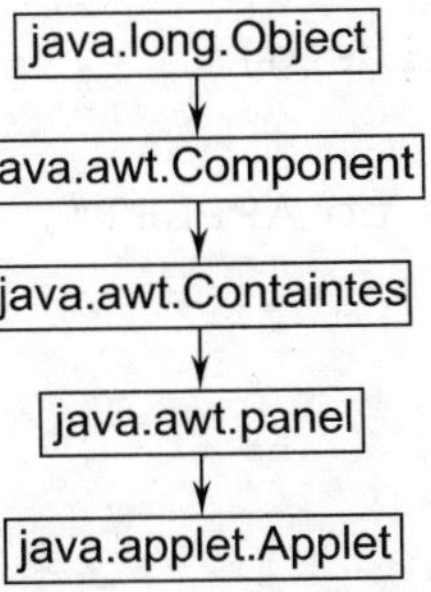

After you enter the program for Myapplet compile it javac Myapplet.java. There are two ways available to run an applet.

1. Executing the applet through HTML within a java compatible browser such as Netscap Navigator, Internet explorer. To executer this method, you need to write a HTML file that contains an appropriate <applet> tag for example.

```
<HTML>
<HEAD>
<TITLE>
MY APPLET PROGRAM <1 TITLE>
<1 HEAD>
<BODY>
<APPLET CODE = "MyApplet.Class" Width= 200 Height=300>
<1 APPLET>
<1 BODY>
<1 HTML>
```

   Type the above program in notepad and save it by the name test-html

   In Internet explorer select the file → open → Browser and select test.html then press OK.

2. Using an appletviewer, which is a standard jdk tool. An appletviewer executes your applet in a window.

   C:\appletviewer test.html.

Without using HTML file to run an Applet

For quick testing of your applet simply include a comment at end of your java source code file that contains applet tag. Here the applet tag and applet source in the same java file

Example ⇒,

```
import java.awt.*;
import java.applet.*;
/ *
 <applet code = "Myapplet 1. class width = 200 height = 200>
 </ applet>
* /
public class Myapplet 1 extends Applet
{
```

```
    public void run (Graphics g)
    {
    g.drawString ("Welcome to APPLET", 30,30);
    }
}
```

Save it — Myapplet1.java

Compile it → javac Myapplet1.java

Run the Applet → appletviewer Myapplet1.java

You will get the output

The APPLET Tag

Square brackets ([and]) that the contents of the brackets are optional

<APPLET

[CODEBASE = codebase URL]

CODE = applet file

[ALT = alternate Text]

[NAME = applet Instance Name]

WIDTH = pixels

HEIGHT = pixels

[ALIGN = alignment]

[V&PACE = Pixels]

[H&PACE = Pixels]

>

[< PARAM NAME = applet Parameter 1 value = value >]

[< PARAM NAME = applet Parameter 2 value = value >]

……..

<APPLET>

paint( ), update( ) and repaint( ) method

The paint method is called each time of your applet's must be redrawn. For example The applet window is minimized and the maximized, paint( ) is also called when the applet begins executions.

Update( ) method is called when your applet has requested that a portion of its window be redraw. This method is used to avoid flickering effect repaint( ) method is causes the entire window to be repainted.

Syntax : void repaint( )

Set Background and Set Foreground( )

set Background method is used to set the Background color of an applet *e.g.,*

Void set Background (Color C1)

set Foreground( ) is used to set the color of an applet text. *e.g.*,

Void set Foreground (Color C2)

C1 & C2 are color constant

Color Constants

Color.black	Color.blue	Color.cyan	Color.darkgray
Color.gray	Color.green	Color.lightgray	Color.mangenta
Color.orange	Color.pink	Color.red	Color.white
Color.yellow			

Font using the font class you can change the default font style and size. The setFont( ) method is used to set the font. *e.g.*, Font *f* = new Font("Times New Roman", font BOLD, 30);

g.setFont(f);

BRIEF SUMMARY OF APPLET LIFE CYCLE

Life Cycle of an Applet: Basically, there are four methods in the `Applet` class on which any applet is built.

- **init:** This method is intended for whatever initialization is needed for your applet. It is called after the param attributes of the applet tag.
- **start:** This method is automatically called after init method. It is also called whenever user returns to the page containing the applet after visiting other pages.
- **stop:** This method is automatically called whenever the user moves away from the page containing applets. You can use this method to stop an animation.
- **destroy:** This method is only called when the browser shuts down normally.

Thus, the applet can be initialized once and only once, started and stopped one or more times in its life, and destroyed once and only once.

For more information on Life Cylcle of an Applet, please refer to The Life Cycle of an Applet section.

When to write Applets vs. Applications

In the early days of Java, one of the critical advantages that Java applets had over Java applications was that applets could be easily deployed over the web while Java applications required a more cumbersome installation process. Additionally, since applets are downloaded from the internet, by default they have to run in a restricted security environment, called the "sandbox", to ensure they don't perform any destructive operations on the user's computer, such as reading/writing to the filesystem.

However, the introduction of Java Web Starthas made it possible for Java applications to also be easily deployed over the web, as well as run in a secure environment. This means that the predominant difference between a Java applet and a Java application is that an applet runs in the context of a web browser, being typically embedded within an html page, while a Java application runs standalone, outside the browser. Thus, applets are particularly well suited for providing functions in a web page which require more interactivity or animation than HTML can provide, such as a graphical game, complex editing, or interactive data visualization. The end user is able to access the functionality without leaving the browser.

Loading Applets in a Web Page

In order to load an applet in a web page, you must specify the applet class with appropriate applet tags. A simple example is below:

Converting Applications to Applets

An application is a standalone program consisting of at least one class with a `main` method. Applets differ significantly from applications. First, applets do not have a `main` method that is automatically called to begin the program. Instead, several methods are called at different points in the execution of an applet. The difference between Java applets and applications lies in how they are run. Applications are usually run by loading the application's main class file with a Java interpreter, such as the java tool in the JDK(TM) 6.

Basic steps to follow to convert an application program into an applet program:

- You need to create a subclass of `java.applet.Applet` in which you override the `init` method to initialize your applet's resources the same way the `main` method initializes the application's resources.
- `init` might be called more than once and should be designed accordingly. Moreover, the top-level `Panel` needs to be added to the applet in `init`; usually it was added to a Frame in `main`. That's it!

You may understand clearly as to how you can convert an application program into an applet, by going through a sample application program SwingUI.java here and its corresponding applet program ApptoAppl.java

When you compare these two programs, you may come up with the following major differences between the two:

- The applet class is declared public so appletviewer can access it.
- The applet class descends from `Applet/JApplet` and the application class descends from `Frame/JFrame`.
- The applet version has no `main` method.
- The application constructor is replaced in the applet by `start` and `init` methods.
- GUI components are added directly to the `Applet`; whereas, in the case of an application, GUI components are added to the content pane of its `JFrame` object.

The rest of this section contains the following to help you get started with applets:

Extending Applet or JApplet

Every applet must define a subclass of the `Applet` or `JApplet` class. In the "Hellow World" applet, this subclass is called `HelloWorld`. Applets inherit a great deal of functionality from the `Applet` or `JApplet` class, including abilities to communicate with the browser and present a graphical user interface (GUI) to the user.

Methods for Milestones

The `JApplet` class provides a framework for applet execution, defining methods that the system calls when milestones — major events in an applet's life cycle — occur. Most applets override some or all of these methods to respond appropriately to milestones.

Methods for Drawing and Event Handling

Applets inherit the drawing and event handling methods of the AWT `Component` class. *Drawing* refers to anything related to representing an applet on-screen — drawing images, presenting user interface components such as buttons, or using graphics primitives. *Event handling* refers to detecting and processing user input such as mouse clicks and key presses, as well as more abstract events such as saving files and iconifying windows.

Methods for Adding UI Components

Applets inherit from the AWT `Container` class. This means that they are designed to hold `Components` — user interface objects such as buttons, labels, pop-up lists, and scrollbars. Like other `Containers`, applets use layout managers to control the positioning of `Components`.

What Applets Can and Can't Do

For security reasons, applets that are loaded over the network have several restrictions. One is that an applet can't ordinarily read or write files on the computer that it's executing on. Another is that an applet can't make network connections except to the host that it came from. Despite these restrictions, applets can do some things that you might not expect. For example, applets can invoke the public methods of other applets on the same page.

Importing Classes and Packages for Applets

The first two lines of the HelloWorld applet import two classes: `JApplet` and `Graphics`.

```
import javax.swing.JApplet;
import java.awt.Graphics;
public class HelloWorld extends JApplet {
   public void paint (Graphics g) {
     g.drawRect (0, 0,
         getSize ( ). width - 1,
         getSize ( ) .height - 1);
     g.drawString ("Hello world!", 5, 15);
  }}
```

If you removed the first two lines, the applet could still compile and run, but only if you changed the rest of the code like this:

Defining an Applet Subclass

The first bold line of the following listing begins a block that defines the `HelloWorld` class.

```
import javax.swing.JApplet;
import java.awt.Graphics;
public class HelloWorld extends JApplet {
   public void paint (Graphics g) {
      g.drawRect (0, 0,
```

```
            getSize ( ) .width - 1,
            getSize ( ) .height - 1);
        g.drawString ("Hello world!", 5, 15);
    }
}
```

Applets inherit a great deal of functionality from the `Applet` or `JApplet` class, including abilities to communicate with the browser and present a graphical user interface (GUI) to the user.

An applet which will be using GUI components from Swing (Java's GUI toolkit) should extend the `javax.swing.JApplet` base class, which provides the best integration with Swing's GUI facilities.

`JApplet` provides the same "RootPane" top-level component structure as Swing's `JFrame` and `Jdialog` components, whereas `Applet` provides just a simple panel. See How to Use Root Panesfor more details on how to utilize this feature.

An applet may extend `java.applet.Applet` when it makes no use of Swing's GUI components. This may be the case if the applet does all its own rendering using the Java graphics libraries (such as with graphing or gaming) and/or uses only AWT components.

The Life Cycle of an Applet

The following is the source code for the `Simple`. The `Simple` applet displays a descriptive string whenever it encounters a major milestone in its life, such as when the user first visits the page the applet's on. The pages that follow use the `Simple` applet and build upon it to illustrate concepts that are common to many applets. If you find yourself baffled by the Java source code, you might want to go to Learning the Java Language to learn about the language.

```
import java.applet.Applet;
import java.awt.Graphics;

public class Simple extends Applet {
     StringBuffer buffer;
     public void init ( ) {
        buffer = new StringBuffer ( );
        addItem ("initializing. . . ");
     }
     public void start ( ) {
        addItem ("starting. . . ");
     }
     public void stop ( ) {
        addItem ("stopping. . . ");
     }
     public void destroy ( ) {
        addItem ("preparing for unloading. . .");
     }
     private void addItem (String newWord) {
```

```
        System.out.println (newWord) ;
        buffer.append (newWord) ;
        repaint ( ) ;
    }
    public void paint (Graphics g) {
        // Draw a Rectangle around the applet's display area.
            g.drawRect (0, 0,
                getWidth ( ) - 1,
                getHeight ( ) - 1);
        // Draw the current string inside the rectangle.
        g.drawString (buffer.toString ( ), 5, 15) ;
    }
}
```

Note: In this example, we extend the `Applet` class, not the Swing `JApplet` class, as we do not need to add Swing components to this applet.

Loading the Applet

You should see "initializing... starting..." above, as the result of the applet being loaded. When an applet is loaded, here's what happens:

- An instance of the applet's controlling class (an `Applet` subclass) is created.
- The applet *initializes* itself.
- The applet *starts* running.

Leaving and Returning to the Applet's Page

When the user leaves the page — for example, to go to another page — the browser stops the applet. When the user returns to the page, the browser *starts* the applet.

Reloading the Applet

Some browsers let the user reload applets, which consists of unloading the applet and then loading it again. Before an applet is unloaded, it's given the chance to *stop* itself and then to perform a *final cleanup*, so that the applet can release any resources it holds. After that, the applet is unloaded and then loaded again, as described in **Loading the Applet,** above.

Quitting the Browser

When the user quits the browser (or whatever application is displaying the applet), the applet has the chance to *stop* itself and do *final cleanup* before the browser exits.

Summary

An applet can react to major events in the following ways:

- It can *initialize* itself.
- It can *start* running.
- It can *stop* running.
- It can perform a *final cleanup*, in preparation for being unloaded.

Methods for Milestones

The `Simple` applet, like every other applet, features a subclass of the `Applet` class. The `Simple` class overrides four `Applet` methods so that it can respond to major events:

`init`

To *initialize* the applet each time it's loaded (or reloaded).

`start`

To *start* the applet's execution, such as when the applet is loaded or when the user revisits a page that contains the applet.

`stop`

To *stop* the applet's execution, such as when the user leaves the applet's page or quits the browser.

`destroy`

To perform a *final cleanup* in preparation for unloading.

Following is the interface for these methods:

```
public class Simple extends JApplet {
    . . .
    public void init ( ) { . . . }
    public void start ( ) { . . . }
    public void stop ( ) { . . . }
    public void destroy ( ) { . . . }
    . . .
}
```

The `init, start, stop,` and `destroy` methods are discussed and used throughout this tutorial. For more information, you can also refer to the `JApplet` API Specification.

Overriding these Methods

Not every applet needs to override every one of these methods. Some very simple applets override none of them. For example, the Hells World applet at the beginning of this section doesn't override any of these methods, since it doesn't do anything except draw itself.

The "Hello World" applet just displays a string once, using its `paint` method (The `paint` method is described on the following page.). Most applets, however, do more.

The init Method

The `init` method is useful for one-time initialization that doesn't take very long. In general, the `init` method should contain the code that you would normally put into a constructor. The reason applets shouldn't usually have constructors is that an applet isn't guaranteed to have full environment until its `init` method is called. For example, the `Applet` image loading methods simply don't work inside of an applet constructor. The `init` method, on the other hand, is a great place to call the image loading methods, since the methods return quickly.

The start Method

Every applet that does something after initialization (except in direct response to user actions) must override the `start` method. The `start` method either performs the applet's work or (more likely) starts up one or more threads to perform the work. You'll learn more about threads later in this trail, in the Threads in Applets section. You'll learn more about handling the events that represent user actions on the next page.

The stop Method

Most applets that override `start` should also override the `stop` method. The `stop` method should suspend the applet's execution, so that it doesn't take up system resources when the user isn't viewing the applet's page. For example, an applet that displays animation should stop trying to draw the animation when the user isn't looking at it.

The destroy Method

Many applets don't need to override the `destroy` method, since their `stop` method (which is called before `destroy`) does everything necessary to shut down the applet's execution. However, `destroy` is available for applets that need to release additional resources.

Using the paint Method

To draw the applet's representation within a browser page, you use the `paint` method.

For example, the `Simple` applet defines its onscreen appearance by overriding the `paint` method:

```
public void paint (Graphics g) {
// Draw a Rectangle around the applet's display area.
         g.drawRect (0, 0,
              getWidth ( ) - 1,
              getHeight ( ) - 1);
        // Draw the current string inside the rectangle.
         g.drawString (buffer.toString ( ) , 5, 15) ;
        }
```

Applets inherit the `paint` method from the Abstract Window Toolkit (AWT) `Container` class.

HANDLING EVENTS

Applets inherit a group of event-handling methods from the `Container` class.

The `Container` class defines several methods, such as `processKeyEvent` and `processMouseEvent`, for handling particular types of events, and then one catch-all method called `processEvent`.

To react to an event, an applet must override the appropriate event-specific method. For example, the following program, SimpleClick, implements a MouseListener and overrides the mouseClicked method.

```
import java.awt.event.MouseListener;
import java.awt.event.MouseEvent;
import java.applet.Applet;
import java.awt.Graphics;
// No need to extend JApplet, since we don't add any components;
// we just paint.
Public class SimpleClick extends Applet
            implements MouseListener
            {
    StringBuffer buffer;
    public void init ( ) {
      addMouseListener (this) ;
      buffer = new StringBuffer ( ) ;
        addItem ("initializing. . . ") ;
    }
    public void start ( )
    {
        addItem ("starting. . . ") ;
    }
    public void stop ( )
    {
        addItem ("stopping. . . ") ;
    }
    public void destroy ( ) {
        addItem ("preparing for unloading. . . ") ;
    }
    void addItem (String newWord) {
        System.out.println(newWord) ;
        buffer.append(newWord) ;
        repaint ( ) ;
    }
    public void paint (Graphics g) {
    // Draw a Rectangle around the applet's display area.
        g.drawRect (0, 0,
          getWidth ( ) - 1,
          getHeight ( ) - 1) ;
      // Draw the current string inside the rectangle.
```

```
        g.drawString(buffer.toString ( ), 5, 15) ;
    }
    // The following empty methods could be removed
    // by implementing a MouseAdapter (usually done
    // using an inner class).
    public void mouseEntered (MouseEvent event) {
    }
    public void mouseExited (MouseEvent event) {
    }
    public void mousePressed (MouseEvent event) {
    }
    public void mouseReleased (MouseEvent event) {
    }
    public void mouseClicked (MouseEvent event) {
        addItem ("click! . . . ") ;
    }
}
```

EXERCISE

1. Write an Applet to illustrate the life cycle of an Applet.
2. Explain the order of Method invocation in an Applet
3. How to convert an Applet to an Application ?
4. What are the interfaces available in Applet class ?
5. What is the use of Applet viewer and show status method ?
6. Explain the following applet Tags.
   - <APPLET >
   - <CODEBASE>
   - <ALIGN>
   - <WIDTH>
   - <HEIGHT>
7. Explain the following Applet method in detail
   - paint()
   - repaint()
   - setBackground()
   - setForeground()
8. What is the default layout of java applet?
9. Explain the life cycle of an Applet.
10. Write the difference between Applet and Application.

17 CHAPTER

AWT AND SWING

AWT FUNDAMENTALS

Graphical User Interfaces

The Java™ programming language provides a class library called the Abstract Window Toolkit (AWT) that contains a number of common graphical widgets. You can add these widgets to your display area and position them with a layout manager.

AWT Basics

All graphical user interface objects stem from a common superclass, Component. To create a Graphical User Interface (GUI), you add components to a Container object. Because a Container is also a Component, containers may be nested arbitrarily.

Each AWT component uses *native code* to display itself on your screen. When you run a Java application under Microsoft Windows, buttons are *really* Microsoft Windows buttons. When you run the same application on a Macintosh, buttons are *really* Macintosh buttons. When you run on a UNIX machine that uses Motif, buttons are *really* Motif buttons.

Basic GUI Logic

There are three steps you take to create any GUI application or applet:

1. Compose your GUI by adding components to Container objects.
2. Setup event handlers to respond to user interaction with the GUI.
3. Display the GUI (automatically done for applets, you must explicitly do this for applications).

When you display an AWT GUI, the interpreter starts a new thread to watch for user interaction with the GUI. This new thread sits and waits until a user presses a key, clicks or moves the mouse, or any other system-level event that affects the GUI. When it receives such an event, it calls one of the event handlers you set up for the GUI.

Note: *The event handler code is executed within the thread that watches the GUI.*

A Simple Example

The following simple example shows some GUI code. This example creates an Applet that contains just an Applet.

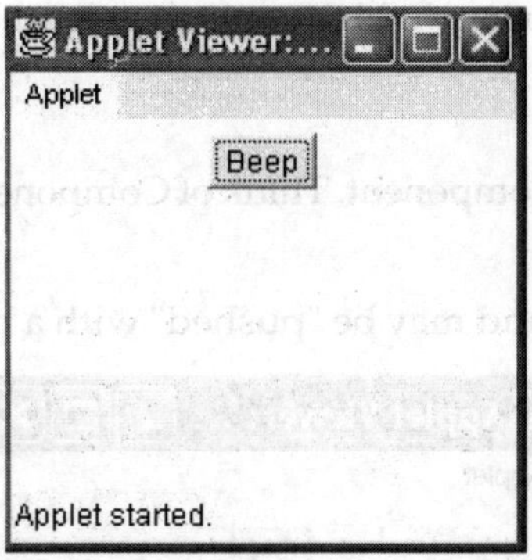


```
import java.awt.Button;
import java.applet.Applet;
public class AButton extends Applet {
  public void init() {
  // STEP 1: Compose the GUI
  Button beepButton = new Button("Beep");
  add(beepButton);
  // Step 2: Setup Event handlers
  beepButton.addActionListener(new Beeper());
  // Step 3: Display the GUI (automatic – this is an applet)
  }
}
```

In step 2, event handling is set up by adding an instance of a *listener* class to the button. When the button is pressed, a certain method in the listener class is called. When the button is pressed, the *button* calls the actionPerformed() method of the listener class.

Suppose you want to produce a "beep" sound when the button is pressed. You can define your event handler as follows:

```
import java.awt.event.ActionListener;
import java.awt.event.ActionEvent;
import java.awt.Component;
public class Beeper implements ActionListener {
  public void actionPerformed(ActionEvent event) {
  Component c = (Component)event.getSource();
  c.getToolkit().beep();
  }
}
```

When actionPerformed() is called, it produces a beep sound on the computer (assuming your system is sound capable).

To see output of this applet in browser window, create a simple HTML page as follows.

<html>

<applet code=AButton.class width=100 height=100>

</applet>

</html>

Open this HTML page in the browser which support at least JRE1.1.

AWT Components

All AWT components extend class Component. Think of Component as the "root of all evil" for AWT.

Buttons

A Button has a single line label and may be "pushed" with a mouse click.

```
import java.awt.*;
import java.applet.Applet;

public class ButtonTest extends Applet {
  public void init() {
  Button button = new Button("OK");
  add(button);
  }
}
```

The AWT button has no direct support for images as labels.

Canvas

The Canvas name derived from a painter's canvas. A Canvas is a graphical component representation of a region where you can draw things such as rectangles, circles, and text strings. You can subclass Canvas to override its default paint() method to define your own components.

You can subclass Canvas to provide a custom graphic in an applet.

```
import java.awt.Canvas;
import java.awt.Graphics;

class DrawingRegion extends Canvas {
  public DrawingRegion() {
```

```
    setSize(100, 50);
  }
  public void paint(Graphics g) {
    g.drawRect(0, 0, 99, 49); // draw border
    g.drawString("A Canvas", 20,20);
  }
}
```

Then you use it like any other component, adding it to a parent container, for example in an Applet subclass.

```
import java.applet.Applet;
public class CanvasPaintTest extends Applet {
  public void init() {
    DrawingRegion region = new DrawingRegion();
    add(region);
  }
```

The Canvas class is frequently extended to create new component types, for example image buttons. However, starting with the JRE 1.1, you can now directly subclass Component directly to create lightweight, transparent widgets.

Checkbox

A Checkbox is a label with a small pushbutton. The state of a Checkbox is either true (button is checked) or false (button not checked). The default initial state is false. Clicking a Checkbox toggles its state.

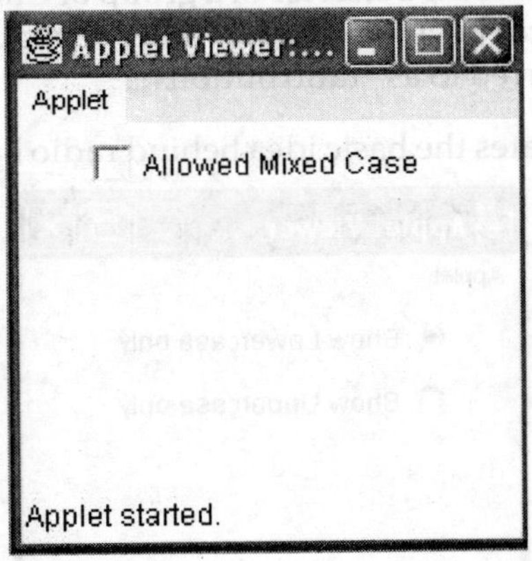


```
import java.awt.*;
import java.applet.Applet;

public class CheckboxSimpleTest extends Applet {
  public void init() {
    Checkbox m = new Checkbox("Allow Mixed Case");
    add(m);
  }
}
```

To set a Checkbox initially true use an alternate constructor:

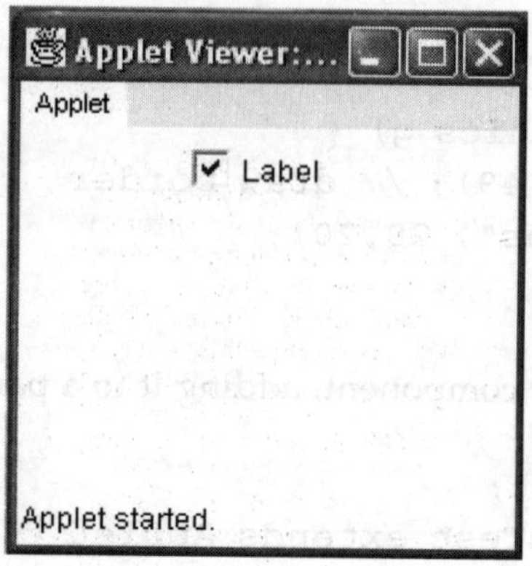


```
import java.awt.*;
import java.applet.Applet;

public class CheckboxSimpleTest2 extends Applet {
  public void init() {
    Checkbox m = new Checkbox("Label", true);
    add(m);
  }
}
```

CheckboxGroup

A CheckboxGroup is used to control the behavior of a group of Checkbox objects. Exactly one of the Checkbox objects is allowed to be true at one time. Checkbox objects controlled with a CheckboxGroup are usually referred to as "ratio buttons".

The following example illustrates the basic idea behind radio buttons.

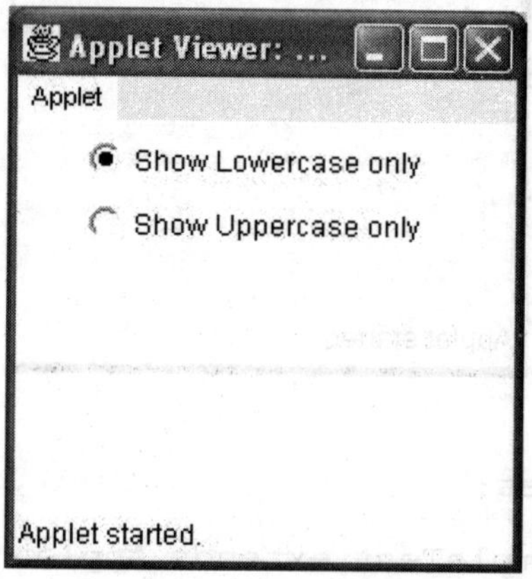


```
import java.awt.*;
import java.applet.Applet;

public class CheckboxGroupTest extends Applet {
  public void init() {
    // create button controller
    CheckboxGroup cbg = new CheckboxGroup();
```

```
    Checkbox cb1 =
      new Checkbox("Show lowercase only", cbg, true);
    Checkbox cb2 =
      new Checkbox("Show uppercase only", cbg, false);
    add(cb1);
    add(cb2);
  }
}
```

Choice

Choice objects are drop-down lists. The visible label of the Choice object is the currently selected entry of the Choice.

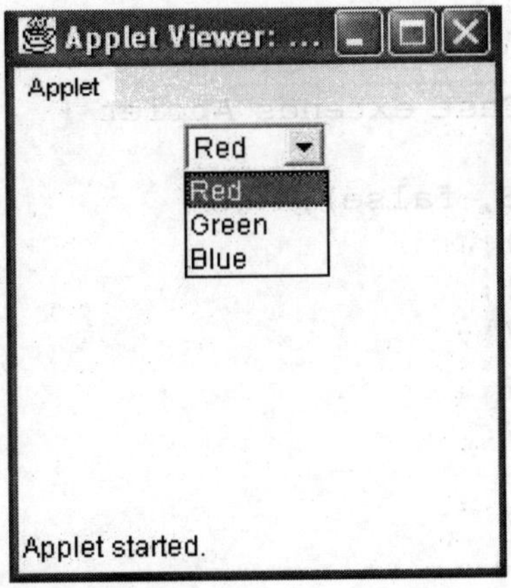


```
import java.awt.*;
import java.applet.Applet;
public class ChoiceSimpleTest extends Applet {
  public void init() {
    Choice rgb = new Choice();
    rgb.add("Red");
    rgb.add("Green");
    rgb.add("Blue");
    add(rgb);
  }
}
```

The first item added is the initial selection.

Label

A Label is a displayed Label object. It is usually used to help indicate what other parts of the GUI do, such as the purpose of a neighboring text field.

```
import java.awt.*;
import java.applet.Applet;
```

```
public class LabelTest extends Applet {
  public void init() {
    add(new Label("A label"));
    // right justify next label
    add(new Label("Another label", Label.RIGHT));
  }
}
```

List

A List is a scrolling list box that allows you to select one or more items. Passing true as the second argument to the constructor may use for multiple selections.

```
import java.awt.*;
import java.applet.Applet;

public class ListSimpleTest extends Applet {
  public void init() {
    List list = newList(5, false);
    list.add("New Delhi");
    list.add("Jalandhar");
    list.add("Chandigarh");
    list.add("Bhatinda");
    list.add("Ludhiana");
    list.add("Patiala");
    list.add("Amritsar");

    add(list);
  }
}
```

The constructor may contain a *preferred* number of lines to display. The current LayoutManager may choose to respect or ignore this request.

Scrollbar

A Scrollbar is a "slider" widget with characteristics specified by integer values that are set during Scrollbar construction. Both horizontal and vertical sliders are available.

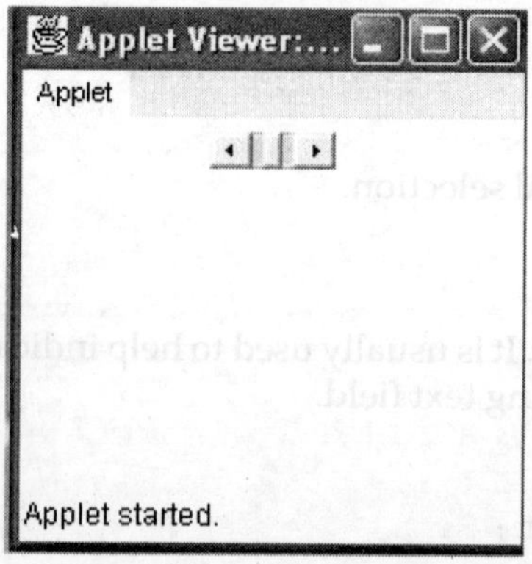

```
import java.awt.*;
import java.applet.Applet;

// A simple example that makes a Scrollbar appear
public class ScrollbarSimpleTest extends Applet {
  public void init() {
    Scrollbar sb =
      new Srcollbar(Scrollbar.HORIZONTAL,
        0, // initial value is 0
        5, // width of slider
        -100, 100); // range -100 to 100
    add(sb);
  }
}
```

The maximum value of the Scrollbar is determined by subtracting the Scrollbar width from the maximum setting (last parameter).

TextField

A TextField is a scrollable text display object with one row of characters. The preferred width of the field may be specified during construction and an initial string may be specified.

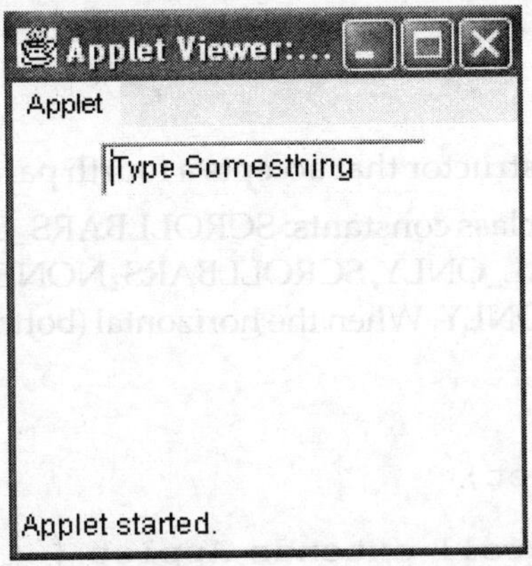


```
import java.awt.*;
import java.applet.Applet;

public class TextFieldSimpleTest extends Applet {
  public void init() {
    TextField f1 =
      new TextField("type something");
    add(f1);
  }
}
```

Tips:

- Call setEditable(false) to make the field read-only.
- The constructor has an optional width parameter.

- This does not control the number of characters in the TextField, but is merely a suggestion of the preferred width on the screen. Note that layout managers may choose to respect or ignore this preferred width.

For password fields:

```
field.setEchoChar('?');
```

To clear/reset:

```
field.setEchoChar((char)0);
```

TextArea

A TextArea is a multi-row text field that displays a single string of characters, where new line ('\n' or '\n\r' or '\r', depending on platform) ends each row. The width and height of the field is set at construction, but the text can be scrolled up/down and left/right.

```
import java.awt.*;
import java.applet.Applet;

public class TextAreaSimpleTest extends Applet {
  TextArea disp;
  public void init() {
    disp = new TextArea("Code goes here", 10,30);
    add(disp);
  }
}
```

There is a four-argument constructor that accepts a fourth parameter of a scrollbar policy.

The different settings are the class constants: SCROLLBARS_BOTH, SCROLLBARS_HORIZONTAL_ONLY, SCROLLBARS_NONE, and SCROLLBARS_ VERTICAL_ONLY. When the horizontal (bottom) scrollbar is not present, the text will wrap.

```
import java.awt.*;
import java.applet.Applet;

public class TextAreaScroll extends Applet {
  String s =
    "This is a very long message " +
    "It should wrap when there is " +
    "no horizontal scrollbar.";
  public void init() {
    add(new TextArea (s, 4, 15,
      TextArea.SCROLLBARS_NONE));
    add(new TextArea (s, 4, 15,
      TextArea.SCROLLBARS_BOTH));
    add(new TextArea (s, 4, 15,
      TextArea.SCROLLBARS_HORIZONTAL_ONLY));
    add(new TextArea (s, 4, 15,
```

```
        TextArea.SCROLLBARS_VERTICAL_ONLY));
    }
}
```

Common Component Methods

All AWT components share the 100-plus methods inherited from the Component class. Some of the most useful and commonly-used methods are listed below:

getSize() - Gets current size of component, as a Dimension.
Dimension *d* = someComponent.getSize();

int height = *d*.height;

int width = *d*.width;

Note: With the Java 2 Platform, you can directly access the width and height using the getWidth() and getHeight() methods. This is more efficient, as the component doesn't need to create a new Dimension object.

If you're using the Java 2 platform, you should only use getSize() if you really need a Dimension object!

getLocation() - Gets position of component, relative to containing component, as a Point.

Point *p* =someComponent.getLocation();

int *x* = *p.x*;

int *y* = *p.y*;

Note: With the Java 2 Platform, you can directly access the x and y parts of the location using getX() and getY(). This is more efficient, as the component doesn't have to create a new Point object.

If you're using the Java 2 platform, you should only use getLocation() if you really need a Point object!

getLocationOnScreen() - Gets the position of the component *relative to the upper-left corner of the computer screen*, as a Point.

Point *p* =someComponent.getLocationOnScreen();
int *x* = *p.x*;
int *y* = *p.y*;
getBounds() –Gets current bounding Rectangle of component.
Rectangle *r* =someComponent.getBounds();
int height = *r*.height;
int width = *r*.width;
int *x* = *r.x*;
int *y* = *r.y*;
This is like a combination of calling getLocation() and getSize().

Note: If you're using the Java 2 Platform and didn't really need a Rectangle object, you should use getX(), getY(), getWidth(), and getHeight() instead.

- setEnabled(boolean) – Toggles the state of the component. If set to true, the component will react to user input and appear normal. If set to false, the component will ignore user interaction, and usually appear *ghosted* or *grayed-out*.
- setVisible(boolean) – Toggles the visibility state of the component. If set to true, the component will appear on the screen *if* it is contained in a visible container. If false, the component will not appear on the screen. Note that if a component is marked as not visible, any layout manager that is responsible for that component will usually proceed with the layout algorithm *as though the component were not in the parent container!* This means that making a component

invisible *will not* simply make it disappear while reserving its space in the GUI. Making the component invisible will cause the layout of its sibling components to readjust!

- setBackground(Color)/setForeground(Color) – Changes component background/ foreground Colors.
- setFont(Font) – Changes font of text within a component.

Containers

A Container is a Component, so may be nested. Class Panel is the most commonly-used Panel and can be extended to partition GUIs. Class Applet is a specialized Panel for running programs within a browser.

Common Container Methods

Besides various methods inherited from the component class, all Container subclasses inherit the behavior of about 50 common methods of Container (most of which just override a method of Component). While the most common method of Container used add(), has already been briefly discussed, if you need to access the list of components within a container, you may find the getComponentCount(), getComponents(), and getComponent(int) methods helpful.

Event Handling

Events

Beginning with the 1.1. version of the JRE, objects register as listeners for events. If there are no listeners when an event happens, nothing happens. If there are twenty listeners registered, each is given an opportunity to process the event, in an undefined order. For example, activating the button notifies any registered ActionListener objects. Consider SimpleButtonEvent applet which creates a Button instance and registers itself as the listener for the button's action events:

```
import java.awt.*;
import java.awt.event.*;
import java.applet.Applet;

public class SimpleButtonEvent extends Applet
  implements ActionListener {
private Button b;

public void init() {
  b = new Button("Press me");
  b.addActionListener(this);
  add(b);
}
public void actionPerformed(ActionEvent e) {
// If the target of the event was our Button
// In this example, the check is not
// truly necessary as we only listen to
```

```
// a single button
  if (e.getSource() = = b) {
    getGraphics().drawString("OUCH",20,20);
  }
 }
}
```

Notice that any class can implement ActionListener, including, in this case, the applet itself. All listeners are always notified. If you don't want an event to be processed further, you can call the AWTEvent.consume() method. However each listener would then need to check for consumption using the isConsumed() method. Consuming events primarily stops events from being processed by the system, after every listener is notified. So, if you want to reject keyboard input from the user, you can consume() the KeyEvent. All the KeyListener implements will still be notified, but the character will not be displayed. Consumption only works for InputEvent and its subclasses.

So, here is how everything works:

- Components generate subclasses of AWTEvent when something interesting happens.
- Event sources permit any class to be a listener using the addXXXListener() method, where XXX is the event type you can listen for, i.e., addActionListener(). You can also remove listeners using the removeXXXListener() methods. If there is an add/removeXXXListener() pair, then the component is a source for the event when the appropriate action happens.
- In order to be an *event handler* you have to implement the listener type, otherwise, you cannot be added, ActionListener being one such type.
- Some listener types are special and require you to implement multiple methods. For instance, if you are interested in key events, and register a KeyListener, you have to implement three methods, one for key press, one for key release, and one for both, key typed. If you only care about key typed events, it doesn't make sense to have to stub out the other two methods. There are special classes out there called adapters that implement the listener interfaces and stub out all the methods. Then, you only need to subclass the adapter and override the necessary method(s).

AWTEvent

Events subclass the AWTEvent class. And nearly every event-type has an associated *Listener* interface, PaintEvent and InputEvent do not. (With PaintEvent, you just override paint() and update(), for InputEvent, you listen for subclass events, since it is abstract.

Low-level Events

Low-level events represent a low-level input or window operation, like a key press, mouse movement, or window opening. The following table displays the different low-level events, and the operations that generate each event (each operation corresponds to a method of the listener interface):

ComponentEvent	Hiding, moving, resizing, showing
ContainerEvent	Adding/removing component
FocusEvent	Getting/losing focus
KeyEvent	Pressing, releasing, or typing (both) a key
MouseEvent	Clicking, dragging, entering, exiting, moving, pressing, or releasing
WindowEvent	Iconifying, deiconifying, opening, closing, really closed, activating, deactivating

For example, typing the letter 'A' on the keyboard generates three events, one for pressing, one for releasing, and one for typing. Depending upon your interests, you can do something for any of the three events.

Semantic Events

Semantic events represent interaction with a GUI component; for instance selecting a button, or changing the text of a text field. Which components generate which events is shown in the next Section.

ActionEvent	Do the command
AdjustmentEvent ItemEvent TextEvent	Value adjusted State changed Text changed

Event Sources

The following table represents the different event sources. Keep in mind the object hierarchy. For instance, when Component is an event source for something, so are all its subclasses:

Low-Level Events	
Component	ComponentListener FocusListener KeyListener MouseListener MouseMotionListener
Container	ContainerListener
Window	WindowListener

Semantic Events	
Button List MenuItem TextField	ActionListener
Choice Checkbox CheckboxMenuItem List	ItemListener
Scrollbar	AdjustmentListener
TextArea	Adjustment
TextField	TextListener

Event Listeners

Each listener interface is paired with one event type and contains a method for each type of event the event class embodies. For example, the KeyListener contains three methods, one for each type of event that the KeyEvent has: keyPressed(), keyReleased(), and keyTyped().

Summary of Listener interfaces and their methods

Interface	Method(s)
ActionListener	actionPerformed(ActionEvent e)
AdjustmentListener	adjustmentValueChanged(AdjustmentEvent e)
ComponentListener	componentHidden(ComponentEvent e)
	componentMoved(ComponentEvent e)
	componentResized(ComponentEvent e)
	componentShown(ComponentEvent e)
ContainerListener	componentAdded(ContainerEvent e)
	componentRemoved(ContainerEvent e)
FocusListener	focusGained(FocusEvent e)
	focusLost(FocusEvent e)
ItemListener	itemStateChanged(ItemEvent e)
KeyListener	keyPressed(KeyEvent e)
	keyReleased(KeyEvent e)
	keyTyped(KeyEvent e)
MouseListener	mouseClicked(MouseEvent e)
	mouseEntered(MouseEvent e)
	mouseExited(MouseEvent e)
	mousePressed(MouseEvent e)
	mouseReleased(MouseEvent e)
MouseMotionLi stener	mouseDragged(MouseEvent e)
	mouseMoved(MouseEvent e)
TextListener	textValueChanged(TextEvent e)
WindowListener	windowActivated(WindowEvent e)
	windowClosed(WindowEvent e)
	windowClosing(WindowEvent e)
	windowDeactivated(WindowEvente)
	windowDeiconified(WindowEvent e)
	windowIconified(WindowEvent e)
	windowOpened(WindoweEvent e)

Event Adapters

Since the low-level event listeners have multiple methods to implement, there are event adapter classes to ease the pain. Instead of implementing the interface and stubbing out the methods you do not care about, you can subclass the appropriate adapter class and just override the one or two methods you are interested in. Since the semantic listeners only contain one method to implement, there is no need for adapter classes.

```
public class MyKeyAdapter extends KeyAdapter {
  public void keyTyped(KeyEvent e) {
    System.out.println("User typed: " +
      KeyEvent.getKeyText(e.getKeyCode()));
  }
}
```

Adapters Example

The following code demonstrates using an adapter as an anonymous inner class to draw a rectangle within an applet. The mouse press signifies the top left corner to draw, with the mouse release the bottom right.

```
import java.awt.*;
import java.awt.event.*;

public class Draw extends java.applet.Applet {
  public void init() {
    addMouseListener(
      new MouseAdapter() {
        int savedX, savedY;
        public void mousePressed(MouseEvent e) {
          savedX = e.getX();
          savedY = e.getY();
        }
        public void mouseReleased(MouseEvent e) {
          Graphics g = Draw.this.getGraphics();
          g.drawRect(savedX, savedY,
                e.getX()-savedX,
                e.getY()-savedY);
        }
      }
    );
  }
}
```

Applications and Menus

GUI-based Applications

To create a window for your application, define a subclass of Frame (a Window with a title, menubar, and border) and have the main method construct an instance of that class.

Applications respond to events in the same way as applets do. The following example, BasicApplication, responds to the native window toolkit quit, or closing, operation:

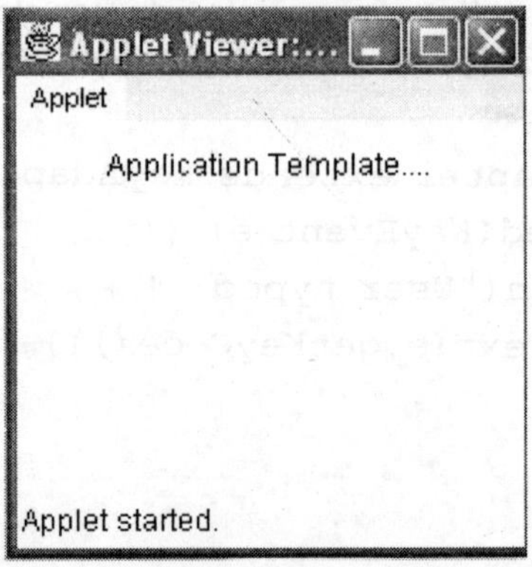

```
import java.awt.*;
import java.awt.event.*;

public class BasicApplication extends Frame {
  public BasicApplication() {
    super("BasicApplication Title");
    setSize(200, 200)
    // add a demo component to this frame
    add(new Label("Application Template...",
                 Label.CENTER),
    BorderLayout.CENTER);
   addWindowListener(new WindowAdapter() {
    public void windowClosing(WindowEvent e) {
      setVisible(false); dispose();
      System.exit(0);
    }
   });
  }
  public static void main(String[] args) {
   BasicApplication app =
            new BasicApplication();
   app.setVisible(true);
  }
}
```

Consider an application that displays the x,y location of the last mouse click and provides a button to reset the displayed x,y coordinates to 0,0:

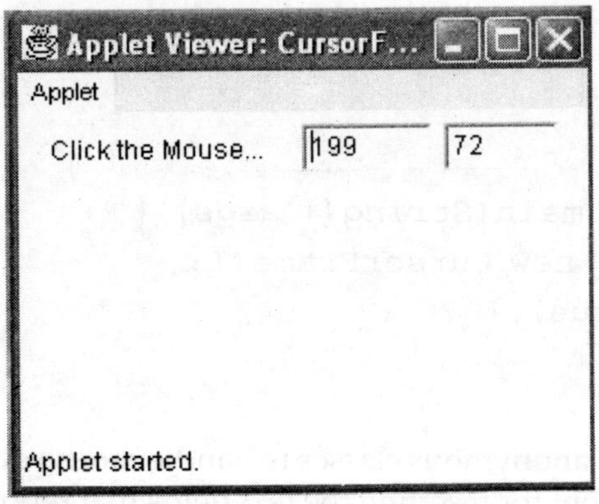


```
import java.awt.*;
import java.awt.event.*;
public class CursorFrame extends Frame {
  TextField a, b;
  Button btn;
  public CursorFrame() {
```

```
    super("CursorFrame");
    setSize(400, 200);
    setLayout(new FlowLayout());
    add(new Label("Click the mouse..."));
    a = new TextField("0", 4);
    b = new TextField("0", 4);
    btn = new Button("RESET");
    add(a); add(b); add(btn);
    addMouseListener(new MouseAdapter() {
    public void mousePressed(MouseEvent e) {
      a.setText(String.valueOf(e.getX()));
      b.setText(String.valueOf(e.getY()));
    ]
  });
  addWindowListener(new WindowAdapter() {
    public void windowClosing(WindowEvent e) {
      setVisible(false);
      dispose();
      System.exit(0);
    }
  });
  btn.addActionListener(new ActionListener() {
    public void actionPerformed(ActionEvent e) {
      a.setText("0");
      b.setText("0");
    }
  });
 }
 public static void main(String[] args) {
  CursorFrame app = new CursorFrame();
  app.setVisible(true);
  }
 }
```

This application provides anonymous classes to handle mouse events, application window closing events, and the action event for resetting the text fields that report mouse coordinates.

When you have a very common operation, such as handling application window closing events, it often makes sense to abstract out this behavior and handle it elsewhere. In this case, it's logical to do this by extending the existing Frame class, creating the specialization AppFrame:

```
import java.awt.*;
import java.awt.event.*;
```

```
public class AppFrame extends Frame
   implements WindowListener {
  public AppFrame(String title) {
    super(title);
    addWindowListener(this);
  }
  public void windowClosing(WindowEvent e) {
    setVisible(false);
    dispose();
    System.exit(0);
  }
  public void windowClosed(WindowEvent e) {}
  public void windowDeactivated(WindowEvent e) {}
  public void windowActivated(WindowEvent e) {}
  public void windowDeiconified(WindowEvent e) {}
  public void windowIconified(WindowEvent e) {}
  public void windowOpened(WindowEvent e) {}
}
```

AppFrame directly implements WindowListener, providing empty methods for all but one window event, namely, the window closing operation. With this definition, applications such as CursorFrame can extend AppFrame instead of Frame and avoid having to provide the anonymous class for window closing operations:

Applications: Dialog Boxes

A Dialog is a window that requires input from the user. Components may be added to the Dialog like any other container. Like a Frame, a Dialog is initially invisible. You must call the method setVisible() to activate the dialog box.

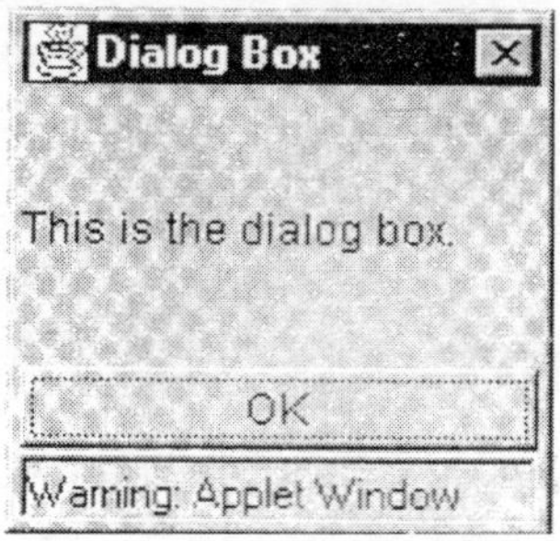


```
import java.awt.*;
import java.awt.event.*;
public class DialogFrame extends AppFrame {
  Dialog d;
```

```
    public DialogFrame() {
      super("DialogFrame");
      setSize(200, 100);
      Button btn, dbtn;
      add(btn = new Button("Press for Dialog Box"),
        BorderLayout.SOUTH);
      d = new Dialog(this, "Dialog Box", false);
      d.setSize(150, 150);
      d.add(new Label("This is the dialog box."),
        BorderLayout.CENTER);
      d.add(dbtn = new Button("OK"),
        BorderLayout.SOUTH);
      btn.addActionListener(new ActionListener() {
        public void actionPerformed(ActionEvent e) {
          d.setVisible(true);
        }
    });
    dbtn.addActionListener(new ActionListener() {
      public.void actionPerformed(ActionEvent e) {
        d.setVisible(false);
      }
  });
    d.addWindowListener(new WindowAdapter() {
      public void windowClosing(WindowEvent e) {
        d.setVisible(false);
      }
    });
  }
    public static void main(String[] args) {
      DialogFrame app = new DialogFrame();
      app.setVisible(true);
    }
  }
MenuBar mb = new MenuBar();
Create a Menu
Menu m = new Menu("File");
```

Create your MenuItem choices and add each to the Menu, in the order you want them to appear, from top to bottom.

```
m.add(new MenuItem("Open"));
```

```
m.addSeparator(); // add a spearator
m.add(new CheckboxMenuItem("Allow writing"));
// Create submenu
Menu sub = new Menu("Options...");
sub.add(new MenuItem("Option 1"));
m.add(sub); // add sub to File menu
```

Add each Menu to the MenuBar in the order you want them to appear, from left to right.

`mb.add(m);   // add File menu to bar` Add the **MenuBar** to the **Frame** by calling the **setMenuBar()** method.

```
setMenuBar(mb);// set menu bar of your Frame
```

The following program, MainWindow, creates an application window with a menu bar and several menus using the strategy outlined above:

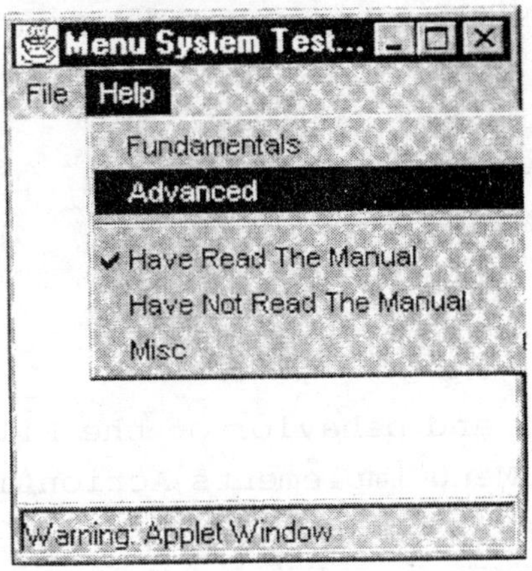


```
  import java.awt.*;
 import java.awt.event.*;

 // Make a main window with two top-level menus: File and Help.
 // Help has a submenu and demonstrates a few interesting menu
items.
 public class MainWindow extends Frame {
  public MainWindow() {
   super("Menu System Test Window");
   setSize(200, 200);
 // make a top level File menu
 FileMenu fileMenu = new FileMenu(this);

 // make a top level Help menu
 HelpMenu helpMenu = new HelpMenu(this);

 // make a menu bar for this frame
 // and add top level menus File and Menu
```

```
    MenuBar mb = new MenuBar();
    mb.add(fileMenu);
    mb.add(helpMenu);
    setMenuBar(mb);
    addWindowListener(new WindowAdapter() {
     public void windowClosing(WindowEvent e) {
      exit();
    }
    });
   }
  public void exit() {
   setVisible(false); // hide the Frame
   dispose(); // tell windowing system to free resources
   System.exit(0); // exit
  }
  public static void main(String args[]){
   MainWindow w = new MainWindow();
   w.setVisible(true);
  }
}
// Encapsulate the look and behavior of the File menu
class FileMenu extends Menu implements ActionListener {
   MainWindow mw; // who owns us?
   public FileMenu(MainWindow m) {
     super("File");
     mw = m;
     MenuItem mi;
     add(mi = new MenuItem("Open"));
     mi.addActionListener(this);
     add(mi = new MenuItem("Close"));
     mi.addActionListener(this);
     add(mi = new MenuItem("Exit"));
     mi.addActionListener(this);
   }
   // respond to the Exit menu choice
   public void actionPerformed(ActionEvent e) {
    String item = e.getActionCommand();
    if (item.equals("Exit"))
     mw.exit();
    else
```

```
    System.out.println("Selected FileMenu" + item);
  }
  // Encapsulate the look and behavior of the Help menu
  class HelpMenu extends Menu implements ActionListener {
   MainWindow mw; // who owns us?
   public HelpMenu(MainWindow m) {
    super("Help");
    mw = m;
    MenuItem mi;
    add(mi = new MenuItem("Fundamentals"));
    mi.addActionListener(this);
    add(mi = new MenuItem("Advanced"));
    mi.addActionListener(this);
    addSeparator();
    add(mi = new CheckboxMenuItem("Have Read The Manual"));
    mi.addActionListener(this);
    add(mi = new CheckboxMenuItem("Have Not Read The Manual"));
    mi.addActionListener(this);

    // make a Misc sub menu of Help menu
    Menu subMenu = new Menu("Misc");
    subMenu.add(mi = new MenuItem("Help!!!"));
    mi.addActionListener(this);
    subMenu.add(mi = new MenuItem("Why did that happen?"));
    mi.addActionListener(this);
    add(submenu);
   }
   // respond to a few menu items
   public void actionPerformed(ActionEvent e) {
    String item = e.getActionCommand();
    if (item.equals("Fundamentals"))
      System.out.println("Fundamentals");
    else if (item.equals("Help!!!"))
      System.out.println("Help!!!"); // etc...
   }
  }
```

Menus

An application (or applet) that constructs a Frame instance and sets up a "File" menu, create a "Help" menu that uses MenuItem objects.

- FileMenu.java
- HelpMenu.java
- TestMenu.java
- MenuTestWindow.java

```
FileMenu.java
import java.awt.*;
import java.awt.event.*;

class FileMenu extends Menu implements ActionListener {
  private MenuTestWindow mw; // who owns us?
  public FileMenu(MenuTestWindow m) {
    super("File");
    mw = m;
    MenuItem mi;
    add(mi = new MenuItem("Open"));
    mi.addActionListener(this);
    add(mi = new MenuItem("Close"));
    mi.addActionListener(this);
    add(mi = new MenuItem("Exit"));
    mi.addActionListener(this);
  }
  public void actionPerformed(ActionEvent e) {
    String item = e.getActionCommand();
    if (item == null)
      item = "null";
    if (item.equals("Exit"))
      mw.exit();
    else
      mw.output.append(
      "Selected File menu item: " + item + "\n");
  }
}
```

```
HelpMenu.java

import java.awt.*;
import java.awt.event.*;

class FileMenu extends Menu implements ActionListener {
  private MenuTestWindow mw; // who owns us?
  Public FileMenu(MenuTestWindow m) {
    super("File");
```

```
  mw = m;
  MenuItem mi;
  add(mi = new MenuItem("Open"));
  mi.addActionListener(this);
  add(mi = new MenuItem("Close"));
  mi.addActionListener(this);
  add(mi = new MenuItem("Exit"));
  mi.addActionListener(this);
 }
public void actionPerformed(ActionEvent e) {
  String item = e.getActionCommand();
  if (item ==null)
    item = "null";
  if (item.equals("Exit"))
    mw.exit();
  else
    mw.output.append(
    "Selected File menu item: " + item + "\n");
  }
 }
```

TestMenu.java

```
import java.awt.*;
public class TestMenu extends java.applet.Applet {
  public static void main(String[] args) {
    MenuTestWindow w = new MenuTestWindow();
      w.setVisible(true);
    }

  public void init() {
    MenuTestWindow w = new MenuTestWindow();
    w.setVisible(true);
  }
}
```

MenuTestWindow.java

```
import java.awt.*;
import java.awt.event.*;
public class MenuTestWindow extends Frame {
  TextArea output;
  public MenuTestWindow() {
```

```
    super("MenuTestWindow");
    setLayout(new FlowLayout());
    setSize(300, 180);

    // make a top level File menu
    FileMenu fileMenu = new FileMenu(this);

    // make a top level Help menu
    HelpMenu helpMenu = new HelpMenu(this);

    // make a menu bar for this frame and add top level menus
    File and Menu
    MenuBar mb = new MenuBar();
    mb.add(fileMenu);
    mb.add(helpMenu);

    setMenuBar(mb);
    add(output = new TextArea(4, 30));
    addWindowListener(new WindowAdapter() {
      public void windowClosing(WindowEvent e) {
        exit();
      }
    });
  }
  public void exit() {
    setVisible(false); // hide the frame
    dispose();  // tell windowing system to free resources
    System.exit();  // exit the application
  }
}
```

INTRODUCTION TO SWING

Introduction

Swing is a library of classes and an architectural framework designed to make it easy to build powerful and attractive graphical user interfaces (GUIs) using Java. Swing supercedes but does not replace the *Abstract Windowing Toolkit* (AWT), Sun's original Java GUI. The relationship between Swing and AWT is a bit complicated, but a fair summary is that Swing re-uses some of the fundamental AWT superclasses and concepts. The "leaf" classes directly used in Swing applications are almost all provided by the Swing toolkit. All Swing classes are prefixed with a "J", e.g. **JButton, JMenu, JPanel,** and forth (Later the Swing class hierarchy is explained in more detail).

Swing essentially consists of two types of objects: containers and components. *Components* are the fundamental objects that comprise GUIs—for example, buttons, menus, an text labels. In Swing, all components are subclasses of **JComponent**, and abstract GUI object. **JComponent** provides the methods and structure common to all concrete components. For example, all components have a size, so size accessor methods are implemented in **JComponent** and inherited by the concrete subclasses that represent actual rendered objects, like buttons.

One more critical part of GUI design in handling user initiated *events*. Examples of events including clicking mouse buttons over parts of the GUI, moving the pointer into and out of a window, or entering text using the keyboard. In Swing, events are processed by *event listener objects*. Without going into the details of event handling, the basics of which are presented later, the general idea is quite simple. Swing's event processing infrastructure keeps track of the objects interested in each type of event. When a event occurs, Swing notifies each interested object by calling a specific standard method. The event handler object is responsible for implementing that method and for registering itself as interested in notification. This is essentially a callback system as used in earlier GUI systems, like X1 1, but the structure of Java makes implementation simpler and more elegant—without sacrificing power and flexibility.

The Simplest Swing Component: A Label

The first step in writing a Swing program is to decide what type of window will be used to display the GUI. Swing provides four basic options in the form of classes that can act as the root of the containment hierarchy. A **JApplet** object is an embeddable Swing applet. A **JFrame** is a stand-alone top level window with the same decorations and basic functionality as a standard platform-specific window, e.g., an X window. A **JWindow** is essentially an undecorated **JFrame**, typically used for splash screens or display of images. A **JDialog** is a popup window typically used to notify the user of some event or to ask a question.

JApplet extends the basic Java **Applet** class, so it inherits **Applet's** four life-cycle management methods. These are four standard methods that the browser or applet viewer calls at certain specific points in thé applet's lifetime:

- **init(),** when the applet is first loaded by the browser;
- **start(),** when the applet should begin executing;
- **stop(),** when the applet should stop executing;
- **destroy(),** when the applet is no longer going to be needed.

The most straightforward way to implement a Swing applet is to extend **JApplet** and then to override whichever of these four methods are appropriate. In many cases, the **init()** method is the only one that has to be coded. (The default, i.e., inherited, behavior of the other methods is usually sufficient.)

Here is a simple applet that creates and displays a text label:

```
// Here we import the necessary Java infrastructure.
import javax.swing.*;
import java.awt.*;
// We extend the basic JApplet, which itself extends
// the Java Applet class, which provides the basic
// init(), start(), stop(), and destroy() life-cycle
// management methods.
public class LabelTest extends JApplet {
  // Don't panic! This is just a hack required because
  // the real world hasn't caught up with Sun's Java2
```

```
    // specs yet. It tweaks a "system" parameter so that
    // a check that always fails and generates an error
    // message won't happen.
    public LabelTest() {
      getRootPane().putClientProperty("defeatSystemEventQueueCheck",
        Boolean.TRUE);
    }
    // Here's the real code. We are overriding Applet's
    // init() class, which is inherited through JApplet,
    // All we do is create a simple label, tell it to center
    // the display text we provided through the constructor,
    // and then add the label to the Applet's display area.
    public void init() {
    JLabel label = new JLabel("A Swing label.");
    label.setHorizontalAlignment(JLabel.CENTER);
    getContentPane().add(label);
  }
}
```

The creation of the label component is straightforward. One of the **JLabel** constructors takes a text string to display as a parameter. Several of **JLabel's** methods, including the one we used to center the text, deal with arranging the display text within the screen area associated with the label. Finally we **add()** our label object to the display area, or **contentPane**, of the **JApplet**.

All Swing components can be created and rendered using the same basic technique: call the constructor, tweak a few things using component methods–for example change the colors or the way that text is aligned–and then add the component to the container that will hold it. In our example we have a single component and we insert it directly into the applet's **contentPane**, which is the root of the **JApplet** containment hierarchy, but in general there will be many components grouped into a variety of intermediate containers.

Containers

Containers store components. They are used to build a *containment hierarchy* that hides some of the details of complicated GUIs and helps simply Swing programming.

Layout Managers

All Swing applications have at least one container—the one that sits at the root of the containment hierarchy. In the case of an applet, this is the JApplet's **contentPane**, which can be accessed using **getContentPane().** We have already seen how to **add()** a component to the **contentPane,** but an obvious question is what happens if we add more components. Where will they appear relative to the first? Do we have control over their arrangement, and if so how?

In general, the on-screen configuration of components in a container is controlled by a *layout manager.* A layout manager is any class implementing the LayoutManager interface. (There is also a subclass, **LayoutManager2,** that adds some functionality and is used for some of the more complicated layout schemes.). Most of the time, the style of layout you will want to use is implemented by a standard layout manager provided with Swing. Here are some examples:

- **GridLayout** chops the container into NxM equal-sized pieces and puts one component into each;
- **FlowLayout** puts the first component on the left and adds subsequent ones to the right;
- **CardLayout** stacks components one on top of the other, with only the top one visible at a time;
- **GridBagLayout** is like **GridLayout** except that the components don't have to be the same size.

Since all standard layout managers implement one of the two layout interfaces, they share some basic methods. Naturally there are also methods particular to each scheme. For example, **GridLayout** provides **setRows(), setColumns(), getRows(),** and **getColumns()** to set and query number of grid slots in the container. **FlowLayout** provides **setAlignment()** to specify how the rows of components should be justified.

To set the layout manager for a container, use the **setLayout()** method, which takes as an argument an object that implements **LayoutManager. SetLayout()** is a method defined by the Java AWT **Container** class, which is a superclass of all Swing containers. (This is an area in which the Swing/AWT class hierarchy becomes somewhat confusing.

Here is a simple applet that arranges four labels in a 2x2 grid:

```
import javax.swing.*;
import java.awt.*;

public class GridTest extends JApplet {
  // Constructor hack omitted for clarity.
  public void init() {
    // Use a 2x2 grid layout in the Applet root contentPane.
    getContentPane().setLayout(new GridLayout(2,2));
    // Add four labels.
    getContentPane().add(new Label("One"));
    getContentPane().add(new Label("Two"));
    getContentPane().add(new Label("Three"));
    getContentPane().add(new Label("Four"));
  }
}
```

A similar version, FlowTest, is exactly the same except the first line of code in init() is:

getContentPane().setLayout(new FlowLayour());

Intermediate Containers

Any substantial GUI is likely to contain many concrete components. In many cases, it is convenient to bind related components into a group and then to manipulate them as a unit. For example, a menu bar is comprised of individual menus, each of which is comprised of menu items. If the programmer and layout manager had to arrange each individual menu item, the layout code would be hideously complex. It is much more convenient to arrange the menu, then encapsulate it as a single object, then to glue it together with other composite menu objects into a single menu bar. In this way, the developer can build up a complicated GUI without having to constantly address the details of each individual component. Another benefit of grouping is that with configurable GUIs, such as those on many web browsers, it is then possible for the user to manipulate the menu bar as a unit.

Once we have internal containers, each comprised of their own components organized by a layout manager, how do we group them into higher level containers? The answer is simple, thanks to the power of inheritance and polymorphism. Containers store generic AWT **Components**. They neither need nor want any detailed information about the type of a component, they simply require generic information such as its preferred size. Likewise for layout managers—they deal with GUI objects by treating them all as **Components**. Thus any subclass of AWT **Component** can be stored in a container and arranged by a layout manager. As we will see when we look at the class hierarchy in detail, AWT's **Component** is a superclass for *all* AWT and Swing classes, including all components and containers. As far as containers and layout managers are concerned, internal containers are no different than simple components. So we can build a containment hierarchy very simply: first create and configure concrete components, then group them into an internal container with the **add()** method, then **add()** the internal container to the root level container's **contentPane**.

The most basic internal container is the **JPanel**, which is simply an undecorated chunk of screen area into which components can be inserted. A more sophisticated container is **JInternalFrame**, which comes decorated similarly to a standard "window" and can be moved around and resized with its parent container. Here is source code for a simple JPanel example. We create two panels, one storing the grid layout from the previous example and one storing the flow layout, and then we place one above the other using a root level 2x1 grid layout. (That's 2 rows, 1 column.) Here is the **init()** method from the source code (the rest remains the same as our previous examples):

```
public void init() {
  // We use a grid layout for the first panel. Note that
  // like many containers the JPanel has a constructor that
  // accepts a layout manager.
  JPanel f1 = new JPanel(new GridLayout(2,2));
  // Add four labels.
  f1.add(new Label("One"));
  f1.add(new Label("Two"));
  f1.add(new Label("Three"));
  f1.add(new Label("Four"));
  // Use a flow grid layout for the second panel.
  JPanel f2 = new JPanel(new FlowLayout());
  // And add four labels here.
  f2.add(new Label("One"));
  f2.add(new Label("Two"));
  f2.add(new Label("Three"));
  f2.add(new Label("Four"));
  // Now use a 1x2 grid layout for the root contentPane.
  getContentPane().setLayout(new GridLayout(1,2));
  // And we add the JPanels to the root pane as
  // if they were simple components.
  getContentPane().add(f1);
```

```
getContentPane().add(f2);
}
```

Swing Events and Event Listeners

Once we know how to create, configure, and manage GUI components, the next step is to support interaction with the user. In Swing (as in most modern GUIs), user interaction is supported through an *event* model. In the abstract, all of the things that can "happen" to a GUI are represented as events. There are two general types: low-level events, and semantic events. *Low-level events* are straightforward "device"events, for example the press of a key or a movement of the mouse. *Semantic* events are more abstract; they represent actions that have a specific meaning associated with a component, for example the press of a button for a ***JButton.*** (Obviously, clicking the mouse to "press" a GUI button involves both a low-level event-the mouse click–and a semantic event—the pressing of the button. One of the services Swing provides is the abstraction away from low-level events and towards semantic events. This helps the programmer by hiding unnecessary details, although the details are still available should the programmer choose to deal with them directly. So in general, a programmer writing code to manage a **JButton** would be concerned only with the semantic button-press event, not with key presses or mouse motion.)

Despite the abstract difference between low-level and semantic events, Swing programs handle both in exactly the same way: with *event listeners*. These are objects instantiated from classes that implement Java *listener* interfaces. For example, one type of semantic event deals with mouse focus. An object that wants to process mouse focus events implements the **FocusListener** interface. This consists of two methods: **focusGained()** and **focusLost().** When the mouse enters the display area associated with a GUI object, Swing calls the **focusGained()** methods for every listener object registered as being interested in focus events. This user-written method will take some action associated with gaining the mouse focus, perhaps changing the color of the GUI object border or issuing a sound. When the mouse leaves the area the **focusLost()** method will be called.

Event listeners are always associated with GUI components (or containers). Each component provides a registration method for each type of listener it supports. For example, when a **JButton** is "pressed", it generates an *Action* event. **JButton** provides the **addActionListener()** method, which takes as an argument any object that implements the **ActionListener** interface. Calling this function is referred to as *registering* the event listener with the component.

In summary, a Swing programmer has to do three things to process an event:

1. Declare that the event listener class *implements* the appropriate listener interface;
2. Write the code that implements each method specified by the listener interface;
3. Register the event listener with the component for which it will process events.

An Example

In practice Swing provides more tools to help simplify the process, and we discuss them later. But first, we look at a simple example: a button whose text changes color when it is clicked.

```
import javax.swing.*;
import java.awt.*;
// Note that we need to import this explicitly.
import java.awt.event.*;
```

```
// We extend JApplet and implement the ActionListener interface.
public class ButtonTest extends JApplet implements ActionListener {
public ButtonTest() {
// First, the hack...
getRootPane().
 putClientProperty("defeatSystemEventQueueCheck",
        Boolean.TRUE);
// Now set the state variable to it's initial value.
isRed = false;
}
public void init() {
 b = new JButton("Change color");
 // Register our listener method. We have made ourselves
 // the action listener, a common idiom for simple programs.
 b.addActionListener(this);
 getContentPane().add(b);
}
// This is the method specified by ActionListener. The
// argument is the actual event, the details of which
// are inconsequential for our purposes.
public void actionPerformed(ActionEvent e) {
 if (isRed) {
  b.setForeground(java.awt.Color.black);
  isRed = false;
 } else {
  b.setForeground(java.awt.Color.red);
  isRed = true;
 }
}
private boolean isRed;
private JButton b;
}
Here is the applet itself:
```

In part because this is such a simple applet, it is its own event listener. That is, the applet itself implements the **ActionListener** interface and provides the **actionPerformed()** method to change colors. This is perfectly acceptable for a small program. If there were lots of components involved then it might make sense to construct specialized event listener objects. But note that this would introduce a complication: the event listener may need to make changes to the internal state of the applet, which is now a different object. For example in our case it records whether or not the button text is currently red. This means that the applet would have to provide a communication mechanism, such as a public method for changing color. One common way to do this is with an inner class that encapsulates event processing but still has access to private fields of its outer class.

There are a couple of other details worth mentioning:

- we need to import "java.awt.event.*", or at least the specific parts of that package that we are going to use–for simplicity we imported the whole thing;
- the **actionPerformed()** method, called when an action (e.g., button press) occurs, is called by the Swing infrastructure with an **ActionEvent** parameter. **ActionEvent** objects contain more details about the action that occurred. For example, if there were more than one button, we would need to determine which one had been pressed. **ActionEvent** provides methods that yield that sort of information. Typically each type of listener has its own event object, e.g., **MouseListener** methods accept **MouseEvent** parameters.

Advanced Topics

A single event listener object can service multiple GUI components, either explicitly or implicitly. To do so explicitly, each component can register the same object as its listener. Implicitly, a **Container** supports many event listener registrations methods, including for example **addFocusListener().** Thus another motivation for grouping components into internal containers is the opportunity to give them all the same behavior with respect to handling some events.

Sometimes, implementing a full listener interface is unnecessarily inconvenient. For example, **MouseListener** specifies five mouse-related methods:

- **mousePressed(),** called when a button is pressed;
- **mouseReleased(),** called when a button is released;
- **mouseClicked(),** called when a button is clicked (i.e. pressed and released);
- **mouseEntered(),** called when the mouse enters the component's screen area;
- **mouseExited(),** called when the mouse leaves the component.

In many cases a mouse listener object is concerned with only a subset of these operations—in some cases perhaps only with a single operation. Because the listener implements **MouseListener**, it is required to provide implementations for each method. Of course, the methods can be empty, but then the program is cluttered with meaningless code and the poor programmer is forced to waste time.

Swing provides an idiom to handle these cases. A class called **MouseAdapter** provides empty implementations of each of the **MouseListener** methods. Now the programmer can simply extend **MouseAdapter** and write only the methods that will be used. (Since Java does not support multiple inheritance this is likely to require creation of a class devoted to event handling-the outer class usually extends **JApplet** or some other top level container. As mentioned above, a common way to do this is to create an inner class that does all the event processing; another possibility is an anonymous class.

Swing Components and the Containment Hierarchy

SwingApplication creates four commonly used Swing components:

- a *frame*, or main window (`JFrame`)
- a *panel*, sometimes called a *pane* (`JPanel`)
- a button (`JButton`)
- a label (`JLabel`)

The frame is a *top-level container*. It exists mainly to provide a place for other Swing components to paint themselves. The other commonly used top-level containers are dialogs (`JDialog`) and applets (`JApplet`).

The penal is an *intermediate container*. Its only purpose is to simplify the positioning of the button and label. Other intermediate Swing containers, such as scroll panes (`JScrollPane`) and tabbed panes (`JTabbedPane`), typically play a more visible, interactive role in a program's GUI.

The button and label are *atomic components*—components that exist not to hold random Swing components, but as self-sufficient entities that present bits of information to the user. Often, atomic components also get input from the user. The Swing API provides many atomic components, including combo boxes (`JComboBox`), text fields (`JTextField`), and tables (`JTable`).

Here is a diagram of the *containment hierarchy* for the window shown by `SwingApplication`. This diagram shows each container created or used by the program, alongwith the components it contains. Note that if we add a window—a dialog, for instance—the new window has its own component hierarchy, unattached to the hierarchy shown in this figure.

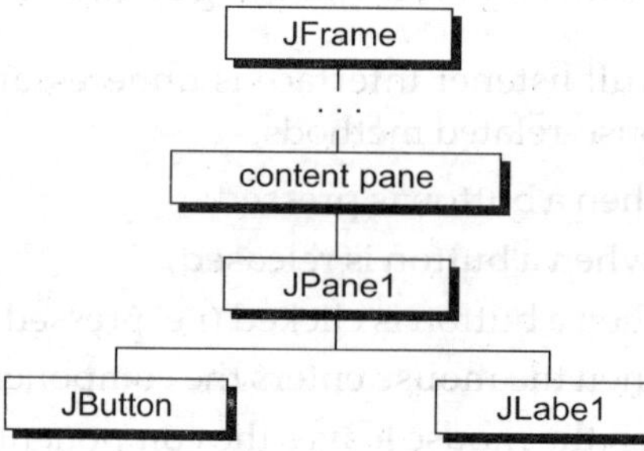

As the figure shows, even the simplest Swing program has multiple levels in its containment hierarchy. The root of the containment hierarchy is always a top-level container. The top-level container provides a place for its descendent Swing components to paint themselves.

Tip: *To view the containment hierarchy for any frame or dialog, click its border to select it, and then press Control-Shift-F1. A list of the containment hierarchy will be written to the standard output stream.*

Every top-level container indirectly contains an intermediate container known as a *content pane*. For most programs, you don't need to know what's between a top-level container and its content pane.

As a rule, the content pane contains, directly or indirectly, all of the visible components in the window's GUI. The big exception to the rule is that if the top-level container has a menu bar, then by convention the menu bar goes in a special place outside of the content pane.

To add a component to a container, you use one of the various forms of the add method. The add method has at least one argument – the component to be added. Sometimes an additional argument is required to provide layout information. For example, the last line of the following code sample specifies that the panel should be in the center of its container (the content pane).

Here is the code that adds the button and label to the panel, and the panel to the content pane:

```
frame = new JFrame ( . . . ) ;
button = new JButton ( . . . ) ;
```

```
label = new JLabel ( . . . ) ;
pane = new JPanel ( ) ;
pane.add (button) ;
pane.add (label) ;
frame.getContentPane ( ) .add (pane,
BorderLayout.CENTER) ;
```

EXERCISE

1. Differentiate between component and container class?
2. What is Intermediate class?
3. How many type of layout a container could have?
4. Explain the layout manager in detail.
5. Explain event listener interface.
6. What is the default layout for Applet, frame and panel?
7. What is the difference between checkbox and checkbox group?
8. What are the different ways of creating Image Object?
9. Write a Java Program using checkbox to display seven wonders of world.
10. Write advantage of swings?
11. Write short notes on JFC?
12. Name the application services that can be used in JFC components.
13. In what way JButton is better than Button class?
14. What is the JRoot Pane? What can it be used for?
15. What are the various layout managers available in JFC? List each of them with their functionality.
16. What is the JFC Container? List according to their functionality.
17. How can you create a button with an image loaded on it and how do you set a tool tip to a button control?
18. Write a Java program to display month names by JList and displaying the days by JCombo Box.
19. Which method of the component class is used to set the position and the size of a component?
20. Which are true about the Container class?
    - The validate( ) method is used to cause a Container to be laid out and redisplayed.
    - The add( ) method is used to add a Component to a Container.
    - The getBorder( ) method returns information about a Container's insets.
    - getComponent( ) method is used to access a Component that is contained in a Container
21. What is a swing?
22. Difference between AWT and Swings.
23. What is a AWT?
24. What are the components provided by AWT?

INDEX